The 2006 ASTD
Organization Development
& Leadership
Sourcebook

Reproducible

- Training Activities
- Assessment Instruments
- Helpful Handouts
- Practical Guides

ASTD Press

Mel Silberman, Editor

Patricia Philips, Assistant Editor

ASTD Press is an internationally renowned source of insightful and practical information on workplace learning and performance topics, including training basics, evaluation and return-on-investment (ROI), instructional systems development (ISD), e-learning, leadership, and career development.

Ordering information: Books published by ASTD Press can be purchased by visiting our Website at store.astd.org or by calling 800.628.2783 or 703.683.8100.

Library of Congress Control Number: 2005939057

ISBN: 1-56286-422-X

Acquisitions and Development Editor: Mark Morrow
Proofreader: Kris Patenaude
Copy Editing and Production: Inkwell Publishing Services
Cover Design: Anna Ilieva

CONTENTS

ASSESSMENT INSTRUMENTS

HELPFUL HANDOUTS

PRACTICAL GUIDES

TOPICAL INDEX
Find a Tool for Your Specific Topic

In place of a traditional index, we present the following classification by topic of the tools found in *The 2006 ASTD Organization Development and Leadership Sourcebook.*

Leadership Development

Team Development

PREFACE

Welcome to the 11th year of *The Leadership and Organization Development Sourcebook*, an annual collection of practical tools for developing teams and organizations.

The *2006 ASTD Organization Development and Leadership Sourcebook* has another great lineup of resources for your professional use. You can customize materials by downloading all of the activity forms, instruments, and handouts from the accompanying CD-ROM.

Along with its companion, *The 2006 ASTD Training and Performance Sourcebook,* this book provides the latest, cutting-edge advice and learning aids on topics important to today's public- and private-sector organizations. While *The Training and Performance Sourcebook* focuses on development and support at the individual level of the organization, *The 2006 ASTD Organization Development and Leadership Sourcebook* emphasizes organization-wide issues.

Having *The 2006 ASTD Organization Development and Leadership Sourcebook* available for instant reference allows you to select printed materials on team and organizational change written by leading experts. In addition, the *Sourcebook* serves as a state-of-the-art clearinghouse of ideas and new practices. It helps you keep up with the spiraling developments in the field of leadership and organization development.

This *Sourcebook* contains activities, assessment instruments, handouts, and practical guides, creating a ready-to-use toolkit for consultants, coaches, trainers, and team leaders. It is also invaluable for team sponsors, managers, and other organizational representatives who are interested in leadership and organization development. Best of all, because these tools are reproducible, they can be shared with your clients and group participants.

We hope you will find *The 2006 ASTD Organization Development and Leadership Sourcebook* to be a one-stop resource you can draw upon again and again in your efforts to facilitate team and organizational effectiveness.

Mel Silberman
Princeton, New Jersey

Patricia Philips
Washington, North Carolina

ACTIVITIES

In this section of *The 2006 ASTD Organization Development and Leadership Sourcebook*, you will find 14 activities. You can use these activities in a variety of settings:

✓ Team-building sessions
✓ Meetings
✓ Retreats
✓ Training programs
✓ Consultations

All the activities featured here are highly participatory. They are designed in the belief that learning and change best occur through experience and reflection. As opposed to preaching or lecturing, experiential activities place people directly within a concrete situation. Typically, participants are asked to solve a problem, complete an assignment, or communicate information. Often, the task can be quite challenging. Sometimes, it can also be a great deal of fun. The bottom line, however, is that participants become active partners in the learning of new concepts or in the development of new ideas.

The experiences contained in the activities you are about to read can be of two kinds: simulated and real-world. Although some may find simulations to be artificial, well-designed ones can provide an effective analogy to real-world experiences. They also have the advantage of being timesaving shortcuts to longer, drawn-out activities. Activities that engage teams in actual, ongoing work can serve as a powerful mechanism for change.

Experience, by itself, is not always "the best teacher." Reflecting on the experience, however, can yield wisdom and insight. You will find that the activities in this section contain helpful guidelines for reflection. Expect a generous selection of questions to process or debrief the actual activities.

All the activities have been written for ease of use. A concise overview of each activity is provided. You will be guided, step-by-step, through the activity instructions. All of the necessary participant materials are included. For your photocopying convenience, these materials are on separate pages. Any materials you need to prepare in advance have been kept to a minimum. Special equipment or physical arrangements are seldom needed.

Best of all, the activities are designed so that you can easily modify or customize them to your specific requirements. Also, time allocations are readily adaptable. Furthermore, many of the activities are "frame exercises"—generic activities that can be used for many topics or areas of subject matter. You will find it easy to plug in the content relevant to your team's circumstances.

As you conduct any of these activities, bear in mind that experiential activity is especially successful if you do a good job as a facilitator. Here are some common mistakes people make in facilitating experiential activities:

1. *Motivation:* Participants aren't invited to buy in to the activity or sold the benefits of joining in. Participants don't know what to expect during the exercise.

2. *Directions:* Instructions are lengthy and unclear. Participants cannot visualize what the facilitator expects from them.

3. *Group Process:* Subgroups are not composed effectively. Group formats are not changed to fit the requirements of each activity. Subgroups are left idle.

4. *Energy:* Activities move too slowly. Participants are sedentary. Activities are long or demanding when they need to be short or relaxed. Participants do not find the activity challenging.

5. *Processing:* Participants are confused or overwhelmed by the questions posed to them. There is a poor fit between the facilitator's questions and the goals of the activity. Facilitators share their opinions before first hearing the participants' views.

To avoid these pitfalls, follow these steps:

I. Introduce the activity.
   1. Explain your objectives.
   2. Sell the benefits.
   3. Convey enthusiasm.
   4. Connect the activity to previous activities.
   5. Share personal feelings and express confidence in participants.
II. Help participants know what they are expected to do.
   1. Speak slowly.
   2. Use visual backup.
   3. Define important terms.
   4. Demonstrate the activity.
III. Manage the group process.
   1. Form groups in a variety of ways.
   2. Vary the number of people in any activity based upon that exercise's specific requirements.

3. Divide participants into teams before giving further directions.

4. Give instructions separately to groups in a multipart activity.

5. Keep people busy.

6. Inform the subgroups about time frames.

IV. Keep participants involved.

1. Keep the activity moving.

2. Challenge the participants.

3. Reinforce participants for their involvement in the activity.

4. Build physical movement into the activity.

V. Get participants to reflect on the activity's implications.

1. Ask relevant questions.

2. Carefully structure the first processing experiences.

3. Observe how participants are reacting to the group processing.

4. Assist a subgroup that is having trouble processing an activity.

5. Hold your own reactions until after hearing from participants.

CONDUCTING EMPLOYEE DEVELOPMENT DISCUSSIONS: A PROBLEM-SOLVING EXERCISE

Shirley Copeland

Shirley Copeland, EdD, *is president of the Learning Resource Group, LLC, a management consulting firm she founded in 1993. Her company specializes in evaluation, instructional systems design, facilitation, and designing certification programs. She has over 20 years' experience and has designed and developed award-winning training materials for the public and private sectors. Shirley is a past contributor to the* **Sourcebooks.**

Contact Information:
2361 Lonicera Way
Charlottesville, VA 22911
434.975.1834
sfcopeland@aol.com

Overview Managers play an important role in the development of employees. Yet they often encounter obstacles in identifying suitable developmental experiences, giving appropriate feedback on developmental assignments, and managing unrealistic employee expectations. This exercise is designed to get managers thinking about these issues. The activity can be used as an opener for a discussion about developing employees or as a problem-solving exercise for real-world application.

Suggested Time 60–90 minutes

Materials Needed ✓ Employee Development Scenarios (Form A)
✓ Guide for the Facilitator (Form B)

Procedure 1. Distribute copies of Form A (Employee Development Scenarios) and introduce the activity.

2. Break the class into five groups of three to five individuals. Assign each group one of the questions. Each group formulates a solution to the question. Each group appoints a spokesperson to report their solution. The groups spend about 10-15 minutes formulating their answers.

3. Ask for volunteers from each team to share their responses.

4. Facilitate the discussion and provide guidance on their responses. See Form B for guidance. Allow about 10-15 minutes of discussion for each group's presentation.

5. Use the discussion as an opportunity to reinforce the following points:

- Managers must use an adaptive approach in coaching and counseling employees about their career development. The manager's role varies according to the situation; managers may be called on to serve as coach, counselor, appraiser, mentor, advisor, referral agent, or advocate.

- Managers need to work to support and facilitate the employee's development while promoting a match of individual and organizational needs.

- The manager should seek to empower employees in taking charge of their development and move beyond being that of just an information provider about career development opportunities.

- Managers need to provide ongoing, timely, constructive feedback.

- Managers should work with the employee to develop realistic goals and to identify appropriate developmental experiences to meet the goals.

EMPLOYEE DEVELOPMENT SCENARIOS   FORM A

Directions: *Work within your group to come up with your solution to the assigned scenario.*

1. You have reviewed your employee's self-assessment and disagree strongly with the employee's evaluation. The employee's performance and capability is far below his or her positive assessment.

   Question: How do you give feedback to the employee?

   _____

   _____

   _____

2. You are in the midst of a discussion with a very ambitious employee. The employee has career aspirations that are well beyond what he or she is capable of achieving.

   Question: How do you respond?

   _____

   _____

   _____

3. You have several employees in your office who have reached a certain level in their career and are not interested in moving up or seeking training opportunities to improve their performance.

   Question: How do you handle the situation?

   _____

   _____

   _____

4. One of your shining stars was given a developmental assignment and failed to complete it successfully.

   Question: How do you counsel and/or coach the person?

   _____

   _____

   _____

5. You have many employees in your office who have reached a career plateau. Opportunities for promotions any time soon are unlikely.

   Question: How do you design developmental opportunities for these employees?

   _____

   _____

   _____

GUIDE FOR THE FACILITATOR   FORM B

Directions: *The following are some key points for each scenario that might be helpful in facilitating the discussion. They provide general guidance about what the manager could do in each situation.*

SCENARIO 1

- Think about how you might have contributed to this discrepancy (i.e., failure to provide specific, useful, timely feedback; failure to address shortcomings in performance, etc.).
- Be prepared to provide specific evidence to support your feedback.
- Work with the employee to design developmental opportunities to improve in the areas where you perceive a discrepancy in his or her positive self-assessment.

SCENARIO 2

- Be cautiously optimistic, but identify specific areas that the employee needs to develop to approach his or her goal.
- Encourage the employee to set realistic goals with measurable outcomes.
- Consider that, in some situations, you might have to refer an employee to other resources in the organization.

SCENARIO 3

- Assess the impact of employees' remaining at their current level of performance to determine how to address the situation.
- Encourage employees to move out of their comfort zone; give them more challenging experiences that will require them to stretch.
- Explore with the employees the consequences of not taking advantage of developmental opportunities.

SCENARIO 4

- Focus on the learning that occurred as a result of the experience. Do not penalize the person, but instead offer words of encouragement.
- Engage the person in a discussion about how he or she would do it differently next time.
- Think about your role in the developmental assignment and how you could have handled it differently.

You can download this handout to your hard drive from the accompanying CD-ROM. The document can then be opened and printed.

SCENARIO 5

- Confer with the employees about potential cross-functional assignments to determine if they would be interested in working on them as a developmental opportunity.

- Identify areas where the employees' experience could be an asset as a coach or mentor to less experienced employees.

- Be creative in thinking about developmental opportunities and ask the employees to take a proactive role in the process.

FACILITATING CONFLICT RESOLUTION: FOUR BEHAVIORAL CORNERSTONES

Jim Andrews

Jim Andrews, PhD, *is a consulting psychologist and practice leader in executive and organizational development, change management, and team development at Hagberg Consulting Group (HCG). Over the past 20 years, HCG has developed an integrated suite of empirical assessment tools that enables senior management to gain a data-oriented view of strategy, leadership, and culture—each taken individually and in relation to the other two. Prior to HCG, Jim was vice president of organizational development at Rusher Loscavio & LoPresto, a national retained executive search firm; and before that he was vice president of human resources and organizational development at Salestar, a telecommunications software company in San Francisco. Jim is the author of "The Intuitive Decision Making Profile" and "Group Consensus Decision Making." He has taught at the University of Tennessee, University of San Francisco, Dominican University, The Haas Business School. Jim was the 2003 and 2004 chair of the San Francisco Chapter of Northern California Human Resource Association and is the 2005 president of the Golden Gate Chapter of the American Society for Training & Development.*

Contact Information:
Hagberg Consulting Group—Senior Consultant
951 Mariners Island Boulevard, Suite 600
San Mateo, CA 94404
650.377.0232 x214
jandrews@hcgnet.com
www.hcgnet.com

Overview The cost of conflict is enormous and is reflected in lost productivity, time, and resources directed at conflict resolution, turnover, and sick leave. This activity helps participants:

- Learn the four fundamental behaviors that are correlated with skill in facilitating conflict resolution.

- Understand how these four key behaviors influence one's perception of others or others' perception of oneself.

- Identify action steps to develop these four behaviors.

Suggested Time   30 minutes

Materials Needed   ✓ Flip chart and markers
                  ✓ Rating Form (Form A)
                  ✓ Action Planning Form (Form B)

Procedure

1. Write the dimensions from the Rating Form (Form A) on a flip chart for all to see.

2. Hand out the Rating Form and ask participants to do the following:

   An employee in XYZ Corporation is viewed as a poor listener, aggressive, defensive, and not open to input. His co-workers are asked to rate this individual on 12 dimensions. Without any further information, what ratings would you predict were given?

3. Ask them to do their rating quietly and individually on Form A.

4. After the participants are finished rating, ask them to break into groups of three or four.

5. Give these instructions:

   • *Compare your predictions.*

   • *How did the four behaviors (nonopenness to input, aggression, defensiveness, and poor listening) influence your predictions?*

6. Ask each group to report their findings to the larger group. Make notes on the flip chart.

7. Share that 22 years of research on 360-degree feedback data show that people who are seen as good listeners, open to input, non-defensive, and assertive are rated higher on *facilitating conflict resolution*. In addition, people who score high on these four behaviors are also seen as adaptable; capable of building relationships and teams; creators of buy-in; able to delegate and empower; possessing emotional control, sensitivity, and consideration; and having overall likeability—while still being seen as having forthrightness and social astuteness.

8. Explain to participants the importance of the fact that these four key behaviors influence the way people see you. Ask them, what can you do develop yourself or develop others in these areas?

9. Distribute Form B (Action Planning Form). Ask participants to complete it.

10. Invite participants to pair up and exchange their action plans. Then reconvene the entire group and obtain a list of specific action steps for each of the four behaviors.

RATING FORM

Directions: *An employee in XYZ Corporation is viewed as a poor listener, aggressive, defensive, and not open to input. His co-workers are asked to rate this individual on 12 dimensions. Without any further information, what ratings (with 1 = poor and 10 = superior) would you predict were given?*

Rating Dimensions	Rating (1–10)
Adaptability	
Building teams	
Creating buy-in	
Delegation and empowerment	
Emotional control	
Forthrightness	
Negotiation competence	
Overall likeability	
Relationship building	
Sensitivity and consideration	
Social astuteness	
Facilitating conflict resolution	

You can download this handout to your hard drive from the accompanying CD-ROM. The document can then be opened and printed.

ACTION PLANNING FORM   FORM B

Directions: *What action steps can you take to develop your competence as someone who is a good listener? As someone open to input? As someone who is nondefensive? As someone who is assertive?*

To become a better listener, I should:

_____

_____

_____

_____

To become more open to input, I should:

_____

_____

_____

_____

To become less defensive, I should:

_____

_____

_____

_____

To become more assertive, I should:

_____

_____

_____

_____

You can download this handout to your hard drive from the accompanying CD-ROM. The document can then be opened and printed.

WISDOM OF THE AGES: A STRUCTURED APPROACH TO IDEA GENERATION

Tracy Fuller

Tracy Fuller *coaches the use of creativity and leadership skills needed to help business leaders approach their tough challenges more effectively. She is an executive coach and managing director of Compio, a coaching partnership that enables business leaders to approach their challenges more creatively and effectively. Prior to founding Compio, Tracy served as vice president of human resources for MetalSite, Inc., an international B2B e-commerce firm.*

Contact Information:
Compio
340 Jefferson Drive
Pittsburgh, PA 15228
412.341.3425
tfuller@compio.net
www.compio.net.

Overview This exercise is intended for use with an intact group. It uses a strength-based approach to idea generation. Group members are encouraged to reflect on and apply catalysts to prior accomplishments to a current challenge facing the group. This process allows for both independent reflection and building on others' ideas. Specific objectives are:

- To approach a challenge from new vantage points.
- To identify new ways to leverage existing insights.

Suggested Time Approximately 90 minutes, depending on the size of the group

Materials Needed ✓ One copy of Wisdom of the Ages Worksheet (Form A) for each participant
✓ One flip chart (or other medium for charting and sharing ideas) and markers for each group
✓ Masking tape, or other method for posting information to be shared

Procedure

1. Clearly define a challenge the group is working to address. State the challenge in the form of a question, such as, how might we ... ? Or how to ... ? If the group contains eight or more members, divide the participants into groups of about four people each. Otherwise, keep the entire group together. Give each participant a copy of the Wisdom of the Ages worksheet (Form A). Place a flip chart and markers near each group.

2. Explain that this worksheet supports a process designed to help groups leverage their strengths in new ways. Each participant first completes his or her own worksheet in private. Participants are then given the opportunity to share the results they choose with each other.

3. Ask the participants to complete the first column, Accomplishments, silently. After allowing several minutes, tell participants they have 10 to 12 minutes to complete the remaining columns. Ask the participants to complete the worksheet silently and independently, starting with each accomplishment and working to the right until finishing the remaining columns before moving down to the next listed accomplishment

4. After the 10 to 12 minutes, give the participants an opportunity to share and build on their Lessons Learned.

   a. Each group chooses a scribe. The scribe writes the challenge statement at the top of the flip chart. Beneath the challenge statement, the scribe creates and titles two columns: Lessons Learned and Links.

   b. One group member shares a lesson learned and how she or he thought of applying it to the challenge at hand. Chart the lesson learned and the links in the appropriate columns.

   c. Give the other group members an opportunity to identify additional ways to apply the lesson learned to the problem. Chart each additional potential solution under Links.

   d. Repeat with the next participant, giving each participant an opportunity to share one lesson learned and to generate links before moving on to the next round.

   e. Continue in a round-robin fashion, giving each participant a chance to either share an additional lesson learned and links or say "pass" until you run out of time or have shared all the lessons learned and links you want to share.

5. If you have conducted the activity with more than one group, convene the total group. Invite each subgroup to post their flip charts of lessons learned and links. Tell the large group they now have 10 minutes to walk around, review, and possibly build on the other groups' work. When anyone sees an opportunity to add to another group's work, he or she adds the idea directly to that group's flip chart.

6. Debrief the activity in two ways: (1) looking at the product and (2) looking at the process.

   a. Emphasizing product:

      • Which ideas did you find most interesting or promising? Why?

      • If you could choose only three ideas to develop further, which might they be? (Variation: Give each participant three sticker dots and have them place them on the three ideas they would like to develop further. Draw the group's attention to the ideas receiving the most dots.)

      • How do we want to act on our most promising ideas?

   b. Emphasizing process:

      • What did you find most challenging in this process? Why?

      • What did you find most rewarding or productive in this process? Why?

      • What, if anything, did you learn about yourself through this exercise? About others?

      • How else might you apply this type of exercise?

Variations
• The worksheet can also be used as an independent brainstorming tool.

• The exercise can also be used during a performance coaching process, as a way to help an employee get past a sticking point.

• The activity can initially be given as a homework assignment to complete between team meetings. After confirming the shared challenge and introducing the worksheet, ask individuals to complete the worksheet before the next meeting. During the next meeting, complete steps 3, 4, and 5.

WISDOM OF THE AGES

Accomplishments	Catalysts	Lessons Learned	Links
List a few of your most significant and satisfying ones, from any stage in your life to date.	What led to this success? Who helped you? How? What prepared you? What did you do differently, or very well?	Note the most valuable insights you gained through this accomplishment.	How might you link what you learned from this accomplishment to the current challenge?

You can download this handout to your hard drive from the accompanying CD-ROM. The document can then be opened and printed.

PIZARRO'S MAP: AN ADVENTURE TEAM AWARENESS EXERCISE

Tony Ventrice and Cindy Ventrice

Tony Ventrice *is a lifelong game designer. He has designed everything from board and computer games to silly social interactions. He currently works with Namco America, where he designs and produces innovative games for your mobile phone.*

Contact Information:
tony@ventrice.com
http://www.ventrice.com/tony/gamedesign.htm

Cindy Ventrice, *the author of* **Make Their Day! Employee Recognition That Works** *(Berrett-Koehler 2003), addresses audiences on issues related to employee relations, engagement, and turnover. She has worked in a wide range of industries including technology, nonprofit, government, health care, service, trade, education, and tourism. A consultant since 1984, Cindy is past president of the Silicon Valley chapter of the American Society for Training & Development and a board member of the Northern California Chapter of the National Speakers Association. Cindy is a past contributor to the* **Sourcebooks**.

Contact Information:
Potential Unlimited
P.O. Box 3437
Santa Cruz, CA 95063
831.476.4224
cventrice@maketheirday.com
www.maketheirday.com
www.potential-unltd.com

Overview   A common complaint of teams is that they have difficulty making decisions. Even after endless meetings to resolve an urgent issue, they can remain stuck in analysis. Clashing personalities, irrelevant side topics, leaders who cannot or will not take charge, and unwillingness to compromise or commit to a plan of action can all contribute to the problem.

This adventure-based activity provides teams with the opportunity to test and assess their ability to work together to solve a problem. The task of the competing teams is to come up with creative solutions, using the supplies they assemble, to meet the challenges presented throughout this jungle adventure. Teams will need to sift through irrelevant details; identify goals, roles, and responsibilities; plan for contingencies; and reach swift, practical solutions.

Suggested Time For two teams of four people:

- 90 minutes to complete the activity
- 15 minutes to an hour to debrief
- 15 minutes overall for each additional team

Materials Needed ✓ One copy for each participant of Participant Worksheet (Form A)

✓ One copy for each participant of Information on Ecuador (Form B, including Pizarro's Map)

✓ One copy for each participant of Supply List (Form C)

✓ Flip chart (to keep score; create a heading for each team)

✓ Four-sided die (optional); if you do not have a four-sided die, you can use a six-sided die and discount any rolls of five and six, or you can cut 12 small slips of paper and number them 1 through 4 (three sets)

Procedure 1. Split the participants into two or more teams, preferably of four people each. Instruct each team to choose an expedition team leader. (For the purposes of role-playing, even if a team has more or fewer actual members, it assumes it has four members.)

2. Distribute one copy each of Form A (Participant Worksheet).

3. Read Form A aloud and encourage participants to ask you questions about its contents.

4. Next, distribute Form B (Information on Ecuador) and give participants enough time to read it carefully. Then, distribute Form C (Supply List). Tell participants that they have five minutes to decide, individually, what supplies the group should bring. Clarify that Form B will not be part of their supplies.

5. Tell the teams that they have 30 minutes to decide, as a group, what to include in each of the four backpacks. Tell teams to list specific items and quantities, not just "food" or "clothing." Remind them that each backpack measures 24×12×12 inches, so space is limited. Also remind them that their supplies cannot cost more than U.S. $3,000. At the end of 30 minutes, ask the teams to read aloud the contents of their packs. Decide if teams are within budget and size limitations.

6. Explain how the journey will take place. Each day the teams will be presented with a situation in which they have to solve a problem using only the supplies they brought, what is available in the jungle, and their own creativity. While success in handling each event means they may progress unhindered, failure may cost them precious time, which will ultimately determine which team finds the lost ruins first. Collect Form B (the teams no longer need it).

7. State the following:

Day One: You are spending the first day traveling the roads east of Quito deep into the jungle. A few hours before nightfall, you abandon the car you are traveling in and enter the jungle itself. The brush is very dense. If you did not have the foresight to bring along machetes or some such means of clearing a path, I am adding two days to your overall travel time right now.

8. Ask teams to tell you what they have packed for dealing with the dense foliage. Record the time lost, if any, on a flip chart. Then state the following:

If you have not packed enough food for four people that lasts at least seven days, your journey will be delayed. I will add one additional day for every day of travel for which you do not have adequate quantities of food. This represents time spent on scavenging edibles under Atlacstal's direction.

Ask teams to read aloud what they have packed in the way of food. Make your decision on whether or not this is a sufficient supply. If you like, you may ask other teams for their opinions before deciding. Record the number of days lost, if any. (You will be the judge of whether a team has brought enough food, remained within their budget, or has found a workable solution to a problem. If a team disagrees with your decision, allow one minute for the team to explain their position. Allow other teams up to a minute for rebuttal. You may change your decision if you choose, but your decision is final.)

9. Next, state the following:

Day Two: Atlacstal informs you that Westerners such as you should not drink the local water; micro-organisms will make you sick. Did you bring enough clean drinking water to last for seven days, or do you have some way to decontaminate the water?

Give each team a few minutes to prepare a response.

Each team offers their solution. Seven days worth of fresh water, a purification kit, or a pot and fire to boil will suffice. Again, if a team has chosen to carry water, the other teams might question whether the quantity is sufficient and if it has adequate room in its packs. If you decide that a team is unprepared, say:

Because you are unprepared, you drink the jungle water and two members of your team fall sick. The team incurs an extra day of travel time as they are slowed by the sick members.

If a team has packed medicine to treat dysentery, reduce the time lost to a half a day.

10. Announce the next event:

Day Three: Atlacstal informs you that he has identified signs that you are approaching the territory of a tribe of magicians that have a blood feud with his own tribe. He concedes that only he is in danger—that the natives would probably not have a problem with the rest of the party. You must decide if you will go a day out of your way to circumvent the territory, as Atlacstal desires, or take the risk and continue directly through.

Give teams a few minutes to decide whether they should go around the territory or through it. Let teams know that disguising Atlacstal or offering any other strategy to change his mind will be rejected by him.

If a team chooses "around," add one day of travel time.

If a team chooses "through," announce that Atlacstal vanishes in the night along with one backpack. (You can throw a die or draw a number from 1 to 4 to select which pack is taken from the team.) Cross the lost backpack off of the team's Supply List. Also tell them the following:

Not only have you lost some of your supplies, but, without Atlacstal to guide you, your progress through the jungle will be slower.

Use a die or draw from slips of paper to determine the time lost (one to four days).

11. Proceed to the next event and state:

Day Four: The dense forest of tall trees breaks to reveal a lazy, murky river, 60 feet wide and 20 feet deep at its center. There is no sign of piranhas or other hostile wildlife more severe than leeches. You need to find some way of crossing it without risking losing your supplies or wasting precious days finding an easier place to cross. How will you cross?

Give teams a few minutes to decide how they will cross the river. Then ask each team to offer its solution. If a team has brought an inflatable raft or can devise some other quick way of crossing with their prepacked supplies, then it may proceed without missing a day. If a team proposes to cut down a tall tree that will stretch over the river (and has the cutting tools necessary), give them a half day penalty. If a team proposes to build a raft that they can make from branches and vines in the area (and has the proper tools), give them a full day penalty. If a team has no solution, it loses four days by traveling two days up and two days back along the river to find a place to cross.

12. Proceed to the next event and state:

Day Five: You are caught in a lengthy downpour that threatens to soak your supplies and most notably your copy of Pizarro's map, as well as any other maps you have thought to bring along. Just 10 minutes or so could render the map completely unreadable as the deluge would smear the ink and degrade the paper. Because the map is a vital reference you realize that, if you have no alternatives, you might need to keep the map safely packed away until the rain abates. What will you do?

Give teams a few minutes to decide what they can do to protect their map. Then, ask each team to offer its solution. If a team waits out the rain to protect their map, it loses one day. Ways of avoiding losing a day include using multiple copies of the map (four or more) and switching as each in turn becomes unreadable, or having laminated or otherwise protected it or putting it in a plastic bag or under the cover of a temporary awning of some sort.

13. Proceed to the next event and state:

    Day Six: You are nearing the site and decide to fan out so as to have a better chance of finding the elusive ruins. You agree to meet again at dusk, but the team is still separated as night falls. You need to quickly relocate each other in almost complete darkness to make camp for the night. What supplies do you have that will help you locate each other?

    Give teams a few minutes to decide how they will find each other. Then ask each team to offer its solution. If a team has not packed four flashlights, it loses one half a day. It loses an additional half of a day if it does not propose an adequate plan for finding each other. Possible solutions include (1) the use of a gun or flare gun to create a rendezvous point (merely yelling is inadequate), or (2) a combination of communication devices, such as walkie-talkies and directional devices such as compasses or GPS locators (cell phones are out of service). Other clever ideas might apply.

14. Announce to the teams that the ruins have been found. Tally the number of days each team took to find the city (seven plus the number of days delayed). Announce which team arrived first.

15. Debrief the activity with any of the following questions:

    • How well did your team prepare for the challenges you faced?

    • How did other teams' lists of supplies compare with your own?

    • How did your team decide which supplies to bring?

    • Did everyone contribute to each decision?

    • Did you feel encouraged or discouraged to participate?

    • What role did the leader play in the decision-making process?

    • How were disagreements resolved?

    • How do unexpected events affect a team's ability to plan or problem solve?

    • How does this activity relate to the issues your team typically faces?

A recently rediscovered manuscript and map, once belonging to the Spanish explorer Francisco Pizarro, provides direction to the location of a lost Incan outpost deep in the jungle near the upper reaches of the Amazon River in Ecuador.

The teams participating in this exercise represent competing factions of researchers and scientists, each eager to locate the site first to claim greater clout over research rights to the lost treasures within the ruins.

Your team must pack quickly but intelligently for an expedition deep into the jungle. The journey will last a minimum of seven days, and many resources are needed for your physical survival and your ability to respond to challenges that might occur along the way. If you are adequately prepared with supplies and are clever in overcoming the obstacles along the way, you will reach the ruins sooner than your competitors. (Note: For simplicity, you do not need to consider packing for the return journey.)

The first day of the trip will be along dirt roads and footpaths. From that point on, you can expect the rest of your journey to be through dense rain forest.

The team you will be sending into the jungle will consist of four members, each carrying one backpack. Each backpack is approximately 24×12×12 inches. *Everything* the team needs for the trip must be stored in these backpacks (no additional packs allowed). (Even if your group is more than four people, you will all virtually make up the four-person team.)

Your funds for the trip are limited to U.S. $3,000. The facilitator will decide if you have stayed within your budget. If you have not, the facilitator will ask you to cut items from your supplies. The facilitator will also decide how well you meet the challenges ahead of you.

For the planning stage, you will be supplied with copies of the map to the location of the ruins and some information about Ecuador.

For the trip itself, your team will have one copy of the map and one native guide, whose name is Atlacstal (*At-lacks-tal*). Atlacstal is extremely short but very sturdy. He is agile, quick, and quiet—well-adapted to the rain forest. Atlacstal is shy and stays in the background as much as possible. At times, he seems a little nervous. He knows the rain forest well and will help you find your way through the dense jungle, but is unfamiliar with the actual location of the ruins.

Your starting place is Quito, the capital city of Ecuador, and you have only one day to assemble your supplies in this bustling city. Look over Form B and think carefully about what your team will need for your expedition into the jungle. You will be hiking for at least seven days. Once you depart, there will be no way to gather any supplies other than what can be found and utilized in the jungle itself.

At the end of the planning session, you will be faced with challenges. Your supplies and ingenuity will determine how long your journey takes.

INFORMATION ON ECUADOR   FORM B

Ecuador is located in the northwest corner of the South American continent and is, aptly, bisected by the equator. It is the smallest country on the Andes mountain range, one of the steepest ranges in the world. On the west side, the rugged peaks leap from the tropical shores of the Pacific Ocean, while on the east they descend into the lush rainforests of the Amazon basin. It is a land rich in the history of the Incan empire and the Spanish colonial explorers.

Since Incan times, the region has been defined by its capital, Quito, the name by which early Spanish explorers knew the region as a whole. Situated high in the Andes, Quito was the magnificent capital of the sprawling Incan empire. Following the murder of his emperor, the Incan general burned the city down rather than relinquish control to the invaders.

The Spanish rebuilt the city. It lives today as a picturesque synthesis of bustling urban center and sweeping panoramic mountain vistas, enjoying year-round springlike weather. The city is divided into a preserved old-town filled with whitewashed colonial relics and an urban new town with modern offices and shopping centers. El Panecillo hill overlooks the city and is the home of the towering statue of the Virgin of Quito, an unmistakable reminder of Ecuador's strong Catholic roots. At the foot of the hill, between the old town and new town, there are expansive plazas that are home to open-air Indian markets.

Although a small country, Ecuador has one overseas holding, the Galapagos Islands, a natural wonder of secluded evolution and the influential seed to Charles Darwin's theory of evolution. The Galapagos sit alone in the Pacific, far to the east of the mainland.

In modern times, Ecuador has seen its fair share of political unrest. Although currently stable, except for a few tumultuous regions in the northeast and west of Quito, it has been the site of political uprisings, military rule, and assassinations as recently as 2001. In recent years, the greatest danger to tourists is the local street crime of larger cities such as Quito and Guayaquil.

Thanks to the decision of an unpopular expresidente, the official currency of Ecuador is the U.S. dollar. Prices in Ecuador are quite cheap by American standards and are even lower for those who can avoid the ubiquitous "gringo tax." A savvy, frugal visitor can get by with food and lodging for as little as U.S. $15 per day and even an indulgence in the most expensive hotels and restaurants would not set you back more than U.S. $150 a day.

Tipping is expected, although not for taxis, and bargaining is expected in the many markets and bazaars.

The eastern half of the country is dominated by the Amazon Basin, a lowland jungle filled with choked rivers, dense vegetation, wild animals, and indigenous tribes. The farther south one travels into the Oriente, or Eastern province, the less the likelihood is of finding paved roads or even roads at all. During the rainy season, large regions of jungle become practically inaccessible.

South of Quito is the Parque Nacional Cotopaxi, home of the Volcan Cotopaxi, the world's tallest active volcano—a 19,000-foot ice-covered monster that dares even the most experienced climbers.

You can download this handout to your hard drive from the accompanying CD-ROM. The document can then be opened and printed.

Statistics:

Full Name: Republic of Ecuador
Area: 283,520 square kilometers
Population: 12 million
Ethnic Distribution: 40 percent Indian, 40 percent mixed, 15 percent Spanish, 5 percent African
Language: Quechua, Spanish
Religion: 90 percent Roman Catholic, plus various Christian denominations
Government: Republic
GDP per capita: Ecuadorian $3100
Industries: Oil, bananas, fish, coffee, textiles, metals, paper, wood, chemicals, and plastics

---

You can download this handout to your hard drive from the accompanying CD-ROM. The document can then be opened and printed.

PIZARRO'S MAP

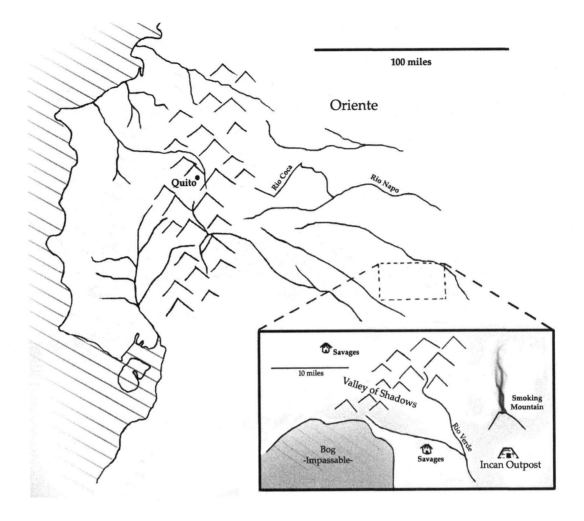

SUPPLY LIST FORM C

Directions:

1. Work by yourself for five minutes and brainstorm the supplies your team will need to reach its destination:

   ____

   ____

   ____

   ____

   ____

2. Work together as a team and identify the supplies to be packed in each of your four backpacks. Be specific about each item and indicate the quantity you need.

   Backpack 1:

   ____

   ____

   ____

   Backpack 2:

   ____

   ____

   ____

   Backpack 3:

   ____

   ____

   ____

   Backpack 4:

   ____

   ____

   ____

You can download this handout to your hard drive from the accompanying CD-ROM. The document can then be opened and printed.

MULTI-PLAST AND GORDI: A NEGOTIATION SIMULATION

Noam Ebner and Yael Efron

Noam Ebner, LLM, *is a conflict resolution specialist, attorney, mediator, and trainer. He is on the faculty at Sabanci University's graduate program on conflict analysis and resolution in Istanbul, Turkey, and teaches negotiation and mediation at Tel-Hai College, Israel.*

Yael Efron, LLM, *an attorney-mediator, specializes in mediation and negotiation training. She teaches conflict resolution and law at the College of Management and at Tel-Hai College, Israel.*

*Yael and Noam codirect Tachlit Mediation Center in Jerusalem, Israel. Specializing in designing conflict resolution simulations and games, their writing on the subject has been accepted for publication in **Negotiation Journal** and **The Creative Problem Solver's Handbook for Negotiators and Mediators.***

Contact Information:
Noam Ebner
43A Emek Refaim Street
Jerusalem, Israel
+972.2.5637482 or +972.523.786996
noam@tachlit.net

Yael Efron
Ficus 3/3
Modiin,71700, Israel
+972.523.557898
yael@tachlit.net

Overview This is a two-team, multi-issue, negotiation simulation/game that can alternatively be used to practice mediation. The simulation/game is designed to introduce participants to the intricacies inherent in negotiating in teams. Participants negotiate in pairs (although team members can be added) and must learn to navigate their intra- and interteam negotiation processes simultaneously. The simulation is based on the following scenario: The mayor of a small town, with financial difficulties and on the eve of a municipal election, is considering solving some of his problems by doubling the municipal taxes on a large factory in town. The factory, the town's largest industry, has its own interests in mind and is not about to take this sitting down. The mayor's team and corporate representatives have to figure out a way to work together before the clock runs out on them.

Although this simulation/game can be used for training dealing specifically with issues of local government and industry relations or environmental conflict resolution, it is designed to be used for any organizational training setting aimed at negotiation skill building.

Suggested Time   180 minutes

Materials Needed   ✓ Instructions for the Mayor of Gordi (Form A)

✓ Instructions for the Town Development Advisor of Gordi (Form B)

✓ Instructions for the General Manager of Multi-Plast, Inc.'s Gordi Factory (Form C)

✓ Instructions for the Head Director of Multi-Plast, Inc. (Form D)

Procedure   1. Divide participants into groups of four, and each group into two teams of two. (See the "variations" section if you do not have a total group size that is divisible by four.)

2. Explain the team formation: One team is composed of the mayor of Gordi and his town development advisor, and the other is composed of Multi-Plast's head director and its local factory manager. Distribute the form that provides instructions for each role.

3. Allow sufficient time to read the instructions carefully.

4. Instruct participants to hold team meetings of up to 10 minutes and decide how they want to proceed. Remind them that they may take private breaks or caucuses in the middle of their meeting with the other team to reassess as they go along. When both teams are ready, have them begin the meeting.

5. Once the negotiations have begun, the participants run the show, taking breaks, changing forums, and so forth, as they see fit.

6. Debrief the activity. The points to be stressed in debriefing vary according to teaching aims and the way the simulation/game is played out. However, the following subjects can invariably be discussed:

Team Negotiation:
Intrateam complexity

• Did team members share information among themselves? Ask whether they would have done anything differently.

• Did team members assume they shared the same interests? Ask whether they would have done anything differently to verify this.

• Do participants think their initial team preparation was sufficient? Ask whether they would have done anything differently.

- Were there obvious differences of opinion or approach between team members?

- Did one team notice differences of opinion or approach between members of the opposite team? How did this affect their behavior and choice of tactics?

Communication

- Who did the talking on each team? Was this predecided, or did it happen naturally? Ask whether they would have done anything differently.

- Did multiple conversations occur simultaneously? If so, what effects did they have?

- How did the status of team members (as defined in roles and as defined by participants' natural interactions) affect communication? What can be learned from this?

- How did time constraints affect the negotiation process? Ask whether they would have done anything differently.

Multiple Issues:

- How much of their information did parties share? Was this intentional (e.g., agreed to in intrateam discussions)? Ask whether they would have done anything differently.

- Were some issues not discussed at all? How might that affect future negotiations between the same parties?

- How did the multi-issue nature of the negotiations affect the different stages of the process: the initial or learning stage, the options stage, and so on?

- How was resolution approached? Did parties seek to solve each issue separately, or did they choose logrolling and packaging? What are the implications of each technique?

Variations
1. If there are more than four participants, several groups can run simultaneously. If there are "spare" participants without roles, they can be designated observers or potential mediators (see below) or assigned ad hoc roles. For example, a participant might be designated a negotiation consultant brought in by one of the parties. His or her employing team decides how to brief the consultant for the upcoming meeting; you can instruct him or her to use the fly-on-the-wall technique, silently observing the meeting and conveying his or her input to the team through notes or caucusing. This introduces participants to a new way of utilizing their negotiation skills, as well as making the intrateam dynamics even more complex.

2. The simulation/game can be structured in such a way that parties meet and discuss the issues for a limited period of time (90–120 minutes). If negotiations are unsuccessful, they can agree on a

future meeting. During the waiting period, a mediator can be appointed (someone who either observed the first meeting or was absent), who can offer his or her services to the parties. This allows participants to observe and compare unmediated and mediated negotiations. A mediator can also be introduced at the beginning of the scenario, for example, as a representative of the state's Local Governance Overview Committee.

3. Depending on teaching aims, different time limits can be imposed on the meetings. It can also be conducted over two separate meetings of 90–120 minutes each.

4. After the meetings, allow parties (or mediators) to send draft agreements to one another by email, until an agreed text is reached. This can be used to show the importance of small details, and the complexities added to a situation by involving different forms of communication.

INSTRUCTIONS FOR THE MAYOR OF GORDI   FORM A

Gordi is a small town of about 30,000 inhabitants. Most of its population is employed locally, in the town's commercial center, at the various small industries in the industrial zone, and at the Multi-Plast factory at the edge of town.

Being mayor is not easy. Sometimes you feel like a juggler trying to keep five balls in the air at once. The most recent example is the issue of the Multi-Plast factory.

Multi-Plast, Inc. is a company specializing in the innovation, design, and manufacture of products made from plastic. Its main asset is the Gordi factory, in which the company manufactures a line of products ranging from toys and lawn furniture to computer casings and automobile parts. The factory complex also holds the company's research and development division, its laboratories, and testing areas. You know that Multi-Plast is a successful company, marketing at the national and international level. The plant has been in Gordi for over five years, having been induced to relocate here by the previous mayor, whose post you inherited.

Although you have nothing against the plant and its manager—and indeed, you see them as an important part of the local economy—recently you have been under pressure from different directions, leading you to change your previous policy toward the plant.

This year's budget did not take into account the fire that damaged many buildings downtown, nor the local safety inspection of the town's football field, which shut down the stadium until all the seating facilities were replaced. The town is, quite simply, U.S. $2,000,000 short of its needs and you are looking for ways to make that up. You considered raising municipal taxes in general, but your political advisors told you you would be looking for a new job if you did. Next you looked at raising taxes on all businesses, but this would be a death warrant for some of the smaller businesses, and they are all owned and staffed by voters.

Different pressure groups have been calling for action against the Multi-Plast factory. Most vocal is the town's small but rapidly growing environmental group, who is sure that the factory is polluting the town's air and water. Another group is the local Commercial Association; the feeling is that the plant imports most of its needs from outside the area, instead of buying from local merchants. You feel you need to show some action on your part to placate these groups.

All these circumstances combined make the idea of raising the factory's municipal taxes appealing. You could alleviate a good portion of the budget pressure simply by doubling Multi-Plast's taxes from U.S. $1 million a year to U.S. $2 million, as well as placating the pressure groups by pointing out how profitable the plant is to the town. You also figure that Multi-Plast, as opposed to other local factories, can afford to pay higher taxes. You will try to cut city spending and enforce strict tax collection to make up as much of the deficit as you can.

The municipal elections will take place in one month, and time is of the essence. You know that your opponent will soon begin criticizing your financial management of the town, and you have to be able to point to some tangible success.

You can download this handout to your hard drive from the accompanying CD-ROM. The document can then be opened and printed.

Last week, you proposed to the city council that a special municipal tax be levied from "industries residing outside the town's designated industrial zones" at a rate double that paid by those in the industrial zone. Multi-Plast, in effect, would be the only business affected. You expect the proposal to be ratified by next week.

It came as no surprise, last week, when your advisor on community and town development received a call from the factory's general manager, asking for a meeting. You invited him to a meeting at your office at town hall.

You can download this handout to your hard drive from the accompanying CD-ROM. The document can then be opened and printed.

INSTRUCTIONS FOR THE TOWN DEVELOPMENT ADVISOR OF GORDI

Gordi is a small town of about 30,000 inhabitants. Most of its population is employed locally, in the town's commercial center, at the various small industries in the industrial zone, and at the Multi-Plast factory at the edge of town.

You are the mayor's advisor on issues related to community and town development. The post covers a wide range of topics, including sports, culture, environment, and local business. The job is not easy; sometimes you feel like a juggler trying to keep five balls in the air at once. The most recent example is the issue of the Multi-Plast factory.

Multi-Plast, Inc. is a company specializing in the innovation, design, and manufacture of products made from plastic. Its main asset is the Gordi factory, in which the company manufactures a line of products ranging from toys and lawn furniture to computer casings and automobile parts. The factory complex also holds the company's research and development division, its laboratories, and testing areas. You know that Multi-Plast is a successful company, marketing at the national and international level. The plant has been in Gordi for over five years now, having been induced to relocate here by the previous mayor, who also gave you your job. You remember listening to the previous mayor promising the world to Multi-Plast if they moved to Gordi, and with good reason: the potential kick to Gordi's sleepy local economy.

Recently the present mayor has been under pressure from different directions, leading him to change his previous policy toward the plant. This year's budget did not take into account the fire that damaged many buildings downtown or the local safety inspection of the town's football field, which shut down the stadium until all the seating facilities were replaced. The town is, quite simply, U.S. $2,000,000 short, and he is looking for ways to make that up. For various political reasons, he does not want to raise municipal taxes in general, but still needs to come up with the money.

Different pressure groups have been calling for action against the Multi-Plast factory. Most vocal is the town's small but rapidly growing environmental group, who is sure that the factory is polluting the town's air and water. Another group is the local Commercial Association; the feeling is that the plant imports most of its needs from outside the area, instead of buying from local merchants. As the town's point of contact on these issues, you are in close contact with both these groups. You feel the environmentalists, just starting out, lashed out at the closest target of opportunity. Although Multi-Plast is certainly a potential polluter, no factual basis has been laid to show this is so. The local business owners certainly have a point; trucks filled with everything from raw materials for the factory to coffee grounds for the cafeteria roll in every day from different parts of the country. Surely the company could do some of its shopping closer to home.

The municipal elections are to be held in one month, and you know the mayor is concerned for his job. You are not a political appointee or a political advisor, and you only have the town's best interests in mind. You would like to see this as the guiding principle of resolving the Multi-Plast issue, but are not sure the mayor will pay more than lip service to the town's good, preferring his personal political needs.

You can download this handout to your hard drive from the accompanying CD-ROM. The document can then be opened and printed.

The mayor thinks he can hit several birds with one stone simply by doubling Multi-Plast's taxes from U.S. $1 million a year to U.S. $2 million. This would alleviate the budget pressure and enable him to placate the local pressure groups by pointing out how profitable the plant is to the town. He also figures that Multi-Plast, as opposed to other local factories, can afford to pay higher taxes. He expects his special municipal tax law, which, in effect, affects only Multi-Plast, to pass next week.

All things taken into consideration, you are not so sure that this is a good idea, and you definitely think that giving Multi-Plast a legislative ultimatum is no way to foster good relations with the town's largest employer. You think he might not have considered what he would do if Multi-Plast packed up and left town. You asked a friend in the municipal tax office to tip off Multi-Plast's general manager. It came as no surprise, therefore, to receive a call from the general manager, asking to arrange a meeting with the mayor. You invited him to a meeting at the mayor's office at Town Hall.

You can download this handout to your hard drive from the accompanying CD-ROM. The document can then be opened and printed.

INSTRUCTIONS FOR THE GENERAL MANAGER OF MULTI-PLAST, INC.'S GORDI FACTORY

Multi-Plast, Inc. is a company specializing in the innovation, design, and manufacture of products made from plastic. Its main asset is the Gordi factory, in which the company manufactures a line of products ranging from toys and lawn furniture to computer casings and automobile parts. The company's motto, "If it's plastic, we make it," reflects the company's diverse range of products as well as the unique effort to design multifunctional production lines and machinery in ways that allow them to shift quickly from one product to another without wasting time, effort, and materials. The factory complex also holds the company's research and development division, its laboratories, and testing areas. The R&D department deals with designing new products as well as exploring possibilities for new "green" (biodegradable and environment-friendly) plastics and plastic substitutes.

You are the factory's general manager, and your job is to make sure everything gets done efficiently and profitably. Recent developments, however, have thrown you into a spin. Last week you received a call from the head of Gordi's municipal tax office, to tip you off on a decision by the mayor to double the plant's municipal taxes from U.S. $1,000,000 to U.S. $2,000,000.

Gordi is a small town of about 30,000 inhabitants. Most of its population is employed locally, in the town's commercial center, at the various small industries in the industrial zone, and at the Multi-Plast factory at the edge of town.

You cannot help feeling angry. You have met the mayor a few times and did not expect this. The factory has been located in Gordi for five years and is a major part of local commerce. Induced to come here by the previous mayor's promises of preferential treatment, the factory employs hundreds of workers from Gordi, estimated at 15 to 20 percent of Gordi's total workforce. Many company employees relocated with the plant when it moved, and have rented or purchased houses in the area. The plant has put the town on the map, and recently three conferences focusing on environment-friendly plastics have been hosted in the town, thanks to your factory. The direct municipal taxes you pay are really only a small part of the effect the plant has on the local economy.

As far as you were able to find out, you are the only business being targeted for a tax raise, and feel that the mayor is out on an unfair fishing expedition. The town has had a rough year financially, but that does not give him the right to reach into your pocket.

Although the plant could pay a bit more taxes without feeling a serious bite—perhaps as much as U.S. $250,000$–300,000—any more would threaten profitability. You are also worried about the precedent this might set.

You can always move the plant to a cheaper area, perhaps saving on taxes and even on rent. This would entail the costs of factory downtime and of moving facilities, production lines, and personnel. It would also mean giving up your investment in building ties with local business owners, suppliers, and interest groups, and hurting your local employees. You personally have put a lot into building the factory in Gordi and tying it into the local infrastructure and community, and would hate to see that go to waste. It goes without saying that you are also personally invested in

---

You can download this handout to your hard drive from the accompanying CD-ROM. The document can then be opened and printed.

INSTRUCTIONS FOR THE GENERAL
MANAGER OF MULTI-PLAST, INC.'S
GORDI FACTORY (CONT.)

FORM C

Gordi: You bought a beautiful house in a quiet neighborhood about three years ago, your spouse owns a bookshop in the town center, and your children attend the local elementary school.

You know from your experience that such matters are always negotiable and that proper pressure put on the mayor (this is an election year ...) might cause him to cancel the tax raise or at least lessen it. You immediately called the mayor's office and asked to meet him, and his advisor set an appointment for you at town hall. You called the company's head office and spoke to the head of the board of directors, briefing him on the situation. You asked him to come out and give you a hand with the developing situation, hoping the additional clout he would add might have some effect on the mayor.

You can download this handout to your hard drive from the accompanying CD-ROM. The document can then be opened and printed.

INSTRUCTIONS FOR THE HEAD DIRECTOR OF MULTI-PLAST, INC.

Multi-Plast, Inc. is a company specializing in the innovation, design, and manufacture of products made from plastic. Its main asset is the Gordi factory, in which the company manufactures a line of products ranging from toys and lawn furniture to computer casings and automobile parts. The company's motto, "If it's plastic, we make it," reflects the company's diverse range of products as well as the unique effort to design multifunctional production lines and machinery in ways that allow them to shift quickly from one product to another without wasting time, effort, and materials. The factory complex also holds the company's research and development division, its laboratories, and testing areas. The R&D department deals with designing new products as well as exploring possibilities for new "green" (biodegradable and environment-friendly) plastics and plastic substitutes. The company's management, marketing, customer-service, and administrative units are located at the company's head office in another part of the country.

You head the board of directors of Multi-Plast, charged with setting company policy, overseeing the profit margin, and protecting the interests of the company's shareholders. With a company market value at U.S. $50,000,000, this is quite a task, and you are well compensated for your success.

Last week you received a call from the factory's general manager, asking you to give him a hand with a developing situation. It seems the town of Gordi has decided to target the plant, the biggest in the area, and double the municipal taxes paid by the plant, from U.S. $1,000,000 a year to U.S. $2,000,000.

Instead of getting angry, you focus on what you know. Although the plant could pay a bit more taxes without feeling a serious bite—perhaps as much as U.S. $250,000–$300,000, but any more would threaten profitability. This is not your first experience with small town greediness, and you also take into account that paying the elevated rate could lead the town to ask for more.

You could always move the plant. Your shareholders do not care where the plant is, as long as it shows a profit. You are sure you can find a locality where taxes would remain at the U.S. $1,000,000 level, and perhaps even be less. On the other hand, this would require moving facilities, production lines, and personnel. It is hard to estimate the cost of relocation, of the factory downtime, and of the cost of hiring and training new workers, but you know it might reach U.S. $3,000,000, even if the plant were relocated to a relatively close area. Still, moving is a definite possibility; you do not feel connected to Gordi in any binding way.

Another possibility is challenging the new tax regulations in court, claiming that it was meant to target you specifically and not factories and businesses in the area in general. However, the outcome of such cases is always unclear, and if the municipality manages to convince the court to shut down production until the case is settled, you would pay a big price.

Another concern is that agreeing to an arbitrary tax raise might set a trend, encouraging the present and future city council to solve whatever budgetary difficulty they might encounter at your expense.

You know from your experience that such matters are always negotiable and that proper pressure put on the mayor might cause him to cancel the tax raise, or at least lessen it. You can only guess what the effect on the city would be if the plant were to pack up and leave, and decide to let him sweat that question out a bit. When in Gordi, you will meet with the factory manager, who knows more about local conditions, and together you will meet with the mayor.

TEAM-BASED PRISONER'S DILEMMA: AN ONLINE CONFLICT RESOLUTION EXERCISE

Albert Widman

Albert Widman, PhD, *is the chair of the Department of Management at Berkeley College's New York City campus. His doctorate was awarded by Pace University in the fields of management and finance. He was the chief operating officer/chief financial officer of a major charitable corporation prior to entering academia. Prior work experience includes executive positions with Haagen-Dazs, Manpower Demonstration Research Corporation, and the Mayor's Office of the City of Syracuse.*

Contact Information:
Berkeley College
3 East 43 Street
New York, NY 10017
718.812.5669 (cell)
adw@berkeleycollege.edu or
DrAlbertWidman@yahoo.com

Overview   The Prisoner's Dilemma game has been played face-to-face and through human-computer iteration for decades. The premise of the game is the opportunity for two prisoners to "rat out" the other in exchange for a lighter sentence. The twist is that players operate in an environment of uncertainty and mistrust, and the game has strong conflict-resolution lessons.

Professor James Owens of American University transformed the game into a fun, team-based exercise called The Blue-Green Game. It enables groups of people to plot strategy and play Prisoner's Dilemma.

Recently, more and more people became involved in distance learning education and online training activities. One of the most popular platforms used is the Blackboard system (*www.blackboard.com*), which is widely used in collegiate, governmental, corporate, and international settings. The following instructions show you how to transform a team-based Prisoner's Dilemma exercise like The Blue-Green Game into a conflict exercise that can be played online using the Blackboard system over a period of five days. This version is known as The Black-Red Game.

Suggested Time

30 minutes	On day one, participants read through an instruction sheet, read an email appointing a group leader, and study a scoring chart.
15–20 minutes daily	For the next four consecutive days, each participant must log on to discuss strategy.
20 minutes daily	One person in each group, designated as the team leader, has increased responsibilities, so his or her time requirement on each of the four days expands by an additional 20 minutes.
30 minutes–1 hour	On the final day of the exercise, each member must allocate time to read the debrief and to share reactions.

Note: The trainer for the exercise needs to spend several hours initially setting up the game and approximately one hour per day of game play. The trainer should also participate in the debrief discussion, which might require several separate log-in sessions of 15 to 20 minutes each on the final day.

Materials Needed

✓ Game Instructions in PowerPoint Format (Form A)

✓ Sample Debrief (Form B)

Procedure

1. Prepare the system by forming multiple teams (an even number of teams) of three to six people per team. Using the Group Discussion Board function of Blackboard (located in Communication Group Pages), establish the teams and designate the members of each team. Remember to add yourself as a member of each team so that you can observe the process!

2. Send each participant an email assigning him or her to one of the teams and designating a team leader for each group. Use identifiers such as Team A1, Team B1, Team A2, Team B2, and so forth.

3. In that email, direct the participants to the Course Documents section of Blackboard to download and watch a PowerPoint presentation that presents the rules of the game. (The author's personal preference is to use Camtasia or Captivate software to present the PowerPoint material as an animated voice annotated file, but this is not necessary and can introduce technical problems in some environments. Form A presents screenshots of the presentation without supplemental voice annotation. It can be freely adapted for your use.)

4. By using the Group Discussion Board, each group can post their thoughts and plan strategy without fear that other groups can see what they are plotting. The team leaders should receive an email stating a particular time on each of four days that they are to email you with a group decision about whether to give their corresponding group a black or a red card.

5. Resist the impulse to enter the discussion or respond to emails reporting confusion about which card to give the other group and how to make that decision. Just refer participants to the instructions and scoring. As a trainer, withholding comment might be stressful for you! Be assured that, after the first one or two rounds, the game becomes increasingly clear to participants and the issues are self-resolved by each team.

6. After groups doing business contact you with their decision, enter the Group Discussion Board to post the results and scoring for their transactions. Also present a quick summary of how the other groups' transactions were concluded and the cumulative score to that point for each group. Each group must have the opportunity to measure their results against the other groups.

7. The groups are not allowed to interact with each other except for an opportunity to pass an email message once after round three, if desired. Send the groups an email informing them of this procedure: Their "negotiation email message" should come to you, and you forward it to the "opposing" team members for a possible response. It is not uncommon for the other group to choose not to respond, and, if that occurs, you should inform the initiating group of their decision.

8. At the conclusion of the final day's transaction, debrief players through a post in the Course Documents section. That debrief should incorporate the actual discussion held by players during the exercise. Follow up with a group discussion using the general Blackboard Discussion Board so that everyone can participate. Form B presents a sample debrief the author used with one group of players.

To Begin....

- ◆ At this point, you have received an email from me appointing you to a team. One of you has been designated as Team Leader for this task.

- ◆ It is the job of the Team Leader to use the GROUP discussion board (not the regular Main discussion board) to discuss with the team about whether to submit a black or a red card during each of the four cycles of the game.

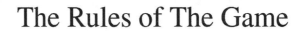

The Rules of The Game

- ◆ I will not take any questions, so no side can claim that the group they conduct business with had an unfair advantage over them.

You can download this handout to your hard drive from the accompanying CD-ROM. The document can then be opened and printed.

Learn the rules

Four groups have been established. They will engage in transactions with each other. To make the game more realistic, we will consider them corporate divisions where group A1 always does business with group B1, group A2 always does business with group B2, etc.

◆ A transaction occurs when one group asks me to pass either a black or a red card to the other group.

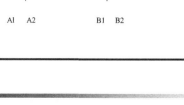

Learn The Rules

◆ All transactions go through me. Neither group knows what color card they will be getting until the exchange is actually made.

◆ The groups are not permitted to interact with each other with one exception described later.

◆ Scoring is done in accordance with the following schedule.

You can download this handout to your hard drive from the accompanying CD-ROM. The document can then be opened and printed.

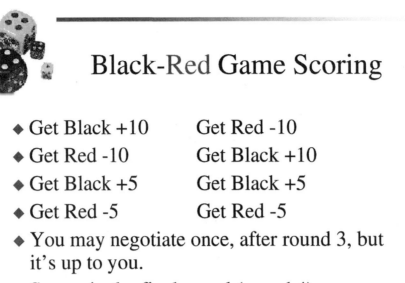

Black-Red Game Scoring

- Get Black +10   Get Red -10
- Get Red -10   Get Black +10
- Get Black +5   Get Black +5
- Get Red -5   Get Red -5
- You may negotiate once, after round 3, but it's up to you.
- Scores in the final round (round 4) are doubled.

Your Resources and Tasks

- You may use the Group Discussion Board to plot strategy with your group members.
- By 9 pm on each of the next four days, your Team Leader is responsible for emailing me with the group decision on whether to give a Black or Red card. Results of the transaction will be posted before 9 am the following morning.

The Black-Red Game game is based on a classic exercise called Prisoner's Dilemma that traces its roots back over 50 years.

So what happened, which group won, and what did it mean?

Well, first I need to tell you that none of you won. Why? Because the organization chart shows that you are all part of the same corporation, just different divisions, so the business goal should have been having each group achieve a positive number. The only way to do that would be by continually giving black cards to ensure everyone's success.

That is often an accurate depiction of business. Don't you think divisions and people within the same company compete with each other? Doesn't one salesperson try to grab business away from another to get the commission? Doesn't Primerica sometimes compete with Smith Barney for business, even though they're both owned by Citigroup?

Back to conflict resolution. The exercise shows that people try to build trust in two primary ways. One is through verbal means and the other is by action.

Verbal promises are weak. Why? Because people lie and communications are imprecise, particularly when they are limited to structured negotiations. I read in some of your group discussions statements like, "Let's promise them a black card and then hit them with a red" or "Let's double-cross them in the last round when the points are doubled." But at least some communications are often better than none. Some of the groups became upset when they sent over a negotiation statement and the other group didn't respond.

Behavior is a better predictor of trust. If someone consistently acts in a certain way, the odds are better that he or she will continue to do so. When there was one second left on the clock and the Chicago Bulls had the ball, they wanted Michael Jordan to take the shot because his past behavior indicated that there was a good chance he would make it.

Companies and specific managers follow certain patterns. Some are known for innovation, others for design, still others for execution. This might make them more consistent business partners because their behavior is more predictable.

So how might you deal with conflict?

There are six main strategies:

1. *Compromise:* You take a little bit less than you asked for and I'll do the same thing. Compromise in this game meant willing to gain only five points rather than delivering cards that might bring you 10.

2. *Bargaining:* We can't seem to reach agreement with the compromises we're suggesting, so you bring an outside item into the negotiation. You want to fly Jet Blue for $99 to California but the fare is $129 and Jet Blue isn't willing to compromise. Suddenly the clerk says, "It's still $129 but we'll enroll you in our frequent flyer program so you'll earn miles toward a future flight." That outside item works for you and you book the flight.

---

3. *Collaboration:* You decide to work together with the other organization. Hewlett Packard, rather than spend millions on a risky venture to make its own music player, agrees to resell the Apple iPod. This was a winning strategy in The Black-Red game.

4. *Fight:* We are going to defend this product at any cost. "We're Sony, we're known for televisions. We must be in the flat screen market."

5. *Flee:* In this model a heavy competitor enters the business and you say, "Cash me out...I'm gone."

6. *Submit:* In this model, a heavy competitor enters the business and you say, "Maybe I can hang on for a while to get rid of my inventory." So you stop advertising, you start watching the pennies, and you pray regularly that someone calls you with a buyout offer.

Aha! Now you get it! Good work.

You can download this handout to your hard drive from the accompanying CD-ROM. The document can then be opened and printed.

OVERCOMING RESISTANCE TO CHANGE: AN EXPERIENTIAL EXERCISE

Jean Barbazette

Jean Barbazette *is the president of The Training Clinic, a training and consulting firm she founded in 1977. Her company focuses on training trainers throughout the United States for major profit, nonprofit, and government organizations. The Training Clinic has three international licensees in the Netherlands, Hungary, and Colombia. Her books include* **Successful New Employee Orientation, 2nd ed.** *(Jossey-Bass/Pfeiffer, 2001);* **The Trainer's Support Handbook** *(McGraw-Hill, 2001);* **Instant Case Studies** *(Pfeiffer, 2003);* **The Trainer's Journey to Competence** *(Pfeiffer, 2005);* **Training Needs Assessment** *(Pfeiffer, 2006); and* **The Art of Great Training Delivery** *(Pfeiffer, 2006). She is a frequent contributor to the* **Sourcebooks.**

Contact Information:
The Training Clinic
645 Seabreeze Drive
Seal Beach, CA 90740
800.937.4698 or 562.430.2484
jean@thetrainingclinic.com
www.thetrainingclinic.com

Overview Often training consultants are asked to implement changes in company policies and procedures. As change agents, training consultants sometimes find themselves the target of hostile reaction. In such cases, they can help employees acknowledge and accept their level of discomfort and anxiety. This activity can help participants work through a "forced" change and identify their own level of resistance. If you acknowledge the resistance, your participants might be more open to new policies and might see training as a means to make a change go more smoothly for themselves. Training consultants can also help managers who act as change agents by making them aware of their employees' anxiety. Managers can empathize better with changes that employees are forced to make.

Suggested Time 45–60 minutes

Materials Needed None

Procedure

1. Ask all participants to stand up and face a partner. If there is an uneven number of trainees, ask three people to form a triad, or you can be someone's partner.

2. Tell partners that they have 60 seconds to memorize every aspect of their partner's appearance. Later they will be asked to make a few small changes, and they will have to identify what's different. (Sixty seconds is a long time to stare at another person. Some will become uncomfortable, but do *not* cut short the time.)

3. Ask the partners to turn their backs to each other and make five changes in their physical appearance. They can be very small or obvious ones. Allow enough time for everyone to make the changes.

4. Before you tell the partners to face each other, explain:

   When I indicate, both of you turn around and each take a turn at identifying the changes your partner has made. Your partner will tell you when you are correct but will not reveal the changes you miss.

   Have partners turn around and begin. After the changes are guessed, tell them *not* to put themselves back to the way they were before.

5. After they have had enough time to guess each other's changes, tell them to turn their backs to each other again, *keeping all the changes they have already made.* Now ask them to make 10 changes from the way they appear right now. (*Hint:* They can put five back and think of five new changes. Do not give participants this hint unless they become very resistant.) It is possible to do this part of the activity without stripping! Before they turn around again, they may not tell a change their partner is unable to guess. Have them turn around.

6. After each partner has had time to guess the changes, tell them it is OK to reveal any change the partner was unable to identify. Thank them for their cooperation and ask them to return to their seats. People automatically begin to put themselves back together. Rarely do they ask permission to do so.

7. Discuss these questions:

   - How did it feel to look so closely at another person for 60 seconds? Elicit several responses. Most will say awkward, uncomfortable, embarrassed, intrusive, and so forth. After they identify these feelings, point out that, when changes are made, often it is very uncomfortable for us (or higher management) to look closely at what we have, before a change is made.

   - Was it easier for you to make five or 10 changes? Why? Allow each option to express a rationale. If they say the five changes are easier to make, it is usually because there are fewer changes to make. When it comes to making 10, many people are asked to risk beyond their level of comfort. I have even had participants refuse to make the 10 changes and withdraw from the activity at this point.

- If the 10 changes were easier to make, it is usually because they were most resistant to making any change at first. After the first change is made, and they see others make similar or minor changes, it becomes easy to make more changes. For some, it is a real challenge and they enjoy trying to hide minute changes from their partner.

- How did you feel when your partner guessed or did not guess your changes? Often we are disappointed if no one notices a change that we have struggled to accomplish. That's also true at work. If you were disappointed that your partner was so successful at identifying all the changes rather than glad for his or her success, there is a message for you in that reaction.

- How did it feel after you had made your 10 changes and then turned around? Most of us feel pretty foolish and awkward. We are often laughing at our appearance and that of others as a way of covering up the embarrassment.

- What did you do at the end of the activity while you were sitting down? Did you put yourself back together? Didn't it feel much more comfortable than when you had just made all 10 changes? When we are asked to make changes, often we feel awkward about doing something that is unfamiliar. We even sometimes deliberately do something the wrong way, go back to the old way, and refuse to do it the new way. We do so because we were comfortable with the status quo.

- For some participants, this is not a low-risk activity. They might refuse to participate in the activity because they will not allow others to see them in an "undignified" appearance. They may pass it off as just a game. Encourage reluctant participants to identify the cause of resistance in themselves as part of the debrief.

8. Ask the participants to identify the difference between ineffective and successful change:

Ineffective change: Change takes place with resistance and whining.

Successful change: Change takes place willingly.

Ask the group to identify what can be done to help make change take place.

9. End with the following words:

If you are being asked to make a change, I want you to know that I recognize your discomfort (anger) at being forced to go through this change. I realize that you would be much more comfortable the way it used to be. However, the change is real, the change is here, and it's not going to be the old way any longer. My role is to try to help you feel more comfortable with the new way of doing things.

If you are a manager asking others to make a change, realize that your employees will feel uncomfortable with change and want to go back to the old way (just as you put yourself back together after the 10 changes). It is up to *you* to help your employees reach a new comfort level to reduce the resistance to the changes. Unless you make them feel comfortable, they'll go right back to the old way or try to defeat the new way.

INTRODUCING TEAM MEMBERS: THE STRENGTH AND PASSION INTERVIEW

Allen Liff

Allen Liff *is the founder of Ronin Marketing and has over 20 years' experience in facilitation and training. He has coauthored a book of strategic thinking exercises, worked as community organizer, and developed training materials (including creating a comic book!) to help prevent migrant farm children from being exposed to pesticides. Allen received training from the Innovation University, a program in which visiting leading-edge, innovative companies learn firsthand how to apply innovation. He is also a certified facilitator with Bottom Line Innovation® Associates, one of the oldest and most respected innovation consulting firms in the country.*

Contact Information:
Ronin Marketing
2901 18th Street NW #612
Washington, DC 20009
202.232.1121
Roninmktg@aol.com
www.Roninmarketing.com

Overview This is a fun and useful warm-up to help introduce team members to each other. It helps to focus people on the strengths and passions they bring to the team's project. The goal is to help team members learn about the skills, experiences, and passions of their fellow team members. The drawing exercise, using one's opposite hand, helps people relax and get into playful mood.

Suggested Time 20–60 minutes, depending on the size of the group

Materials Needed ✓ Masking tape (to post drawings on the wall).
✓ Interview Worksheet (Form A)
✓ Instructions: The Strength and Passion Interview (Form B)
✓ Instructions: Our Shared Strengths and Passions (Form C)
✓ Strengths and Passions Worksheet (Form D)

Procedure

1. Pass out Forms A and B. Explain the process of the interview.

2. Ask participants to pair up. If there is an odd number, one group can have three people.

3. Tell pairs that they have 10 minutes to complete the drawing and interviewing process. Each interview should take about five minutes. (After five minutes, remind the group it is time to switch.)

4. When the interviews are complete, post the drawing on the wall to create a fun gallery of team members.

5. Gather the participants around the gallery. Then ask each person to introduce his or her partner.

6. Break up into small groups of four to six people. Distribute Forms C and D to each group. Explain the activity.

7. Give the groups about 10 minutes to complete their work.

8. When the groups have finished, add the new drawings to the gallery on the wall.

9. Gather the participants around the gallery. Then ask each group to explain their drawing and the shared strengths and passions.

10. Invite participants to share their reactions to the overall activity.

INTERVIEW WORKSHEET

FORM A

- Your assignment is to learn about the strengths and passions of your partner.

- Write in the name of your partner on Form B.

- Begin in a fun and unusual way. Using your opposite hand (i.e., right-handers use your left hand, left-handers use your right hand), draw a picture of your partner inside the box. Don't worry, everyone's drawing will be equally amusing!

- Now switch back to your normal hand.

- Ask your partner what his or her work-related passions might be. What brings satisfaction? What types of tasks or projects are motivating? What is it about this project that he or she finds exciting? Write these down in the left-hand column on Form B.

- Now ask your partner about his or her strengths. What skills and experiences does this person bring to the project? Write these down in the right-hand column on Form B.

You can download this handout to your hard drive from the accompanying CD-ROM. The document can then be opened and printed.

INSTRUCTIONS: THE STRENGTH AND PASSION INTERVIEW

_____

NAME

WORK-RELATED PASSIONS

STRENGTHS

You can download this handout to your hard drive from the accompanying CD-ROM. The document can then be opened and printed.

INSTRUCTIONS: OUR SHARED STRENGTHS AND PASSIONS

- Your assignment is to answer the questions:

  Among all the participants here today, what sets of strengths and passions do we share?

  As a large group, what are we best at?

  What do we care the most about?

- Begin by identifying the top two or three shared passions. Write those in the left-hand column on Form D.

- Next, identify the top two or three shared strengths. Write those in the right-hand column on Form D.

- Then imagine what type of person or animal (real or fictional) has those strengths and passions.

- Give that person or animal a name.

- Have a member of your group draw a picture of that person or animal. (*Note:* This time you can use the hand you normally write and draw with.)

STRENGTHS AND PASSIONS WORKSHEET   FORM D

_____

NAME

OUR SHARED PASSIONS

OUR SHARED STRENGTHS

You can download this handout to your hard drive from the accompanying CD-ROM. The document can then be opened and printed.

CONNECTIONS AND TENSIONS: EXPLORING PROJECT ISSUES

Becky Saeger and Chris Saeger

Becky *and* **Chris Saeger** *have been creating simulations and interactive learning experiences since 1985. Their work has won awards from ASTD, Lakewood Publications, and the International Society for Performance Improvement— Potomac Chapter. They are regular presenters at ISPI, the North American Simulation and Gaming Association, and other conferences. They improve performance through learning in nonprofit, manufacturing, information technology, and health care organizations. Becky and Chris are frequent contributors to the* ***Sourcebooks***.

Contact Information:
4231 Peekskill Lane
Fairfax, VA 22033
703.322.9592
info@learninglandscapes.com

Overview   Sometimes in a planning meeting, we say these things:

- What are the critical success factors for our project?
- What values and principles do we agree to in working together?
- What are the conditions for success in this project?

Then, we make a list, prioritize it somehow, and move on. This approach results in what some systems thinkers call "laundry-list thinking." The list has interdependent variables and a simple priority order will not do.

Connections and Tensions is a way to explore issues from a more holistic perspective and generate a deeper discussion about the planning topic.

Suggested Time: 60–90 minutes

Materials Needed   ✓ Flip chart for recording ideas
✓ A large spool of ribbon, string, or yarn
✓ Large name tags

Procedure

1. Say to the group:

   What are the top three conditions for success in this project? Please jot them down on a piece of paper.

   One person might write, for example, top management support, adequate resources, and clear expectations.

2. On newsprint, make a composite list of all the conditions written down by participants individually. To accomplish this, go around the group and invite each participant to share one item not previously stated by someone else. Continue the process until all ideas are recorded.

3. Ask each person to go to the newsprint and select a success condition and create a name tag with the one chosen. (Only one person may select any success condition. Not all items must be selected.)

4. Give this instruction:

   Become the success condition that you selected and go around the room and talk to the other conditions. See how you relate to one another. Does one idea form the foundation for the other?

   For example, a person with *top management support* might talk with someone with *open communication* and agree that open communication is needed to build management support.

5. Stop the conversations after people have had the opportunity to interact with all or most of the participants. Then say:

   I heard a lot of interesting discussions. Give me a short headline about the condition for success you represent and how you related it to other ideas.

6. Then ask the group to form into a loose circle and say:

   Let's build a web of all these relationships. Sounds to me like _____ comes first in your minds. [Insert the condition for success that seems to come first in the prior discussion, such as open communication.] Is that what I am hearing?

7. If the group agrees, unwind some ribbon from a spool and give the end of the ribbon to the person bearing the name tag of that success condition. Then, while holding on to the spool, say:

   From _____ [the condition just chosen], who should get the ribbon next, or how does it relate to others?

8. Pass the spool to the person representing the success condition chosen next. Continue the process of building a web by asking how ideas are related to one another. Continue moving the spool until all are connected. (Some ideas might be mentioned several times and that person ends up holding several loops of ribbon.)

9. Point to people who are holding several loops of ribbon and ask for thoughts from the group.

10. Then, ask:

What are some possible tensions among the ideas?

Someone might point out that *speed* and *quality* (two of the ideas mentioned) might be in tension. Ask for thoughts from the group about how to reconcile these ideas. For example, someone might say that *quality* can reduce the need for rework and actually improve *speed*. Then ask:

What would happen if an idea were missing?

Request that a person who represents one of the ideas with few wraps of ribbon to drop his or her ribbon, and then ask the group to step back to pick up the slack and tighten the web. Comment on how people have to pick up the slack for the project to be successful. Continue this process with ideas with fewer loops.

11. Then, ask a person representing one of the ideas with many loops to drop the ribbon. Continue that process until the web becomes too unstable to hold together. Comment on how these ideas seem to be higher leverage and that losing these ideas may cause the project to fail. Then ask everyone still holding on to the ribbon to drop it.

12. Debrief the exercise with questions such as:

- How did you experience the activity? How are you feeling?
- What did you observe during the activity?
- What is your view of the ideas you identified at the beginning?
- How can we use this in our teamwork?

13. Guide the group to the realization that they have a new view of the original list and have a new sense of which of the items might be a lever for producing results in several areas. They might also see where they need to explore some tension among the ideas. From dropping parts of the web, they now have the view that for the whole to succeed, all of the items must be attended to because none is operating in a vacuum.

14. Thank the group for their observations and being such great ideas. Throughout the rest of the meeting, the team refers to the leverage areas and looks for opportunities to reconcile potential tensions in the project.

PEOPLE ARE TALKING: A GAME FOR COLLABORATIVE LEARNING

Mark Casey, Patrick Lockett, and Shawn Redfern

Mark Casey *is a consultant with AARP, where he helps internal clients target performance solutions for their staff. He is an active presenter for both NASAGA and CBODN. He is currently developing a community of practice to discuss visual cues and interpretations in Web-based and virtual learning environments. Mark was a contributor to both* **2005 Sourcebooks**.

Contact Information:
AARP
601 East Street NW
Washington, DC 20049
202.434.3395
mcasey@aarp.org

Patrick Lockett *is an instructional designer at Kadix Systems LLC in Arlington, Virginia, where he develops multimedia language training for government clients. He has over eight years of experience as a training professional. He has designed and delivered training programs for national audiences at the American Dietetic Association's national headquarters in Chicago and the Red Cross national headquarters in Washington, D.C.*

Contact Information:
Kadix Systems
4245 N. Fairfax Drive
Suite 700
Arlington, VA 22203
703.236.3015
plockett@kadix.com

Shawn Redfern *is a learning program manager with The Nature Conservancy, Worldwide Office, where he develops and delivers online, self-study, and instructor-led training and performance improvement products for Conservancy staff. He specializes in the development of active learning exercises, such as interactive games and simulations that are engaging and fun and that improve performance.*

Contact Information:
The Nature Conservancy
Worldwide Office
4245 N. Fairfax Drive, Suite 100
Arlington, VA 22203
703.841.4252
sredfern@tnc.org

Overview   When employees come across a problem, many times they struggle to determine the best strategy or to identify whom they can speak to about the problem. People Are Talking is a game that enables employees to share success stories, lessons learned, and best practices in a collaborative environment.

The object of the game is to be the person who provides the best response to Problem Statement Cards and collects those that satisfy all the color categories associated with their Employee Role Card. The game uses Problem Statement Cards depicting blockades and obstacles that often interfere with their work. Game participants get the opportunity to create some of the Problem Statement Cards about daily office issues. The cards are collected and incorporated into game play. During the game, a player picks a Problem Statement Card and reads it aloud to the game table. Each player then has one minute to provide a solution to address the issue on the Problem Statement Card. Once each player has responded, the participant who read the card aloud awards it to the person he or she felt provided the best response.

Organizational development teams can also use People Are Talking as a tool for basic qualitative data collection to draw out issues that relate to departments, information systems, and administration.

Suggested Time   45–60 minutes, depending on the length of the debrief

Materials Needed   ✓ Sample Card Statements (Form A)
✓ Game Directions (Form B)
✓ One-minute egg timer (one for each team or table)
✓ Employee Role Cards (one set for each team or table)
✓ Deck of Generic and Blank Problem Statement Cards (one set for each team or table)

Procedure

Before the Activity Begins

1. Create a deck of Generic Problem Statement Cards and Blank Problem Statement Cards. This deck makes up the bulk of the required game materials and can be created using a printable, perforated business card stock product such as those made by Avery Inc. (http://www.avery.com). Each of the two problem card types is

color-coded and maps to an associated category. Problem Statement Cards (both Generic and Blank) are broken into six categories:

- Black: Information Technology
- White: Administrative/Paperwork
- Yellow: Communications
- Red: Resource/People Management
- Green: Office Culture
- Blue: Company Policies

Make up the game deck using three Generic Problem Statement Cards and five Blank Problem Statement Cards for each problem statement type. For example, create three Generic Communication Cards and five Blank Communications cards. This creates a deck of 48 cards for the game.

2. *Making Generic Problem Statement Cards:* These cards provide the player with a common issue associated with one of the six categories. See Form A for sample generic problem statements and Figure 1 for an example of a Problem Statement Card layout.

3. *Making Blank Problem Statement Cards:* These cards are similar to their Generic counterpart, but they provide a space for the player to enter a unique problem statement he or she has actually encountered (related to the category type). This statement should address an issue the participant was unable to resolve.

4. *Making Employee Role Cards:* Employee Role Cards are subdivided into five key staff roles, with each card displaying a nondescript silhouette on the front, and a corresponding job description containing the key knowledge, skills, and abilities typically associated with that role on the back (see Figure 2). In addition to the job description are five colored boxes. These boxes correlate to the types of activities and responsibilities making up the listed position type. Employee Role Cards can include:

- Program Analyst
- Office Administrator
- IT Support/Information Technology
- Middle Management
- Senior Director

Figure 1

> ■ **Culture**
>
> *Staff is reluctant to attend group meetings, stating that meetings are too long and often nothing gets accomplished anyway.*

Figure 2

> ■ **Program Analyst:**
> The company "worker bee," the PA is tasked with administering programs and is the direct link from the customer base to the main office.

When creating the Employee Role Cards, feel free to tailor the cards' titles and descriptions to roles that are relevant to your organization. For example, your company might not contain a Program Analyst, but utilize a Development Specialist, who performs a similar responsibility.

During the Activity

1. Table groups for this game consist of between four and six players. You can play the game with as little as one table group. If you have more than one table group, have one set of materials for each table. At the conclusion of the game, you can bring the entire room back together for the debrief.

2. Once the table groups have been set up, pass out the game materials. Assign one Employee Role Card to each participant. Separate the Blank Problem Statement Cards and divide them among the table group, giving approximately five to 10 minutes to fill them out. Inform participants that they can look at the Generic Problem Statement Cards for examples of what you are looking for.

   Note: An alternative is to fill out the blank cards ahead of time. This gives you time to print out the examples, providing anonymity for individuals who feel their card might be "recognized."

3. Once time is up, collect the Blank Problem Statement Cards and shuffle them back into the deck.

4. Review Form B with participants. Use the following guide to present the game rules:

   • *Start the game play:* Start with [*insert Employee Role*] and move clockwise around the table.

   • *Draw a Problem Statement Card:* At the beginning of your turn, draw a Problem Statement Card from the deck and read it aloud to the group.

   • *Turn over the timer and respond:* Starting with the player to the left of the person who drew the card, each individual turns over the one-minute timer and provides a personal best practice, lesson learned, or success story he or she utilized to resolve the problem on the card. Encourage responses that offer potential solutions ("I placed a basket next to the printer so that we could always keep a fresh supply of paper handy..."), rather than placing blame ("The printer is always out of paper, and I don't think I should have to chase some down"). Once time is up, the player must end the response and pass the timer to the next player.

   Note: Players can respond either as themselves or in the role listed on the card. Having participants respond in their role can allow individuals to be more open to viewing problems from multiple perspectives. You can also have players start the game responding as themselves, switching to their roles halfway through the game.

You can then use the debrief as an opportunity to discuss the differences in playing the game in both formats.

- *Award response:* Once all responses are completed, the player who drew the card awards the Problem Statement card to the best solution, providing a statement as to why he or she selected the solution.

- *Play continues:* The next player draws a card and play continues.

- *Winning the game:* The winner is the first player to obtain one each of their associated color type card.

- Check for any final questions or confusion about the game.

5. Once you have reviewed the game rules and answered any last-minute questions, begin the activity. During game play, capture any game process information or information related to the cards. Look for loaded cards and assess trends in the various table groups. Use this information to prepare a targeted debrief discussion.

6. Let participants know when about five minutes are left to the end of the session. Once the time is up, ask teams to finish playing their final card and identify a winner. If appropriate, award fabulous prizes to the individuals who won the game.

7. Once the game is complete, facilitate a discussion to bridge between the activity and the debrief.

- The sharing of success stories with other teams and groups provides a great way for employees to get acquainted with each other.

- Lessons learned and best practices gained during the activity provide the opportunity for participants to:
  - Develop empathy with other units.
  - Work to solve common problems collaboratively.
  - Develop a personalization of problems.
  - Gather stories that provide support and solutions for problem statements.
  - Communicate services their team or department can provide to the rest of the organization.

8. Lead a discussion about the general results from the game as well as participant reaction. Using the following questions, conduct a debrief:

- How do you think the game went? What interesting things happened during the game?

- What are the advantages or disadvantages of using self-created cards? How did you feel when your card was pulled? How would the game have been different if we had only Generic Problem Statement Cards?

- What dynamics, if any, did you notice developing during game play? How do these dynamics relate to dynamics present in a workplace or organization?

- What best practices or lessons learned came out of your game?

- [*If you had individuals answer in their roles ...*] What differences did you notice, if any, when participants answered in their assigned role? Did you find there was more learning when you wore your own hat or when you wore your assigned role hat?

9. Upon completion of the debrief, conclude the session by summarizing any key points that came up and by providing a participant evaluation form (if required). Upon completion of the activity, collect the Bank Problem Statement Cards for use in the development of future editions of the game.

Variations The game can be used as a data collection tool. Blank cards provide a good opportunity to do basic data collection on a variety of organizational issues. Multiple sessions with a variety of participants help you develop a large data pool.

SAMPLE CARD STATEMENTS

FORM A

Directions: *The following is a list of sample problem statements you can use when creating your Generic Problem Statement Cards. We suggest you create your cards using a printable, perforated business card stock product, such as those made by Avery (http://www.avery.com).*

CULTURE

1. Key project partners from inside the company refuse to attend joint staff meetings, stating they see little or no relevance to their jobs.

2. There is a persistent "us versus them" attitude between the field sites and national office staff.

3. You hear through the grapevine that one of the "in" departments received incentive bonuses and remote control cars as a reward for completing a project—coincidently, the same project you worked on.

INFORMATION TECHNOLOGY

1. Laptops keep disappearing.

2. The shared public drive is replete with information that is both outdated and obsolete, making it difficult to navigate and locate necessary files.

3. The Helpdesk is consistently backlogged with requests for assistance.

PEOPLE MANAGEMENT

1. You have a major milestone for your project due Friday. A key developer works a flextime schedule and is not scheduled to be in the office. Worse yet, he has already put in over a hundred hours in the past two weeks.

2. Everybody on the team uses shared calendar software, like Outlook, to schedule meetings and appointments, and to log their time in and out of the office—everyone except the program coordinator, who just does not see the value.

3. The project manager constantly assigns you tasks without a real understanding of the scope of work, giving you a third of the hours required to complete the task.

COMMUNICATIONS

1. The client has provided a list of messages that must be incorporated into the final product. The messages do not in any way meet audience expectations and will more than likely result in product failure.

You can download this handout to your hard drive from the accompanying CD-ROM. The document can then be opened and printed.

2. You run into one of your clients in the hallway who is upset because the project team manager never returns emails or phone calls.

3. You, along with everyone else in the company, receive the new "productivity'" report via email, which states who is working above capacity ... and who is not!

POLICY

1. You must pay your vendor three months in advance because it is the end of the fiscal year, even though there are still four months left in the contract. This makes you a bit concerned about the vendor delivering the product on time ... if at all.

2. The business development team is pursuing business outside the company's scope of expertise.

3. Each department maintains its own Website, creating a very inconsistent look, feel, and overall message for the company.

ADMINISTRATION

1. New hires brought in by HR are not meeting requirements, and they usually leave after six months on the job.

2. Your pay is being held up until your boss can sign the approval paperwork. Ironically, the same thing has happened to three of the past four new hires.

3. Whom do I talk with to purchase new software around here?

GAME DIRECTIONS

Directions: *You are going to play a game today called People Are Talking. Use the following guide as a review of the game rules and directions.*

GAME OBJECTIVE

The object of the game is to be the person who provides the best response to Problem Statement Cards and collects cards that satisfy all the color categories associated with your Employee Role Card. The color categories correlate to the types of activities and responsibilities that typically make up the listed position type. For example, if you look at an Information Technologist Employee Role Card, you might see the following: three black squares, one yellow square, and one green square. To win the game, you need to be awarded the following Problem Statement Card Types:

- Three black Problem Statement Cards [Information Technology]
- One yellow Problem Statement Card [Communications]
- One green Problem Statement Card [Office Culture]

You should try to win as many of the Problem Statement Cards as possible, but only the color categories associated with your specific Employee Role count toward your winning the game.

START THE GAME PLAY

Start with the Employee Role the facilitator has identified and move clockwise around the table.

Step 1: Draw a Problem Statement Card: At the beginning of your turn, draw a Problem Statement Card from the deck and read it aloud to the group.

Step 2: Turn over the timer and respond to the Problem Statement Card: Starting with the player to the left of the person who drew the card, each player turns over the one-minute timer and provides a personal best practice, lesson learned, or success story that resolved the problem statement. Responses must offer potential solutions rather than placing blame.

Step 3: Award response: Once all players at the table group have answered, the person who drew the card awards the Problem Statement Card to the best solution and makes a brief statement as to why he or she selected the solution.

Step 4: Play continues: The next player draws a card, and play continues as described in steps one through three.

WINNING THE GAME

The first player to obtain one each of the associated color type card wins.

You can download this handout to your hard drive from the accompanying CD-ROM. The document can then be opened and printed.

68 ACTIVITIES

PICK ME! PICK ME! USING COALITIONS TO GET YOUR MESSAGE HEARD

Matt DeMarco

Matt DeMarco *is a professional trainer with a particular interest in the intersection of professional and personal development. In his current position as the director of leadership development for the American Farm Bureau Federation, he conducts workshops for state staff and volunteer groups around the country. His career has also included work as a career counselor at Johns Hopkins University School of Advanced International Studies. Matt served as a teacher and trainer with the U.S. Peace Corps in Western Samoa. He currently lives in Washington, D.C.*

Contact Information:
American Farm Bureau Federation
600 Maryland Avenue SW, Suite 800
Washington DC 20024
202.406.3635
mattd@fb.org

Overview   What if the time and energy that interest groups spent competing with one another were used to devise strategies to creatively work together? Instead of fighting to be the best individual advocates, interest groups could form teams and work together. Sound too good to be true? Maybe not, if you expand your traditional definition of teams to include coalitions.

Coalitions are a unique form of teams. They are often formed on a temporary basis to accomplish a finite goal or to influence decision makers on a particular issue. A coalition can form between individuals or currently existing groups.

In this activity, participants experience the benefits of forming coalitions. As advocates for manufacturers of different types of fasteners, they have the opportunity to compete as individuals, as small coalitions, and as large coalitions. As the size of the coalition increases, so does the availability of resources and improved relationships with decision makers. By weighing the pros and cons of forming coalitions, participants will determine the most effective way to work together to get their voice heard.

This activity requires a minimum of 12 participants.

Materials Needed ✓ Four types of fasteners in different sizes and colors (paper clips, safety pins, binder clips, and string)

✓ Flip chart

✓ 8$\frac{1}{2}$ ×11-inch cardstock

✓ Markers in assorted colors

✓ Ribbon or certificate awarded in round one

✓ Chocolate coins as prizes in rounds two and three

Suggested Time 60–90 minutes

Procedure 1. *Introduction*

    a. Before the group arrives, place one of the four types of fasteners at random on each seat.

    b. Upon arrival, instruct participants to carefully examine the items on their seats. They should closely study the item's characteristics and feel comfortable explaining why it would be a good item to use as a fastener. Give participants two minutes to write down the features and benefits of using their items as fasteners (for example, safety pins lock so items will not come apart, binder clips can hold a large number of pages, and so on).

    c. Share with the group that the goal of today's activity is to examine how coalitions form and to identify some of the benefits that arise from forming coalitions. During the activity, their role will be to advocate on behalf of their fastener.

2. *Round 1: Individuals*

    a. Tell participants they have been hired by the manufacturers of their item to advocate on the manufacturer's behalf. The National Fastening Board (NFB) wants to make a U.S. $25,000,000 deal with one manufacturer. Each participant has the opportunity to try to sell his or her item to the NFB representative. In this activity, you as the facilitator play the role of the NFB representative.

    b. Ask participants to review their list of features and benefits they identified for their fastener. Tell participants they will have 45 seconds to try to attract your attention and have their item considered. Everyone is allowed to speak at the same time. Advocates are allowed to do whatever possible to attract your attention except move from their spot in the room. No one is allowed to move from their original location.

    c. As the representative of the NFB, stand in middle of the room.

    d. After the 45 seconds, make a *conditional* offer to the individual who was most successful in lobbying. (Stress that this is a conditional offer since participants will be competing again in the second round. Also acknowledge the winner with some sort of prize, such as a ribbon or a certificate. This helps to fuel the competition in the room and draw attention to the inequities involved in the process, such as the winner standing on the chair or just being the person closest to you.)

3. *Round Two: Small Coalitions*

   a. Announce to participants that because a multimillion-dollar deal is at stake, the NFB has agreed to reopen the bidding to include small associations as a way of ensuring that the right decision is made.

   b. Point out that some of the participants have the same fastener, though it might differ in size or color. For example, there are large and small paper clips and/or paper clips of different colors.

   c. Instruct the group that, during this round, they have the opportunity to form a coalition with participants who have the same item. All coalitions formed will receive additional resources.

   d. To qualify for a coalition participants must:
      ❑ Have the same item, though it may differ in its features such as color and size.
      ❑ Agree to share the $25,000,000 deal equally among all participants in the coalition

   e. Instruct participants that, once they have formed a coalition, members should raise their hands and they will receive one piece of cardstock and two markers.

   f. Share with the group that in this round anyone who forms a coalition will also be allowed to move around the room and can approach you as the NFB representative directly.

   g. Make the group aware that participants do not have to form a coalition. However, they do not receive any additional resources if they choose to advocate as individuals, and they are not allowed to move from their original place in the room.

   h. Give participants five minutes to find other coalition members and prepare a visual aid using the cardstock and markers.

   i. At the end of the five minutes, stand in the middle of the room and give groups and any individual advocates another 45 seconds to petition you as the NFB representative for consideration. Remind them that anyone who has remained an individual advocate cannot move.

   j. Ask the group to return to their places in the room and announce the winner of the second offer. Award them the $25,000,000 in the form of chocolate coins to be divided among the members of their group.

4. *Round Three: Large Coalitions*

   a. Explain to the group that the NFB staff spends a significant portion of their time meeting with different advocate groups. When possible, they try to improve their decision-making process to make it more focused and efficient. One way to do that is to look for credible, representative voices that they trust. Sometimes, the voices are individuals or small coalitions of similar manufacturers, as in rounds one and two. However, sometimes these voices are larger coalitions representing a variety of manufacturers.

   b. Tell the group that in the last round a second deal is being offered but the NFB is soliciting offers only from large coalitions. The award in this case will be larger than the first but still must be shared equally among coalition members.

   c. Instruct the group that in the last round they have the opportunity to gain a private audience with the NFB staff by forming a large coalition and advocating on behalf of a group of manufacturers.

   d. To form a large coalition, participants must:

      ❑ Have two or more different items represented.

      ❑ Have the majority of the total members holding that item represented.

      For example, you could have paper clips and string form a coalition, but, of all the people in the room with paper clips and string, you must have the majority of them represented.

   e. Share with the participants that, in forming a large coalition, they receive additional resources in the form of one piece of flip chart paper and five colored markers. They will also receive a private two-minute audience with the vice president of the NFB.

   f. As in round two, participants do not have to join a large coalition. However, they are not allowed to participate as individuals or as smaller, item-specific associations. A maximum of two invitations are extended to meet with the vice president. People who do not join a large coalition sit the last part out.

   g. Give the participants five minutes to form their coalitions, create a visual aid, and prepare a two-minute presentation.

   h. In the last role, you will play the role of vice president of the NFB. Allow each coalition up to two minutes to present. Award the second prize of chocolate coins to the winning team and instruct them to share it equally among the members.

   i. Debrief.

   j. Have everyone return to their seats and ask them the following questions:

❑ *What was the first process like when you advocated as an individual?*

— It was frustrating because there were too many people talking at one time.

— It was exciting because there was a lot of energy in the room.

— It was pointless because they could not hear me.

— It was high pressure to try to figure out how to get myself heard.

— It was discouraging because only the people close to the representative could really be heard or could talk to the representative.

❑ *Were you successful advocating as an individual? Why or why not?*

No:

— No one could hear me or see me.

— They did not pick my item.

— I could not make a personal connection with the representative.

Yes:

— They picked my item.

❑ *Based on this activity how would you define a coalition?*

❑ *What makes a coalition unique from other teams?*

— It might be temporary.

— It will sometimes compete with the other team members.

❑ *How did the experience change when you could form coalitions?*

— We were able to talk through ideas and come up with a way to grab the representative's attention through a catch phrase or a stimulating visual.

— Resources became available for us to get our idea across.

— We had time to prepare something.

— There was less competition because there were fewer voices.

— We could move around the room and actually approach and meet the representative.

❑ *What factors did you consider when deciding to form a coalition? What were the advantages and disadvantages?*

— Additional resources were available.

— I could cooperate with other people of similar interests.

— I did not have to do it by myself.

— One unified voice, instead of many voices, were talking at the same time.

—I could not argue for one individual commodity.

—I still compete with other people for time and attention.

❏ *What were the advantages and the disadvantages of a large coalition over smaller ones?*

—Private audience

—More resources and time to prepare what to say

—Felt valued and trusted with one-on-one interaction

—Felt like the person really wanted to hear what I had to say

—Everyone's products encompassed by one voice

❏ *Why would people choose to remain an individual during the second or third round?*

—The want to have their individual product selected and not have to join with other manufacturers.

—They feel defeated by the process because they had not been selected earlier.

—They did not want to "play the game."

❏ *Do you think this is an accurate portrayal of what really happens? Why?*

—Coalitions have additional resources available to get their message out, and larger associations have more resources. This most often means money—for lobbying, public relations, marketing, programs and products, services to members, and so forth. It also means numbers, in that larger associations have more members and therefore more people who can get involved.

—The real world is about connections. People with more connections can get their message heard. Large coalitions mean a larger infrastructure of people who go out and cultivate relationships in individual communities, states, and countries.

—It makes more sense for organizations who share common interests to form coalitions to achieve what they want. By the same token, individuals with common interests, needs, and challenges can work more efficiently and accomplish more when they join groups that represent their interests and help them accomplish their goals.

—When people join associations, they benefit from additional resources and connections but they do not stop fighting for their individual interests.

—Government agencies and members of Congress want reliable connections to industries and stakeholders. They use associations and coalitions as representative voices for industries. Although it is easier to give an audience to an association to make its case, the information does not seem credible or reliable if it cannot be authenticated by the actual members.

k. Summarize for the participants the effectiveness of coalitions:
- ❑ Access to resources
- ❑ Unified voice
- ❑ Opportunities to meet and discuss issues with decision makers
- ❑ Shared skills

l. Award prizes to the group that made the most convincing argument for their items.

YOUR BEST GUESS: PLAYING WITH ASSUMPTIONS

Brian Remer

Brian Remer *is a designer of interactive strategies for training, facilitation, and performance improvement. He blends information, discussion, games, and participant input to ensure maximum involvement and commitment. Brian has worked with businesses and organizations in Egypt, Zaire, Ecuador, and throughout the United States. He is a member of the International Society for Performance Improvement and has served on the board of directors and as chairman and president of the North American Simulation and Gaming Association. Brian is noted for his ability to create a low-pressure, high-impact learning environment.*

Contact Information:
The Firefly Group
339 Bullock Road
Guilford, VT 05301
802.257.7247
brian@thefirefly.org
www.thefirefly.org

Overview How often do our assumptions get in the way of effective communication or lead to negative, unhelpful actions? We all have our favorite assumptions that we use every day to make decisions and to make sense of the world. We make our observations and add them to our experience, our values, and our worldview to draw conclusions. Often, our conclusions are correct, but sometimes they are not. The problem occurs when we make an assumption and generalize it for all situations. When we do this without considering other interpretations of the observed data, we are opening ourselves to faulty thinking.

In this game, players read a brief description of an observed event and try to think up a plausible explanation for it. It is an opportunity to expose a few of our common assumptions and get practice in identifying alternative conclusions that might be just as valid. When we are able to see the possibility that any of several options might be true, we are in a better position to figure out which option or assumption is most valid. And we are less likely to pigeonhole other people, fall back on stereotypes, or revert to outdated prejudices.

Suggested Time   45–60 minutes

Materials Needed   Forms A, B, C, D printed on card stock and cut in quarters. (Or use 8½ × 11-inch, perforated postcards. Form D can be printed on the backs of the other forms.) Make one deck of 12 cards for each pair of players.

Procedure

1. Ask participants to choose a partner and distribute a deck of cards to each pair. Play begins with one person drawing a card from the deck and reading the observation out loud. The other person must give an explanation for the observation.

2. The first player then compares the explanation given with those on the card. If the explanation is similar to one of the explanations on the card, the person gets the number of points indicated by the number at the beginning of the explanation. More creative explanations are worth more points. However, all explanations must be plausible (e.g., no aliens, superheroes, or Elvis sightings!). (*Note to facilitator*: The most stereotypical answer always receives zero points. Once participants realize this, they tend to be more creative.)

3. Players alternate reading cards, keeping track of their own points. Let the partner groups play for 20 minutes and then stop for a discussion of what they have learned.

4. Debrief the game with any of these questions:

   • How does this game challenge our common assumptions?

   • What assumptions did you make?

   • What is the basis of some of your most noteworthy assumptions?

   • To what extent did your explanations for the observations become more creative and less stereotyped as you played the game?

   • How do you explain the fact that different people can come up with such different explanations for the same situations?

   • Some people have difficulty thinking of more than one explanation for each situation. Why do you think that might be?

   • If you were going to write ambiguous situations of your own, what would you do to make sure they touched on people's common assumptions?

   • What types of situations in the workplace lend themselves to misinterpretation?

   • Give an example of an assumption you made at work or at home that turned out to be false. What was the result? How did you recover from the wrong assumption?

   • What are the implications of what you have learned about assumptions for your work and your personal life?

Variations   •   Draw cards and think of plausible explanations, like the preceding ones, but challenge the person guessing to come up with as many alternatives as possible in just 30 seconds.

•   Divide participants into groups of three to six. Let them take turns reading cards. When each card is read, all the other members of the group write their own explanations on slips of paper. The person who read the observation is the judge of which is the most creative explanation.

•   Combine this game with an exploration of the concept of Mental Models, as discussed in *The Fifth Discipline Fieldbook* by Peter Senge (New York: Currency Publishing, 1994). The game has direct application to The Ladder of Inference and The Left Hand Column.

FORM A

1. **Observation:** A married woman goes to a single man's apartment two nights of every week for three hours. What is your explanation?

   0 = The two are having an affair.

   1 = She is his housekeeper.

   2 = She is his mother and is caring for him while he is sick.

   3 = He is a music teacher and she goes there for piano lessons.

   4 = Any answer that is more creative.

2. **Observation:** Two police officers visit your next-door neighbor's house. What is your explanation?

   0 = The police officers are questioning your neighbors about some dreadful crime they have committed.

   1 = The police officers are visiting the house because the neighbors are their friends.

   2 = The neighbors are, themselves, police officers.

   3 = The police officers are asking questions about you!

   4 = Any answer that is more creative.

3. **Observation:** A person smelling of stale liquor is buying aspirin at 6 a.m. What is your explanation?

   0 = The person was out all night and has a headache as a result.

   1 = The person is buying aspirin for his or her partner who has the flu.

   2 = The person works in Johnny's Blues Bar and has just finished the late shift.

   3 = The person spilled a bottle of rum when trying to reach the breakfast cereal, bumping his or her head on the open cupboard and has a headache.

   4 = Any answer that is more creative.

4. **Observation:** When you get home you find your brother's car is dented on the right side. What's your explanation?

   0 = Your brother had an accident.

   1 = The car has always been like that and you never noticed.

   2 = Old Volkswagens always look like that. It is the same on the other side.

   3 = The car is full of rust. This was bound to happen.

   4 = Any answer that is more creative.

You can download this handout to your hard drive from the accompanying CD-ROM. The document can then be opened and printed.

ACTIVITY 12: YOUR BEST GUESS: PLAYING WITH ASSUMPTIONS   **79**

FORM B

5. **Observation:** You see a man chasing a woman down an alley. What is your explanation?

0 = You are witnessing a case of domestic violence.

1 = She is a shoplifter; he is a plainclothes officer.

2 = They are trying to catch their dog.

3 = The two are in a marathon.

4 = Any answer that is more creative.

6. **Observation:** A teenager carrying a heavy backpack runs out the door of a convenience store. What is your explanation?

0 = The teenager just robbed the store.

1 = The teenager is late for class.

2 = The teenager is a track star and runs everywhere.

3 = The store is on fire.

4 = Any answer that is more creative.

7. **Observation:** Two clean-cut young men wearing dark slacks and white shirts ring your doorbell. What is your explanation?

0 = They are proselytizing for a religious group.

1 = They are asking for directions.

2 = They are canvassing the neighborhood for a voter registration effort.

3 = They are members of the high school choral group with information about their next performance.

4 = Any answer that is more creative.

8. **Observation:** It is dinnertime and the phone rings. A pleasant person on the line asks for you but mispronounces your name. What is your explanation?

0 = It is a telemarketer interrupting your dinner.

1 = It is your Malaysian friend who always mispronounces your name.

2 = It is a call from your friend, a practical joker always giving you a hard time.

3 = You are waiting outside a popular restaurant and the hostess is calling on your cell phone to tell you your table is ready.

4 = Any answer that is more creative.

You can download this handout to your hard drive from the accompanying CD-ROM. The document can then be opened and printed.

FORM C

9. **Observation:** Last week a mechanic fixed the vibration in your car's front end. Now you feel the vibration again. What is your explanation?

0 = The mechanic did a poor job.

1 = You recently drove through wet, sloppy dirt roads and mud is now caked on the suspension system.

2 = You are driving over those bumpy warning strips in the road.

3 = Your teenager damaged the tires while learning to parallel park.

4 = Any answer that is more creative.

11. **Observation:** You are driving down the street when a car in a side driveway suddenly cuts in front of you. What is your explanation?

0 = The driver is an aggressive, rage-filled road warrior.

1 = The sun was in the driver's eyes so you could not be seen.

2 = The driver is inexperienced using a clutch.

3 = The car was hit from behind and pushed into your lane.

4 = Any answer that is more creative.

10. **Observation:** Your boss and the director of personnel are moving boxes out of your friend's office. What is your explanation?

0 = Your friend just got fired.

1 = Your friend got a promotion and is moving to another part of the building.

2 = Your boss has decided not to keep company documents in your friend's office any longer.

3 = The boxes should have been delivered to the personnel director's office.

4 = Any answer that is more creative.

12. **Observation:** You are sitting in the airport waiting for a flight. When you reach for your newspaper, the person next to you is reading it. What is your explanation?

0 = The person has stolen your newspaper.

1 = The person thought the paper had been abandoned.

2 = The person thought the paper belonged to his or her friend.

3 = The paper belongs to the other person. Yours is still in your carry-on!

4 = Any answer that is more creative.

Your Best Guess

Your Best Guess

Your Best Guess

Your Best Guess

INQUIRY AND FEEDBACK: A TEAM ACTION LEARNING AND PROBLEM IDENTIFICATION EXERCISE

Diane L. Dunton and Debra Carpenter

Diane L. Dunton, *president of Potential Released Consulting Services, has over 25 years of business and human resource experience. She designs and implements development programs and systems to assess individuals, groups, and organizations to identify the strategies to meet business demands and individual needs. Diane has extensive experience in organizational development. She has received specialized training with National Training Labs, the Gestalt Institute, the Center for Creative Leadership, the University of Michigan's Organizational Career Development, and the Center for Reengineering Leadership programs. Diane is a frequent contributor to the* **Sourcebooks***.*

Contact Information:
57 Tandberg Trail
P.O. Box 1000
Windham, ME 04062
207.892.9292
dldunton@potentialreleased.com

Debra Carpenter, *president of Learning Quest, Inc., has been developing and building teams for 15 years in executive, marketing, and sales organizations. Her success there led her into the leadership development field, where she uses Action Learning to help teams overcome the inherent barriers of politics, micromanagement, too little management, faulty goals and metrics, and poor team communications.*

Contact Information:
14 June Street
Portland ME 04102
207.409.0545
dcarpenter@maine.rr.com

Overview   Why does it take so long to get a team to work on an issue? Someone brings a problem or opportunity, and quickly the meeting is full of hot air, tangents, and advice. Opinions and turf battles squeeze out dialog.

Weeks later, everyone finally understands what the issue is and gets to work—or worse, the idea is buried.

Most team members respond to an idea or opportunity from their own perspective. Marketing people turn it into a marketing issue, finance people turn it into a financial issue, and so on. With everyone seeking to be the expert with the best idea, the issue becomes clouded, confused, and complicated. Motivation is sapped, and the benefits seem small compared to the fog the team must go through.

The Action Learning exercise, a process of teaching teams to teach themselves, shows how to quickly identify the real issue. The facilitator—called a coach—gives up control over the group's improvement and instead allows the team to self-correct through controlled feedback.

The exercise is designed for a group of four to eight people, who can be an actual team or individuals who do not work with each other.

Suggested Time   2–3 hours

Materials Needed
✓ Introduction to Action Learning (Form A)
✓ Flip Chart Graphic (Form B)
✓ Observer's Sheet (Form C)
✓ Flip chart and markers

Procedure
1. Distribute Form A and introduce the concepts of Action Learning.

2. Ask one participant to identify a current issue in his or her job or, if participants are from the same organization, a companywide issue. An example to share might be: "Our parent company does not understand how we do business here."

3. Ask the team to list what they think the issue is, how to solve it, what is important about it, and so forth.

4. List their responses on a flip chart. Examples are communication with the parent company, how to build an educational relationship with the parent company, lack of negotiation skills, how smaller organizations can create clout within a larger conglomerate.

5. Display the graphic on Form B on a flip chart.

6. Ask the person who volunteered an issue to indicate to the team how relevant their ideas and thoughts are to the issue, as he or she sees it:
   • One—not relevant
   • Two—has some relevance, but is not really the topic
   • Three—has quite a bit of relevance, "getting warmer"
   • Four—right on target

7. The rating will probably be low. The group members may show surprise that their best effort did not immediately help the person.

Point out that strategizing and problem solving are impossible without understanding the core issues.

8. Explain that some questions lead the group to the issues while others lead away from them.

9. Ask another person in the group to be a volunteer to talk about an issue.

10. Assign two observers and give them copies of Form C.

11. The rest of the group are consultants.

12. Explain the process:

    - The volunteer states and explains the issue and answers questions.

    - The consultants ask questions, interact with the issue, and simply do what comes naturally to them.

    - The observers check which types of questions and behaviors they see, using Form C.

    - The facilitator pauses the group after a few minutes and:

        ❑ Asks the observers for feedback on the questions.

        ❑ Asks the volunteer to rate the relevance of the discussion using the target.

        ❑ Starts the process again.

13. Allow the volunteer to begin to tell the story of the issue. As you see the consultants beginning to get into the interaction (about five minutes), ask everyone to pause.

14. Ask the observers to identify the types of questions and behaviors they are seeing, based on Form C.

15. Ask the volunteer to rate how close they are to the real issue, by using the target flip chart.

16. Encourage the consultants to improve their rating, but without giving them pointers or advice.

17. Give the observers fresh copies of Form C.

18. Allow the process to roll forward again, again pausing as you sense the questions are not leading to the real issue. Repeat this process until the volunteer says they are getting very close to the real issue.

19. Ask, "How could you have gotten to the real issue even faster? How different was the real issue from your first impression of it?"

20. Change volunteers, consultants, and observers until three or four people have had a chance to volunteer, observe, and ask questions.

21. Debrief the group: What were their personal ahas about how they ask questions? Which questions got at the real issue best? How might they use this technique on their problems?

22. Ask the group to list the benefits they see, and list them on the flip chart.

INTRODUCTION TO ACTION LEARNING   FORM A

ACTION LEARNING

- A small group working on real problems, taking action, and being responsible for its own learning
- A process of holding oneself and the other team members accountable for communication and results, thus building leadership in each member of the team or group

COMPONENTS OF AN ACTION LEARNING PROGRAM

1. A current and important project, challenge, task, or problem
2. Group of four to eight people
3. Processes of reflective questioning and listening to zero in on the real issue
4. Development of strategies
5. Commitment to learning
6. Learning coach/facilitator

In this exercise, we work on steps one, two, and three, and experience how a learning coach works.

YOU WILL BE LEARNING TO

- Get at the core issue quickly.
- Accept and give feedback.
- Adapt to what you have learned and improve group communications.

You can download this handout to your hard drive from the accompanying CD-ROM. The document can then be opened and printed.

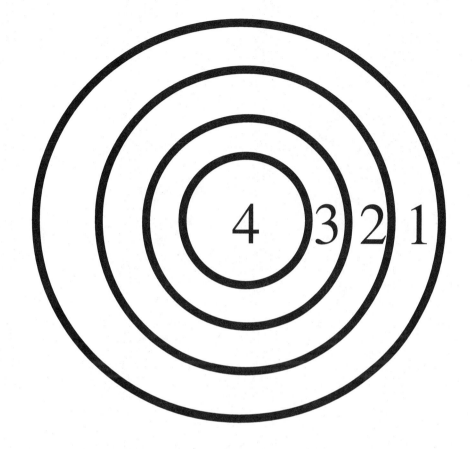

One—not relevant, "getting colder"

Two—has some relevance, but isn't really the topic

Three—has quite a bit of relevance, "getting warmer"

Four—right on target

Getting Colder	Getting Warmer
Consulting Behaviors *That Lead Away from the Issues*	*Consultant Behaviors* *That Help Identify the Core Issues*
❏ Make comments from their own department: Marketing people seeing it from a marketing point of view, HR seeing it from a personnel point of view, etc.	❏ Focus on the volunteer: What is most important about this to you?
❏ Recount personal experiences of the same type of issue: When I was in this situation	❏ Listen and reflect what the volunteer is saying: You're saying there is no way to control the parent company.
❏ Give advice: Have you tried ...?	❏ Help the volunteer see the whole picture: What outcomes are on the line? What if we do nothing? Who all needs to be involved?
❏ Ask technical questions in a rapid-fire way.	❏ Explore the impact of the idea or issue: Is the value to add profit or reduce costs, or what?
❏ Give opinions: Parent companies are always out of the real world.	❏ Uncover resistance areas: Where do you expect to have resistance? Where will support most likely come from?
❏ Take the conversation on tangents and dominate the flow.	❏ Summarize: So, it's not the parent company, and it doesn't seem to be an educational issue.

Questions for Observers:

What did you notice about the relationship between the volunteer and consultants?

At any point, did you get especially interested? Bored? How does that correlate with behaviors from the "colder" or "warmer" columns?

You can download this handout to your hard drive from the accompanying CD-ROM. The document can then be opened and printed.

THINKING OUT OF THE BAG: A GROUP BREAKTHROUGH THINKING EXERCISE

Yael Schy

Yael Schy *is a consultant, facilitator, trainer, and coach with over 20 years of management experience, known for her creative approach to organizational learning. She is principal of Dramatic Strides™ Consulting, specializing in leadership development, communication skills, team building, and creative decision-making techniques that help people and organizations move forward by leaps and bounds. Yael brings a unique perspective by incorporating her improvisational theater and dance experience into active interpersonal skills training in the workplace. She has a demonstrated track record in assessing communication needs of both individuals and organizations and in developing innovative strategies that meet personal and business goals.*

Contact Information:
Dramatic Strides™ Consulting
1849 Drake Drive
Oakland, CA 94611
510.339.2404
yael@pobox.com
www.DramaticStrides.com

Overview In our fast-paced work lives, we rarely take the time to use our creative, right-brain thinking capacity in facing challenges. Instead, we are often forced into a linear, logical, left-brain orientation to problem solving. In addition, too often we spend all our time focusing on solving problems rather than on building on our strengths. Finally, we are often faced with solving problems alone, rather than utilizing the power and creativity of group thinking.

A recent study by Teresa Amabile, who heads the Entrepreneurial Management Unit at Harvard Business School, found that, "The most creative teams are those that have the confidence to share and debate ideas. But when people compete for recognition, they stop sharing information. And that's destructive because nobody in an organization has all of the information required to put all the pieces of the puzzle together." Amabile's study also challenged the common myth that only certain people are creative. She found that "anyone with normal intelligence is capable of doing some degree of creative work," and that "Creativity depends on a number of things: experience, including knowledge and technical skills; talent; an ability to think in new ways; and the capacity to push through uncreative dry spells."[1]

This training activity uses a creative, group thinking approach in dealing with challenges in organizations. Participants learn how to focus on their creative strengths rather than on obstacles and barriers. They also learn how the use of random objects (as well as drawings, music, movement, etc.) can help to utilize right-brain thinking and stimulate creative solutions.

By the end of this activity, participants will:

- Identify and discuss a personal success story of creative thinking.
- Practice group brainstorming and prioritizing skills.
- Identify a group challenge for further discussion.
- Engage in a creative thinking exercise using random objects.
- Discuss applications of this exercise to the workplace.

Suggested Time   2 hours

Materials Needed   ✓ Reflection Questions (Form A)

✓ Brainstorming Guidelines (Form B)

✓ Chart paper and easel

✓ Marking pens

✓ Paper and pens for participants

✓ Adhesive dots (one color, three per participant; a second contrasting color, one per participant)

✓ Large paper bag ("Grab Bag")

✓ Assorted collected objects from around the home, office, or outdoors (enough for each participant to have one object) placed in the paper bag

✓ Music (optional)

Procedure   1. Ask participants to take a few minutes to individually write down their answers to the questions on Form A:

- Think of a time when you were at your most creative. Describe the situation, and why you feel it was creative. How did it affect you?
- What resources (from yourself or others) helped you to be creative?
- What obstacles did you face in achieving that creative moment? How did you overcome them so that you could succeed?

[1]Bill Breen, "The 6 Myths of Creativity," *Fast Company* (December 2004): 89, p. 75.

- What did you learn from this experience that can help you face future challenges creatively?

- What is a current challenge that you are facing in your work that you would like to resolve more creatively?

2. Next, ask the participants to pair up with someone they don't know well and ask them to interview each other about their answers to the preceding questions. Allow 15 minutes for each of the two interviews.

3. Bring the full group of participants together to discuss their answers to the interview questions:

- What are some examples of shining moments of creativity in this group?

- What obstacles did you face in your most creative moment? How did you overcome them?

- What did you personally do to make the creative solution possible?

- How can you deal with obstacles in the future?

- What creative challenges are you currently facing in your work?

4. Say:

There's an old saying that "two heads are better than one." And more heads are even better! When dealing with a problem or challenge on our own, we can often get stuck in old patterns of thinking. By involving others in a group problem-solving session, we open ourselves up to new ideas and perspectives on the challenge, and increase the likelihood of coming up with an innovative solution.

The technique of brainstorming allows groups to get everyone's ideas on the table for consideration, without evaluating them, as a jumping-off point for group discussion. A facilitator asks for spontaneous ideas and suggestions on the topic at hand, and either charts them or asks for a volunteer to record them on a chart. After everyone's contributions have been made, the group can begin the process of prioritizing and narrowing down the list of ideas.

5. Distribute Form B (Brainstorming Guidelines) and review the guidelines.

6. Engage the participants in a group brainstorming session on a single work challenge for which they would like to find a creative solution, and on which the group will focus in the next activity. If participants are all from the same organization, they need to focus on one challenge currently facing their organization. If they are from different organizations, they need to reach consensus on an issue of relevance to all of them.

7. First, have the participants generate as many issues as possible for five minutes, without editing or disputing any of the ideas, and record the ideas on chart paper.

Then, ask the participants to decide individually which of the challenges identified they feel is the most pressing or which they want to focus on.

8. Give each participant three adhesive dots, all the same color. Each participant uses the three dots to "vote" for the challenge(s) he or she feels are most important by placing the dots on the chart paper next to the issue(s) chosen. They can vote for three separate challenges, put all three dots on one challenge, or split them between two challenges. If no one challenge clearly receives the most dots, then repeat the dot voting process, using one dot (of a contrasting color) and one vote per person this time. The goal is to identify a single challenge of greatest importance to the group.

9. Ask the participants to sit in one large circle. Walk around the circle, holding the paper Grab Bag filled with objects. Ask each participant, one at a time, to take an object from the Grab Bag, without looking in it.

10. Ask the participants to think quietly for a moment about how their object personifies the work challenge identified in the previous brainstorming activity. Then ask each participant to share their thoughts with the group about how the object represents the group challenge. You can either go around the circle round-robin style with each participant speaking in turn, or ask people to speak in any order until all have spoken.

11. Now, invite the participants to move around the room, trading objects with each other as music plays, until the music stops or until the facilitator says, "Stop." Have the participants sit back down in the circle, holding their new objects. Ask them each to think quietly for a moment about how the new object represents a possible *solution* to the challenge identified by the group.

12. Ask each participant in the circle to share their thoughts with the group about how these objects represent solutions to the group challenge.

13. Engage the participants in a full group discussion:

    • How did the use of objects help you to think outside the box? Were you able to come up with ideas for dealing with this challenge that you would not have thought of otherwise?

    • Although you each had a different object in the second round, as a group they were still the same objects. What changed to make these objects represent solutions, instead of problems? (Answer: Only the participants' *perception* of the objects changed!)

    • What ideas did you get as a result of this exercise that you can actually implement in your work to address the challenge you identified?

    • How can you look at future challenges in a way that helps you to see opportunities and solutions, instead of problems?

- How can you draw on your personal and professional strengths that you identified in your creativity success stories, when dealing with future work challenges?

- How can you use this creative thinking exercise in your daily work to deal with potential challenges?

REFLECTION QUESTIONS

- Think of a time when you were at your most creative. Describe the situation, and why you feel it was creative. How did it affect you?

- What resources (from yourself or others) helped you to be creative?

- What obstacles did you face in achieving that creative moment? How did you overcome them so that you could succeed?

- What did you learn from this experience that can help you face future challenges creatively?

- What is a current challenge that you are facing in your work that you would like to resolve more creatively?

You can download this handout to your hard drive from the accompanying CD-ROM. The document can then be opened and printed.

BRAINSTORMING GUIDELINES   FORM B

- **Don't Judge**
  There are no "bad" ideas! Don't evaluate each other's ideas, and don't censor your own ideas. The repetition of ideas is OK.

- **Be Creative**
  Anything goes! Every contribution is worthwhile—even weird, way-out ideas, even confusing ideas, and especially silly ideas.

- **Go for Quantity**
  Try to generate as many ideas as possible. Later, the group can narrow them down.

- **"Piggyback" on Others' Ideas**
  Listen carefully to each other's ideas and allow them to "spark" new ones for you.

You can download this handout to your hard drive from the accompanying CD-ROM. The document can then be opened and printed.

ASSESSMENT INSTRUMENTS

In this section of *The 2006 ASTD Organization Development and Leadership Sourcebook*, you will find five assessment instruments. With these instruments, you will be able to answer these questions:

✓ Do your behaviors promote a culture of inclusion?

✓ Do your leadership teams work together?

✓ Is your organization a generative place to work?

✓ Are your team's values aligned for optimal productivity?

✓ How effective is your feedback?

The instruments are designed both to evaluate training and performance issues and to suggest areas for improvement. Most are not for research purposes. Instead, they are intended to build awareness, provide feedback about your own specific situation, and promote group reflection.

In selecting instruments for publication, a premium was placed on questionnaires or survey forms that are easy to understand and quick to complete. Preceding each instrument is an overview that contains key questions to be assessed. The instrument itself is on a separate page(s) to make reproduction more convenient. All the instruments are scorable and some contain guidelines for scoring interpretation. Some include questions for follow-up discussion.

Many of these instruments can be utilized as activities in training sessions. Participants can complete the instrument you have selected prior to or during the session. After completion, ask participants to score and interpret their own results. Then, have them compare outcomes with other participants, either in pairs or in larger groupings. Be careful, however, to stress that the data from these instruments are not "hard." The data suggest rather than demonstrate facts about people or situations. Ask participants to compare scores to their own perceptions. If they do not match, urge them to consider why. In some cases, the discrepancy may be due to the crudeness of the measurement device. In others, the discrepancy may result from distorted self-perceptions. Urge participants to open themselves to new feedback and awareness.

Other instruments will help you and others to assess future training needs. Again, it would be useful to show and discuss the data that emerge with others involved in the area under evaluation.

You may also wish to use some instruments as a basis for planning retreats or staff meetings. Have participants complete the instruments prior to the session. Then, summarize the results and open them up to team discussion.

If you choose this option, be sure to state the process clearly to respondents. You might want to use the following text:

> *We are planning to get together soon to identify issues that need to be worked through in order to maximize our future effectiveness. An excellent way to begin doing some of this work is to collect information through a questionnaire to feed back information for group discussion.*
>
> *I would like you to join with your colleagues in filling out the attached questionnaire. Your honest responses will enable us to have a clear, objective view of our situation.*
>
> *Your participation will be totally anonymous. My job will be to summarize the results and report them to the group for reaction.*

You can also share the instruments with others in your organization who might find them useful for their own purposes. In some cases, merely reading through the questions is a valuable exercise in self- and group reflection.

DO YOUR BEHAVIORS PROMOTE A CULTURE OF INCLUSION?

Frederick A. Miller and Judith H. Katz

Frederick A. Miller *is the CEO and lead client strategist of The Kaleel Jamison Consulting Group, Inc. Fred joined Kaleel Jamison and KJCG in 1979. He was president and CEO of KJCG from 1985 to 2004 and has been CEO and lead client strategist since 2004. In his 30-plus years of experience, he has worked with numerous CEOs and senior level executives from renowned companies, such as ExxonMobil, Dupont, Toyota, and Apple Computers. He was on the board of directors for Ben & Jerry's Homemade, Inc. for eight years.*

*Fred is currently on the boards of directors for Day & Zimmerman, Seton Health Systems, and The Sage Colleges and is a member of the Social Venture Network (SVN). He is a former board member of NTL Institute, American Society for Training & Development (ASTD), and the Organization Development Network (ODN). Fred is coauthor, with Judith H. Katz, of **The Inclusion Breakthrough: Unleashing the Real Power of Diversity** (Berrett-Koehler, 2002), contributes regularly to publications in the organizational development and leadership fields, and is a speaker at national conferences. Fred is also a frequent contributor to the **Sourcebooks**.*

Judith H. Katz, EdD, *became a partner in The Kaleel Jamison Consulting Group, Inc., in 1985 and currently serves as executive vice president. Judith is a speaker and internationally known author. The 25th anniversary of her book, **White Awareness: Handbook for Anti-Racism Training** (University of Oklahoma Press, 1978, 2003) has been celebrated with the publication of a revised edition. Her courageous autobiographical work, **No Fairy Godmothers, No Magic Wands: The Healing Process after Rape** (R & E Publishers, Inc., 1984) is widely used in assisting rape survivors in the recovery process. She is coeditor of **The Promise of Diversity** (McGraw-Hill, 1994) and coauthor, with Frederick A. Miller, of **The Inclusion Breakthrough: Unleashing the Real Power of Diversity** (Berrett-Koehler, 2002). Judith has also published over 50 articles and is a frequent contributor to the **Sourcebooks**.*

Judith serves on the boards of directors for Social Venture Network and The Group for Cultural Documentation. She is also a member of the Diversity Collegium. Judith is the recipient of the 2003 DTUI Cultural Competency Professional Award and the 2004 American College Personnel Association Voice of Inclusion Medallion.

Contact Information:
Frederick A. Miller
The Kaleel Jamison Consulting Group, Inc.
279 River Street, Suite 401
Troy, NY 12180
518.271.7000
familler@kjcg.com
www.kjcg.com

Judith H. Katz
The Kaleel Jamison Consulting Group, Inc.
279 River Street, Suite 401
Troy, NY 12180
518.271.7000
judithkatz@kjcg.com
www.kjcg.com

Overview Creating an inclusive culture can seem like a long and difficult process. Eliminating biases and changing people's attitudes usually require a great deal of education and widespread changes in organizational policies and practices. Inclusion is a product of behavior and the result of conscious daily decisions by individuals.

The following behaviors, if used consistently, are an effective starting point in creating the practice of inclusion and giving people the experience of inclusion. With the support of other organizational practices and policies, in addition to commitment and effort at the individual and organizational levels, these behaviors promote a culture of inclusion that leverages diversity for higher performance.

ELEVEN BEHAVIORS TO ENCOURAGE A CULTURE OF INCLUSION

1. *Greet others authentically:* From the moment people arrive at work, they must feel that they are part of the organizational community. Too often people are in such a hurry to get to their emails or voicemails that they miss contact with the people they work with. A simple hello to acknowledge people and team members is a key first step to creating a more inclusive work environment. The more diverse the group is, the more important hellos become, because people who are new or different from the traditional group often feel excluded from acknowledgment.

   • Take the time to say hello or check in with each team member during the course of the day. At meetings, greet each individual by name. Introduce yourself to people you do not know. Show genuine interest in others.

   • Make contact (e.g., respectful eye contact; shake hands; say, "Hi, how are you?" and listen attentively to the response).

- When it is appropriate, begin meetings with a "check in." Depending on time constraints and group needs, it can be a report on project status or a personal update.

2. *Create a sense of "safety" for yourself and team members:* Creating safety does not mean creating a risk-averse environment. It means fostering an environment of respect for and acknowledgment of people's differing needs and approaches. The goal is to create an environment in which people feel physically safe from harm and emotionally safe to share their perspectives, thoughts, and ideas— even if they differ from others. If people's ideas are frequently attacked or ignored, they are reluctant to share their thinking and their contributions are diminished. People must also feel safe enough to take risks, which are essential for growth and innovation; if people are afraid to make mistakes, they are reluctant to practice new skills or voice new ideas.

   - Think about the language you use. Avoid language that diminishes or ridicules people or their efforts.
   - Be careful with the use of humor. Make sure that no one is the object of demeaning humor.
   - Give honest, constructive feedback without attaching blame or personal judgments.
   - Evaluate and critique actions, not people.
   - Inquire about what people need to do their best work. You cannot assume or guess.

3. *Address misunderstandings and resolve disagreements:* When people with different backgrounds and perspectives fully participate in an organization, the potential for conflicts and disagreements increases. The challenge is to avoid suppressing disagreements and differences and to engage and leverage them to provide break-throughs in thinking and ideas. Disagreements help build the creative tension that, when worked through, enables teams to over-come barriers and exceed expectations. Many people feel unsafe in acknowledging or engaging in conflicts, but, over time, unresolved issues damage a team's ability to effectively work together.

   - Deal with misunderstandings and disagreements as soon as possible.
   - Use disagreements as a catalyst for learning.
   - Avoid discussing the problem with others unless you need a third party to help mediate or clarify how to deal with the problem.
   - Develop team mechanisms that make it OK to raise disagree-ments as a normal part of decision making and problem solving.

4. *Listen carefully to the person speaking until she or he feels under-stood:* Being understood does not mean being in agreement, but it

is required for being included. Too often, after a person voices a new or different perspective, the next speaker immediately gives an opposing perspective or changes the subject, and the group moves on as if the original remark had no value. Inclusion requires two-way communication, and that means acknowledging and making an effort to understand the speaker's contribution before offering a new or different perspective. When each individual feels heard and understood, the communication process can move from argumentative to additive, as each speaker overtly bridges to and/or responds to others' ideas, thoughts, and perspectives.

- Before you respond, it is sometimes helpful to paraphrase what you think you have heard so the speaker can correct any miscommunication.

- Recognize and acknowledge that all ideas, as well as the people who contribute ideas, add value to the discussion.

- Build on the thoughts and ideas of others, whenever possible, as a way to let them know they have been heard and that you were influenced by what they shared.

5. *Communicate clearly, directly, and honestly:* Clear communication is essential for a team or organization to be successful. This involves giving honest and unambiguous feedback to people. In many organizations, people have learned to guard their information and to be "politically correct" instead of being candid and honest in what they say. When people are afraid to be the bearers of bad news, leaders and others often do not hear what is really going on in an organization, which can lead to their basing decisions on faulty information. When individuals do not get candid information about their performance, their ability to improve their performance and be successful is impaired.

- Give and accept honest feedback.

- Avoid sarcasm, put-downs, name-calling, or judgmental remarks.

- Use "I" language. Do not attribute your thoughts and opinions to others. For example, say, "I feel," not "Everyone feels."

6. *Solidify the team's vision of its task and its relationship to the organization's mission:* At its core, an inclusive organization creates an environment in which all people can do their best work and add value. To do this, all individuals and teams must understand their roles in contributing to the organization's success. They must be able to establish goals that will help the organization achieve its mission. One of the most inclusive things an organization can do is to ensure that people have, and are supported in, meaningful work.

- Make sure everyone on the team understands how each person's role is essential to the achievement of the team's work and the organization's mission.

- Reevaluate projects and processes to ensure that they are consistent with the team's objectives and the organization's goals.

7. *Hear all voices and allow for all options:* Part of the aspiration of creating a more inclusive environment is enabling all people in the organization to contribute. When making a decision or forming a work team, a diverse group of voices must be heard, whether they are in the room or not. Including all stakeholders at the front end saves time, money, and future resources. A team should ask itself, have we heard from everyone? Who else needs to be included in this decision to make sure all the bases are covered? Each different idea can spark a new train of thought or chain of ideas. If everyone is of one mind, people cannot learn from each other and nothing new can be achieved.

   - Actively solicit ideas from all members present and discuss each option before making decisions. Getting all views allows for a 360-degree perspective.

   - Invite the quiet members of the team to speak and give them the assurance that their contributions are essential.

   - Vary processes for how ideas are shared to allow for a variety of styles and approaches (e.g., share agenda items prior to the meeting and/or allow people to submit their ideas in writing).

8. *Ask others to share their thoughts and experiences and accept their frame of reference as true for them:* Communication styles vary among individuals. Realize that differences in communicating do not reflect on the value of the other person's information or ideas. Although another person's frame of reference may be different from your own, it is no less valid. As more voices are heard in an organization and different perspectives enter the conversation, new opportunities for learning, creativity, and growth present themselves.

   - Ask for clarification when concepts seem unfamiliar. Treat speakers as experts of their own experience.

   - Have curiosity about the experiences of other people, particularly if their experiences are different from your own.

   - Be open to learning why and how people have reached their conclusions and ideas.

9. *Speak up when people are being excluded:* When people are excluded, ideas are excluded, and the entire team suffers. Unfortunately, exclusive behaviors and attitudes are deeply ingrained in most organizations, and it takes a concerted effort to change established patterns of thinking and acting. The assumption that everyone will speak up if he or she has something to say is incorrect. If the objective is to encourage new ideas and ensure the richest and best thinking, all members of the team have to be responsible for the team's efforts.

- Actively intervene when someone is being discounted or ignored.

- Use inclusive language (e.g., be aware of using acronyms, "insider" language, and/or metaphors that some people may not understand).

10. *Make careful choices about group actions and schedules:* Be respectful of everyone's time, and make sure the scheduling of meetings and tasks takes into account that each person's participation is critical to the success of the project. In too many organizations, meetings are held without much consideration of people's differing needs. (Does Harry have to pick up his children from day care at 4:30 p.m.? Does Sue have a parent care situation that keeps her from arriving at the office before 9 a.m.?) Being mindful of team members' needs sends the signal that each person counts and each person's contribution is not only welcome but necessary.

   - Carefully consider how the team's time can be best spent to further its task or mission, and regularly reevaluate the process used by the team in meeting its goals.

   - Ask the question, is this the best use of our time right now? If the answer is no, modify the workflow by scheduling an alternative time to deal with the current issue.

   - Start and end meetings on time as a matter of respecting people's other commitments.

11. *Be brave:* To create an inclusive work culture, each person must deal with the discomfort of change and take the risk of challenging norms. If people are to adopt new behaviors, work processes, and strategies, they must have the courage to speak out, learn, grow, and work differently. As individuals, they must work to break through the barriers inherent in their old behaviors, just as the organization must work to break through patterns and processes at the systems level. Be prepared to make some mistakes along the way, and value mistakes as learning opportunities for the team and the whole organization.

   - Accept mistakes as a necessary part of the learning process.

   - Recognize that sometimes resistance is feedback from people who feel excluded from the change process. Seek their help in finding ways to include them.

   - Find partners with whom to share your vision, mission, burdens, and successes.

   Inclusion is all about partnership.

   The self-assessment instrument that follows will help you determine which of the 11 behaviors you are currently using and which behaviors you need to start practicing.

ELEVEN BEHAVIORS FOR INCLUSION
SELF-ASSESSMENT
Frederick A. Miller and Judith H. Katz

Directions:

Part A: *Consider each of the following statements and assess your day-to-day behavior at work. Share only what you choose to share with others in the room.*

For each behavior, indicate how frequently you practice it.

Please circle the number that most accurately reflects your day-to-day workplace behavior.

Part B: *After completing the self-assessment, respond to the three questions.*

Part C: *Respond to the two questions relating to leveraging diversity and inclusion.*

Part A

1.   Greet others authentically.

0	1	2	3	4	5	6	7	8	9	10
Never		Seldom			Sometimes		Almost Always			Always

2.   Create a sense of "safety" for yourself and team members.

0	1	2	3	4	5	6	7	8	9	10
Never		Seldom			Sometimes		Almost Always			Always

3.   Address misunderstandings and resolve disagreements.

0	1	2	3	4	5	6	7	8	9	10
Never		Seldom			Sometimes		Almost Always			Always

4.   Listen carefully to the person speaking until she or he feels understood.

0	1	2	3	4	5	6	7	8	9	10
Never		Seldom			Sometimes		Almost Always			Always

5.   Communicate clearly, directly, and honestly.

0	1	2	3	4	5	6	7	8	9	10
Never		Seldom			Sometimes		Almost Always			Always

6.   Solidify the team's vision of its task and its relationship to the organization's mission.

0	1	2	3	4	5	6	7	8	9	10
Never		Seldom			Sometimes		Almost Always			Always

7.   Hear all voices and allow for all options.

0	1	2	3	4	5	6	7	8	9	10
Never		Seldom			Sometimes		Almost Always			Always

8. Ask others to share their thoughts and experiences and accept their frame of reference as true for them.

0	1	2	3	4	5	6	7	8	9	10
Never		Seldom			Sometimes		Almost Always			Always

9. Speak up when people are being excluded.

0	1	2	3	4	5	6	7	8	9	10
Never		Seldom			Sometimes		Almost Always			Always

10. Make careful choices about group actions and schedules.

0	1	2	3	4	5	6	7	8	9	10
Never		Seldom			Sometimes		Almost Always			Always

11. Be brave.

0	1	2	3	4	5	6	7	8	9	10
Never		Seldom			Sometimes		Almost Always			Always

Part B

1. What do you see as your three key strengths? _____

_____

_____

2. What do you see as your three key areas for improvement? _____

_____

_____

3. Identify one or two inclusive behaviors that you will practice.

_____

_____

Part C: Leveraging Diversity and Inclusion: Key Steps to Higher Performance

1. Discuss with your supervisor what you see as your strengths, areas for improvement, and behaviors you will practice. Agree on how you will monitor your commitment to practice inclusive behaviors. _____

_____

2. Find someone who is different from you in some way (gender, race, age, religion, life style, function, tenure with the company, or the like).

• Have a conversation with and get to know the person.

• What are some things you have in common?

• In what ways are you different?

DO YOUR LEADERSHIP TEAMS WORK TOGETHER?

Dean Anderson and Linda Ackerman Anderson

Dean Anderson *and* **Linda Ackerman Anderson** *are cofounders of Being First, Inc, a change leadership development and transformational change consulting firm. These founding leaders in the field are highly sought-after speakers and consultants. They specialize in helping organizations plan and execute transformational changes that deliver the business results they need while simultaneously affecting the people and culture of the organization. Together they coauthored two books in the field of change leadership,* **Beyond Change Management: Advanced Strategies for Today's Transformational Leaders** *(Jossey-Bass, 2001) and* **The Change Leader's Roadmap: How to Navigate Your Organization's Transformation** *(Jossey-Bass, 2001).*

Contact Information:
Being First, Inc.
1242 Oak Drive DW2
Durango, CO 81301
970.385.5100
deananderson@beingfirst.com

Overview   Every change effort has a number of teams working on it that can impact its success. Typical teams include the Executive Team, Change Leadership Team, Change Project Team, and any other group of people working on some aspect of the effort. If any of these teams is not working well, their negative performance can severely impede the overall success and pace of the change. All the teams leading or contributing to the change must work effectively and expediently on behalf of producing the desired outcomes of the effort.

Do yours? If your teams are being created anew, a well-designed team start-up process expedites their launch. If the people on the team have been working together, it is very useful to assess their current effectiveness so that it can be strengthened to serve the change. The first step in assessing a team's performance and effectiveness is, of course, getting the members' agreement to address their behavior and performance to identify ways to improve and have a more positive impact on the change.

This tool helps to assess the operating and relationship effectiveness of a functioning team. It is used to surface areas where a team needs to improve on behalf of fulfilling its role on the change. This assessment can be facilitated by a change consultant or the change process leader. Teams can fill this tool out together by discussing each point and determining a consensual view, or each team member can fill it out individually and the scores of all tallied. You might also consider having people who are affected by the team's performance fill it out based on their observations of the team, similar to 360-degree feedback. If the team is just beginning, use the items in the assessment to set ground rules and goals for their effective start-up.

INSTRUCTIONS

Step 1

Consider each of the following statements, and rate your team's performance by circling the number on the rating scale based on whether you "agree," "tend to agree," "don't know," "tend to disagree," or "disagree." In some cases, it might be difficult to decide. Do not spend a great deal of time considering each statement. Simply make your decision, and move on to the next statement. Do not split hairs and attempt to answer based on a more refined scale, such as 3.7 or 4.2. Be honest with yourself, and select a number from the given five-point scale.

Step 2

The Score Sheet for the assessment follows the questions. After completing the instrument, transfer the resulting number (1 through 5) for each statement to a vertical column on the Score Sheet. If more than one person has completed the assessment, put each person's name at the top of one of the columns, then transfer each person's results into the appropriate column on the Score Sheet. Once the score sheet is completed, add all the numbers across each horizontal row, and place the results in the Total column. The highest scores indicate areas of concern. The lowest scores represent areas of strength.

Step 3

Present and explore your results with the team.

Step 4

Have the team members collectively discuss the areas requiring improvement for the change effort to succeed. Identify specific actions to take to accomplish this improvement, and begin them as soon as possible. For developmental plans that will take place throughout the change, incorporate them into the change effort's Implementation Master Plan.

Step 5

If this team has close interactions with any other teams on behalf of the change, consider using this assessment with the other teams as well. Focus attention on the quality of the working relationships and communications between the various teams.

CHANGE LEADERSHIP TEAM ASSESSMENT WORKSHEET
Dean Anderson and Linda Ackerman Anderson

1. The team charter is understood and agreed on by all team members.

1	2	3	4	5
Agree	Tend to Agree	Don't Know	Tend to Disagree	Disagree

2. Conditions for success for high performance are developed and agreed to by all team members.

1	2	3	4	5
Agree	Tend to Agree	Don't Know	Tend to Disagree	Disagree

3. Team member roles are clearly defined and accepted.

1	2	3	4	5
Agree	Tend to Agree	Don't Know	Tend to Disagree	Disagree

4. Task processes (goal or outcome oriented) for the team are in place and effective.

1	2	3	4	5
Agree	Tend to Agree	Don't Know	Tend to Disagree	Disagree

5. Group processes (interaction oriented) for the team are in place and effective.

1	2	3	4	5
Agree	Tend to Agree	Don't Know	Tend to Disagree	Disagree

6. The team has the time and resources it needs to function optimally to produce its results for the change effort.

1	2	3	4	5
Agree	Tend to Agree	Don't Know	Tend to Disagree	Disagree

7. The team has a range of diversity and uses its members' different strengths well.

1	2	3	4	5
Agree	Tend to Agree	Don't Know	Tend to Disagree	Disagree

8. The team has a clearly defined decision-making process and uses it effectively.

1	2	3	4	5
Agree	Tend to Agree	Don't Know	Tend to Disagree	Disagree

9. All team members are highly committed to the success of the team, its charter, and its deliverables for the change effort.

1	2	3	4	5
Agree	Tend to Agree	Don't Know	Tend to Disagree	Disagree

10. All team members are skilled in two-way coaching and facilitating others' learning.

1	2	3	4	5
Agree	Tend to Agree	Don't Know	Tend to Disagree	Disagree

You can download this handout to your hard drive from the accompanying CD-ROM. The document can then be opened and printed.

11. All team members are skilled at giving and receiving feedback.

1	2	3	4	5
Agree	Tend to Agree	Don't Know	Tend to Disagree	Disagree

12. The team is able to identify and resolve conflicts well.

1	2	3	4	5
Agree	Tend to Agree	Don't Know	Tend to Disagree	Disagree

13. The team has and uses a well-defined course correction process for both behavior and results.

1	2	3	4	5
Agree	Tend to Agree	Don't Know	Tend to Disagree	Disagree

14. The negative politics within the team are minimal.

1	2	3	4	5
Agree	Tend to Agree	Don't Know	Tend to Disagree	Disagree

15. The team has a clear accountability process and actively uses it to hold each other and staff support accountable for their behavior and results.

1	2	3	4	5
Agree	Tend to Agree	Don't Know	Tend to Disagree	Disagree

16. The relationships between this team and other teams supporting this change are effective.

1	2	3	4	5
Agree	Tend to Agree	Don't Know	Tend to Disagree	Disagree

17. Team members have a high degree of trust of each other.

1	2	3	4	5
Agree	Tend to Agree	Don't Know	Tend to Disagree	Disagree

18. The team has good spirit and energy.

1	2	3	4	5
Agree	Tend to Agree	Don't Know	Tend to Disagree	Disagree

19. Team members can openly discuss their operating norms, values, mind-sets, and underlying assumptions that may be negatively impacting the team's collective ability to produce results.

1	2	3	4	5
Agree	Tend to Agree	Don't Know	Tend to Disagree	Disagree

20. The team is committed to doing whatever is necessary to improve its performance on the change effort and its members' satisfaction with its way of operating.

1	2	3	4	5
Agree	Tend to Agree	Don't Know	Tend to Disagree	Disagree

You can download this handout to your hard drive from the accompanying CD-ROM. The document can then be opened and printed.

SCORE SHEET

Team _____

Directions: *Place each team member's name who has done the assessment in a vertical column, along with his or her scores. Add all the numbers across each horizontal column, and place the results in the Total column. The lowest scores represent areas of strength for the team. The highest scores indicate problem areas.*

										Total
1. Team Charter										
2. Conditions for Success										
3. Roles										
4. Task Processes										
5. Group Processes										
6. Time and Resources										
7. Diversity										
8. Decision Making										
9. Commitment										
10. Coaching										
11. Feedback										
12. Conflict Resolution										
13. Course Correction										
14. Politics										
15. Accountability										
16. Links With Other Teams										
17. Trust										
18. Spirit and Energy										
19. Openness										
20. Improvement										

IS YOUR ORGANIZATION A GENERATIVE PLACE TO WORK?

Stewart Levine

Stewart Levine *works with individuals, couples, partners, and small and large organizations of all kinds. His models for problem solving, collaboration and conflict resolution were endorsed by the House Judiciary Committee. He has worked for American Express, Chevron, ConAgra, EDS, General Motors, Oracle, University of San Francisco, and the U.S. Departments of Agriculture and the Navy. His book* **Getting to Resolution: Turning Conflict into Collaboration** *(Berrett-Koehler, 1998) was an Executive Book Club Selection, featured by Executive Book Summaries, and named one of the 30 Best Business Books of 1998. It has been translated into Russian, Hebrew, and Portuguese. He has also written* **The Book of Agreement** *(Berrett-Koehler, 2003) and is a frequent contributor to the* **Sourcebooks**.

Contact Information:
ResolutionWorks
9015 Golf Links Road
Oakland, CA 94605
510.777.1166
resolutionworks@msn.com

Overview   Organizational culture plays a critical role in the success and quality of any enterprise. The question is, what makes a particular culture unique? I believe that *culture* is a function of the quality and character of the web of relationships in the organization and, in many ways, the relationships are the organization. Another question is, what determines the quality of the relationships? The answer is the quality of agreements among individuals and between individuals and the organization.

Many personal skills, organizational factors, and other variables enable functional agreements between collaborators. This instrument is an attempt to recognize the importance of the variables, their specific presence, and their participation in designing and creating the relationships that are effective in realizing the goals of the organization. Given the different functions that organizations serve, an instrument might be more useful if it is tailored to measure the factors a particular organization believes will result in the most effective culture rather than using this generic instrument.

The instrument does not come with any statistical validation at this time. It is not intended to evaluate an organization for an award. Its best use is to serve as a place to start a conversation about an organizational culture, as well as whether and how it might be changed. As training and development professionals, your thoughts and responses are most welcome.

CULTURAL ASSESSMENT
Stewart Levine

Directions: *Circle the response that most accurately reflects your organization. At times you might be torn between two or more answers; make the selection that* **best** *reflects your assessment. Your candor is most important.*

1. The prevailing attitude of people toward others in the organization is:

   (1) I will defeat you.
   (2) I will use you.
   (3) You scratch my back, I will scratch yours.
   (4) We are partners.
   (5) We are for each other and for the whole.

2. The prevailing philosophy of most people in the organization is:

   (1) Do unto others before they do unto you.
   (2) Do unto others because everyone is doing it.
   (3) Do unto others in a way that is fair.
   (4) Do unto others as you would have them do unto you.
   (5) Do for all in a way that best serves all.

3. The prevailing belief system in our organization is:

   (1) Might makes right; winning is everything.
   (2) It is a tough competitive world.
   (3) We need to compromise.
   (4) Strategic partnerships are possible.
   (5) All stakeholders serve means-sustainable growth.

4. The quality of our agreements and keeping promises is:

   (1) Tacit, dysfunctional, hostile, codependent.
   (2) Legalistic and/or haphazard.
   (3) Intent, roles, and promises clear.
   (4) Intent, roles, promises clear, and effective accountability loops in place.
   (5) Intent, roles, promises clear, and effective self-improving and self-evolving accountability loops in place.

5. The quality of response when other people speak in our organization is:

   (1) Stereotyping and discounting.
   (2) Distracted and impatient.
   (3) Focused and nonjudgmental.
   (4) Active and appreciative.
   (5) Draws out the genius in others.

You can download this handout to your hard drive from the accompanying CD-ROM. The document can then be opened and printed.

6. The quality of inquiry is:

    (1) Punitive.
    (2) Like a cross-examination.
    (3) One of purposeful exploration.
    (4) Clarifying and integrity evoking.
    (5) Co-creatively escalating.

7. The quality of speaking in our organization is:

    (1) Attacking, blaming, alienating.
    (2) Confusing.
    (3) People speak their truth without blame or judgment.
    (4) Clarifying and integrity evoking.
    (5) Elicits breakthroughs.

8. The mood in our organization is:

    (1) Forceful and uncertain.
    (2) Wasteful and convoluted.
    (3) Polite and aloof.
    (4) One of concern for others.
    (5) Alive with enthusiasm and respect.

9. Our business results are:

    (1) Exploitative for the good of the few.
    (2) Subtly exploitative.
    (3) Value-adding for all.
    (4) Consistently high-performing from additive synergy.
    (5) Radical sustainable growth from exponential synergy.

10. The level of trust in our organization is best described as:

    (1) Fear is palpable.
    (2) Communication is constrained by unspoken fear.
    (3) Surface politeness prevails.
    (4) Truth telling is rewarded
    (5) Mutual trust and respect are at the highest levels.

11. The level of mutual respect and caring is:

    (1) Focused on the worst in others, blaming.
    (2) "Dissing"—disrespect, discounting, dishonesty, discouraging.
    (3) Perceptive of others as limited and in need of development.
    (4) A mind-set of appreciation and concern for the well-being of others.
    (5) Committed to unleashing others' gifts and potential.

You can download this handout to your hard drive from the accompanying CD-ROM. The document can then be opened and printed.

CULTURAL ASSESSMENT (CONT.)

12. The discomfort and group conflict with others are used:

    (1) As an opportunity for denial and counterattack.
    (2) To generate denial and defensiveness.
    (3) As a signal to minimize others' discomfort.
    (4) As an important signal for action and dialogue.
    (5) As an opportunity to generate a vital feedback loop.

13. Our organizational energy is characterized by:

    (1) Unhealthy stress; uncertainty and fear; blaming and attacking.
    (2) Reacting; defending; escaping; gossiping.
    (3) Analysis, planning, and design.
    (4) Exploration and discovery; reflection and practice.
    (5) Learning and teaching; co-creation and innovation; truth telling and deep listening; risk taking.

14. Our organizational mood is characterized by:

    (1) Reinforcement of vicious cycles.
    (2) Fear of making waves.
    (3) Reinforcement of status quo.
    (4) Exploring new pathways.
    (5) Spawning of generative spirals.

15. Our organizational performance is:

    (1) Worst in class.
    (2) Borderline.
    (3) Reasonably effective and efficient.
    (4) Best in class, a standard-setter.
    (5) Masterful and innovation spawning.

16. The quality of our agreements is:

    (1) Unconscious and dysfunctional.
    (2) Unclear and/or unkept.
    (3) Mostly implicit.
    (4) Mostly explicit.
    (5) Self-sustaining; self-regulating; always renegotiating.

You can download this handout to your hard drive from the accompanying CD-ROM. The document can then be opened and printed.

17. Our organizational processes are:

    (1) Malfunctioning.
    (2) Of uncertain reliability.
    (3) Minimally meeting standards—errors within tolerance.
    (4) High integrity, continuous improvement.
    (5) Self-improving and evolving.

18. Our communication pathways are:

    (1) Personal and systemic denial.
    (2) Crisis driven; subtly exploitative.
    (3) Developmental work is marginally value adding.
    (4) Highest reliability and predictability.
    (5) Spirit- and soul-enhancing.

19. Our interactions can be described as:

    (1) Attacking; blaming; grossly exploitative.
    (2) Dissing—disrespect, discounting; discouraging.
    (3) Polite on the surface; conflict suppressing.
    (4) Open, trusting, and respectful at the highest levels.
    (5) Alive and aware.

20. Our energy is characterized by:

    (1) Pervasive palpable fear.
    (2) Fear-driven high energy.
    (3) Moderation and evenness.
    (4) High levels for many.
    (5) Collaboration and generative ability.

21. Our collaborative problem-solving ability is:

    (1) Nonexistent.
    (2) On a path of diminishing results.
    (3) Cooperative when essential.
    (4) Masterful.
    (5) Innovative.

22. Generally, employees are part of the organization until they:

    (1) Burn out.
    (2) Find something more tolerable.
    (3) Retire.
    (4) Stop learning and move on.
    (5) Find something they love more.

You can download this handout to your hard drive from the accompanying CD-ROM. The document can then be opened and printed.

CULTURAL ASSESSMENT (CONT.)

23. Our people go to work every day because they:

    (1) Have not looked for something they like and they need a paycheck.
    (2) Do not have the initiative to change.
    (3) Are satisfied with their basic competence and they are comfortable.
    (4) Have the opportunity to solve problems and express creativity.
    (5) Continually exhibit masterful, innovative productivity.

24. We believe our products and/or service offerings are considered to be of _____quality?

    (1) Inferior
    (2) Marginal
    (3) Adequate
    (4) Above-average
    (5) Leading-edge

25. Our organization has a reputation in the community of being:

    (1) Exploitative.
    (2) No place special.
    (3) An OK place to work.
    (4) Top quality.
    (5) One of the best places to work.

26. Our skills in the area of collaboration and conflict resolution are:

    (1) Not part of our employee development.
    (2) Considered important, but not part of our formal training.
    (3) Part of employee development.
    (4) Considered an essential competence for all employees.
    (5) Encouraged, valued, and rewarded.

27. Our dominant organizational conversation on the availability of resources (people, equipment, expenses) is one of:

    (1) Scarcity.
    (2) Not enough.
    (3) We have enough.
    (4) We have more than enough.
    (5) We have an abundance of resources.

You can download this handout to your hard drive from the accompanying CD-ROM. The document can then be opened and printed.

28. Our organizational performance in terms of using resources is that we:

    (1) Waste a lot of resources.
    (2) Waste some of our resources.
    (3) Do not think much about using resources.
    (4) Are effective in our use of resources.
    (5) Are efficient in our use of resources.

29. As a dominant organizational mind-set, we:

    (1) Always talk about how bad things are instead of working.
    (2) Talk about problems and issues but work anyway.
    (3) Do not waste time talking about what we believe cannot be changed.
    (4) Are open to doing things differently to resolve our challenges.
    (5) Proactively use our creativity and focus on solutions to our challenges.

30. Our communication habits and processes:

    (1) Foster polarization and unproductive fighting and bickering.
    (2) Ignore conflict that everyone is aware of.
    (3) Have little impact on the ultimate resolution.
    (4) Contribute to resolving the conflict because we have had some training.
    (5) Foster resolution because we have been trained and having good agreements is one of our organizational values.

31. When we get into conflicts, we step into a mind-set of:

    (1) Righteous bravado and posturing.
    (2) "I am right."
    (3) Making believe it does not exist.
    (4) Sharing information.
    (5) Openness, willingness to be educated, and learning.

32. In conflict situations, we perceive other(s) as:

    (1) Short-term adversaries.
    (2) "I do not trust them."
    (3) "Prove to me you are trustworthy."
    (4) "I want to trust you."
    (5) Prospective partners in long-term collaborations.

33. We use _____ to resolve our differences.

    (1) Personal power
    (2) Our position
    (3) Logical thinking in our conversations
    (4) Feelings and intuition based on experience in our conversations
    (5) Logic, feelings, and intuition in our conversations

You can download this handout to your hard drive from the accompanying CD-ROM. The document can then be opened and printed.

34. Our communication is filled with:

    (1) Purposeful secrecy and withholding of information.
    (2) Providing information when asked or required.
    (3) Providing some information.
    (4) Full disclosure of information.
    (5) Full disclosure of information and feelings.

35. Our first thoughts when we have a disagreement are that:

    (1) Winning is everything and I act accordingly.
    (2) Winning is important and I will show them why I am right.
    (3) Having dialogue will be helpful.
    (4) What I learn and what I can teach about our different perspectives.
    (5) How can we develop a new agreement that takes care of everyone's needs.

36. When dealing with difficult situations, it is essential to:

    (1) Let someone else take responsibility for the outcome.
    (2) Heavily rely on the advice and counsel of experts.
    (3) Seek expert information as a guide.
    (4) Rely on the experts and use your own opinions and experience.
    (5) Take personal responsibility to resolve the situation using all available resources.

37. When we do not know the answers, we rely on:

    (1) Frenetic energy to find the solution.
    (2) What we already know.
    (3) What we know and the input of others.
    (4) Input from discerning sources.
    (5) All available resources including our own grounded intuition.

38. Most people in our organization understand that we learn the most when we are:

    (1) Speaking.
    (2) Listening to ourselves.
    (3) Listening to others.
    (4) Listening to others and ourselves.
    (5) Listening to others with our hearts.

You can download this handout to your hard drive from the accompanying CD-ROM. The document can then be opened and printed.

39. When we begin a new initiative, project, team, or reporting relationship, we:

    (1) Quickly move into action without consultation.
    (2) Touch base quickly with others involved.
    (3) Make sure we have a similar vision for the outcome.
    (4) Spend the time to make sure we have an alignment of heart and mind going forward.
    (5) Spend the time to make sure we have alignment of heart and mind going forward as a matter of standard practice.

40. When a project runs into conflict and challenges, we immediately:

    (1) Look for ways to protect and insulate ourselves from blame or fault.
    (2) Talk about who is not performing to everyone but the person we believe is responsible.
    (3) Ask a supervisor to step in and fix the problems.
    (4) Open frank conversations with the people involved.
    (5) Have a comprehensive common standard conversational process to follow.

41. As an organization we have:

    (1) No consciousness about the value of differences or the cost of conflict.
    (2) A general awareness of value of differences and the costs of conflict.
    (3) An awareness of the real costs of seemingly unresolvable differences that result in a work-stopping conflict.
    (4) A process in place to constructively address differences so as to quickly resolve costly conflicts.
    (5) A process in place to prevent differences from becoming costly conflicts.

42. Most people in our organization immediately access the following processes used to resolve conflict:

    (1) Grievance process.
    (2) Informal conferences.
    (3) Ombudsman process.
    (4) Mediation.
    (5) What they believed was the best process for the situation.

43. When it comes to training in interpersonal skills, our organization provides:

    (1) No education.
    (2) Some education as part of employee or management development.
    (3) Basic communication skills training, including listening, speaking, and presentation skills.
    (4) Advanced communication skills, including role-plays and other exercises.
    (5) Practicum and a learning program with comprehensive skills training.

CULTURAL ASSESSMENT (CONT.)

44. Our comprehensive learning programs enable employees to deal with the emotions of others because they include:

    (1) Little emotional learning as a group because it is looked upon as too touchy-feely.
    (2) Some basic sensitivity training.
    (3) Some training in the area of emotional intelligence.
    (4) Personality typing, such a MBPA or DISC, and how to deal with differences effectively.
    (5) The requirement to be certified in "emotional intelligence."

45. In terms of productivity and reaching goals, we understand that it is all about:

    (1) Working harder.
    (2) Working much harder.
    (3) Working smarter.
    (4) Synergy in our collaborative efforts.
    (5) Synergy in our collaborative efforts that begins with a shared vision and an agreement on how to achieve it.

46. When we have conflict, we understand how important it is to:

    (1) Get everyone back in action quickly.
    (2) Quickly get a new agreement in place even when there is disagreement.
    (3) Get the people who disagree to compromise.
    (4) Make sure the people who disagree go along with the new agreement and promise not to undermine the new agreement.
    (5) Have alignment and true resolution (no "chatter") about the new agreement.

47. We understand how critical it is to have the "difficult" conversations quickly and:

    (1) Unfortunately most of them are never had.
    (2) People usually have them with themselves, but they are rarely public.
    (3) People are beginning to say what needs attention, and their personal integrity is demanding that the tough questions be asked and answered.
    (4) We usually have the difficult conversations, although things could be addressed in much greater detail.
    (5) We regularly and with detail have the difficult conversations with ourselves, our supervisors, our teams, and our futures.

You can download this handout to your hard drive from the accompanying CD-ROM. The document can then be opened and printed.

48. The leaders in our organization are _____ available to engage in thoughtful dialogue.

    (1) Never
    (2) Sometimes
    (3) Often
    (4) Most of the time
    (5) Always

49. Our organizational commitment to individual and organizational learning is:

    (1) A platitude of empty words.
    (2) Available to everyone but not rewarded within our culture.
    (3) Reflected in our robust catalogue of educational offerings.
    (4) Reflected in the generativity that "learners" bring to their work.
    (5) Explicitly recognized and rewarded by our organization.

50. As an organization, we are optimistic about our future because:

    (1) It is part of our value statement.
    (2) Everyone runs around quickly and is very polite.
    (3) We have a proven track record and measurable results.
    (4) Many people in the organization can take charge of a project, develop a joint vision, and drive to a desired result.
    (5) Most people in the organization can take charge of a project, develop a joint vision, and drive to a desired result.

You can download this handout to your hard drive from the accompanying CD-ROM. The document can then be opened and printed.

SCORING

Directions: *Total all the numbers you have circled. Take the total score and use the instrument not so much as a grade, but as a basis for reflection, discussion, aspiration, and planning.*

0–25	You have a great deal of work to do to create a generative organization.
26–50	D: At least you are looking at the game board.
51–75	D+: You are getting onto the game board of generativity.
76–100	C–: You are on the generativity game board with a great deal of work to do.
101–125	C: Welcome to the low end of mediocrity.
126–150	C: Welcome to the high end of mediocrity.
151–175	B: You are doing some generative work, but there is room for improvement.
176–200	B+: You should feel real good about the generative place you work in.
201–225	A: Congratulations on being in a very generative work space.
226–250	A+: Congratulations on being in a highly generative place to work.

For all the 1 and 2 responses, you have much work to do. Where you have 3s, do you want to settle for ordinariness? Where you have 4s, what small incremental improvements can you make to get to 5? And for all the 5s, be proud and inspired to use the same skills in other areas.

ARE YOUR TEAM'S VALUES ALIGNED FOR OPTIMAL PRODUCTIVITY?

Ed Andriessen

Ed Andriessen *has trained and coached thousands of people in a broad range of topics, including management, sales, presentations, and team building. His unique perspective on these topics includes models and techniques from the field of neurolinguistic programming, a school of thought that involves strategic thinking and an understanding of the mental processes behind behavior. Ed is the codirector of the Princeton Center for NLP, which he founded with his partner in 1999. His clients have included Time, Inc., American Express Co., United States Postal Service, State Farm Insurance, Texaco, IBM, American Cyanamid, McGraw-Hill Companies, U.S. Department of Agriculture, and K. Hovnanian Homes. He has been a featured speaker for SAP America and the National Association of Homebuilders.*

Contact Information:
The Princeton Center for NLP
4599 Main Street
Kingston, NJ 08528
609.689.3748
nlpprinc@optonline.net
www.nlpprinceton.com

Overview   A team's productivity can be easily observed. Are the team members communicating effectively? Are the team members supporting each other? Is the team producing results? If the answer to these questions is no, a manager can spend an enormous amount of time coaching and correcting to improve the situation.

This assessment is designed to be conducted with all the team members present. The purpose is to allow the members to identify the desired values within the team structure and the specific behaviors needed to support these values. The team needs time to discuss the values, agree on the most important one, and share strategies for supportive behaviors.

When the team has agreed on appropriate values, individual team members invest the time and resources to support the values. Team members become "self-regulating" toward the values, and individuals adjust their capabilities and behavior to adhere to group norms.

LOGICAL LEVELS OF CHANGE AND LEARNING

The assessment is based on a model of learning and change initially formulated by Gregory Bateson and adapted by Robert Dilts in the mid-1980s. The model describes a hierarchy of levels of a group or individual. Each level affects the level below it and, by changing a higher level, you automatically produce changes in the lower levels. These levels include (in order of highest to lowest):

Level	Questions	Corresponds to:
System	For whom?	Organization or workgroup purpose
Identity	Who?	Individuals role or mission
Beliefs and values	Why?	Motivation
Capabilities	How?	Goals and plans
Behavior	What?	Actions and results
Environment	Where? When?	Constraints and opportunities

Because most organizational systems are established and individual roles are defined within these organizational systems, a group or individual can generally do little to initiate change at these levels.

However, beliefs and values can be identified and adjusted to meet a specific mission or vision. This assessment allows a team to select the most appropriate combination of values to create a positive impact on the team's motivation. When the team works at the level of beliefs and values, the team's selected levels then automatically affect the levels below, that is, capabilities, behavior, and environment.

TEAM VALUES ASSESSMENT
Ed Andriessen

Directions: *The first 12 rows identify values that most teams have identified as important and desirable. The three additional blank rows are for values that you might choose to include, such as thoroughness, accuracy, friendliness, and the like.*

Step 1. Write in additional values that you believe are important.

Step 2. Rank the values in order of importance, such as Respect is #1, Honesty is #2, and so forth.

Step 3. Rate how frequently team members demonstrate the value. Rating scale:
1 = Never, 2 = Seldom, 3 = Occasionally, 4 = Often

Rank	Value	Rating Scale
	Responsibility	
	Accountability	
	Integrity	
	Respect	
	Communication	
	Support of each other	
	Enthusiasm	
	Dedication	
	Honesty	
	Punctuality	
	Pride of workmanship	
	Reliability	

You can download this handout to your hard drive from the accompanying CD-ROM. The document can then be opened and printed.

POSTASSESSMENT DISCUSSION

1. Prior to the assessment, duplicate the values list on a chart board or white board where the participants can see them. If you cannot prepare the chart board ahead of time, ask the person who finishes the assessment first to duplicate the assessment values list.

2. The first objective of the postassessment discussion is to identify the top five values that the team agrees are the most important. With a small group of five or less, chart each individual's ranking and determine the top five values from the responses. With a larger group, ask for a show of hands to determine how many participants ranked a value in the top five. Use *M* for many (more than half), *S* for some (30 to 50 percent), *F* for few (less than 30 percent).

3. The second objective of the postassessment discussion is to have the team explore ways to integrate the values into team interactions. After the top values have been identified, initiate a discussion of the values rating by introducing this question:

   If the value is demonstrated less than often, how should we behave to demonstrate the value, and how often should we engage in the behaviors?

   With a smaller group, the discussion can be round-robin. A larger group can be broken into teams, with each team working on a different value.

4. Capture all suggestions. Either record on a chart board each participant's contributions, or distribute 3×5-inch cards and ask each participant to write at least three suggestions for how team members should support the values. Review and discuss the contributions with the participants.

   Examples:

   Responsibility

   - Participate and say what you believe.
   - Do what you say you are going to do when you say you are going to do it.
   - Take initiative!

   Respect

   - Actively listen to what I am saying.
   - Say thank you and please; be polite.
   - Speak to me in a respectful tone.

   Communication

   - Let people know immediately if there is a problem; do not wait till tomorrow.
   - If you have to write more than two paragraphs in an email, pick up the phone and call instead.
   - Ask, who else needs to know about this?

DISCUSSION POINTS

- If the team insists on having more than five values, include the additional values. Selecting a number of values is a way to stimulate a discussion about why specific values are important and the hierarchy of their importance. When team members have established the importance and hierarchy, they are more likely to support the values and take responsibility for their behavior.

- Avoid discussing the reasons for the current lack of specific values; this often leads to blame and focusing on what is not there. Concentrate the discussion on the benefits of having appropriate and resourceful values and what needs to be done to support them.

REFERENCES AND RELATED READING

Bateson, G. *Steps to an Ecology of Mind.* New York: Ballantine Books, 1972.

Deering, A., Dilts, R., and Russell, J. *Alpha Leadership.* New York: John Wiley & Sons, 2002.

Dilts, R. *Visionary Leadership Skills.* Capitola, CA: Meta Publications, 1996.

Dilts, R., and Bonissone, G. *Skills for the Future.* Capitola, CA: Meta Publications, 1993.

HOW EFFECTIVE IS YOUR FEEDBACK?

Hank Karp

Hank Karp *is an associate professor of management at Hampton University in Hampton, Virginia, and owner of Personal Growth Systems, a consulting firm that has offered training, conflict management consultation, and executive development to large corporations and government agencies, such as the Smithsonian Institutions, General Dynamics, and Chaparral Steel, for the past 27 years. He has authored over 75 publications, including four books, the most recent of which is* **Bridging the Boomer-Xer Gap: Creating Authentic Teams for High Performance at Work** *(Davies-Black Publishing, 2002), which won the ForeWord Gold Medal for Best Book in Business and Economics for 2002, and Soundviews Executive Summaries, One of the Top Thirty Books in Business for 2002. He is also a frequent contributor to the* **Sourcebooks.**

Contact Information:
Personal Growth Systems
4932 Barn Swallow Drive
Chesapeake, Virginia 23321
757.488.3536
pgshank@aol.com

Overview Giving constructive feedback is essential to subordinates, but it is fraught with problems when you do not know how to give it effectively. This instrument and the included material help you determine the effectiveness of your feedback and strategies for developing the skills in the areas that could use improvement.

FEEDBACK EFFECTIVENESS INSTRUMENT
Hank Karp

Directions: *Each of the following examples is an attempt to provide feedback. If you agree that the statement provides effective feedback, place an* A *next to it under the Individual column. If you partially agree, or disagree, place a* D *by it. When you have completed the items, attempt to reach a consensus with your group on each item, by placing your responses under the Group column. If you cannot reach agreement on a particular item, place a question mark (?) next to it.*

	Individual	Group
1. I like the way you're working.	_____	_____
2. The last three units were wrong. I'm disappointed in your performance.	_____	_____
3. Your attitude has been improving over the last six weeks.	_____	_____
4. I'm pleased to tell you that you made every deadline last quarter.	_____	_____
5. According to this record, you were late several times last month.	_____	_____
6. I am really sorry to have to tell you that your performance has been deteriorating.	_____	_____
7. You were very hostile toward Charlie in the meeting today.	_____	_____
8. You did it right but you didn't get in on time.	_____	_____
9. It seemed to me that you were shouting at Janet and I saw her flinch. What might have worked better would have been . . .	_____	_____
10. Oh by the way, I wanted to let you know that that complex revision you suggested was the key factor in our getting the Miller contract. Way to go.	_____	_____

SCORING

Item	Answer	Guideline Violated
1	D	1
2	D	3
3	D	2
4	A	OK
5	D	4
6	D	10 (7)
7	D	2
8	D	6
9	A	OK
10	D	5

Note: A case can be easily made for some of the statements to have violated more than just the one designated and the possibility might be the source of a good discussion. The emphasis here is on the *major* violation.

THE IMPORTANCE OF EFFECTIVE FEEDBACK

Feedback is probably covered more than any other specific topic in management development programs. Obviously, any feedback is better than none at all; however, the difference between any old feedback and *effective* feedback is monumental. Although most things about feedback are already known, the critical elements are often forgotten. For feedback to be truly effective on an ongoing basis, only a few simple assumptions and guidelines need to be remembered.

The Assumptions

Three assumptions about feedback need to be stated clearly at the very beginning.

1. There is no such thing as negative feedback.
2. Effective feedback is an essential element for human motivation and development.
3. Feedback is the *only* tool available to the manager to *constantly control* behavior in the work setting.

1. No Such Thing as Negative Feedback

With a continuing move toward more humanistic and progressive strategies in today's organizations, the thrust for most enlightened managers is to create "positive" work environments. Also, the common view is to look at feedback as being either positive or negative. Once this view is taken, positive feedback becomes a good thing to give and to hear, and negative feedback becomes a bad thing. In many cases, people do not get the negative feedback because of an unwillingness to listen on their part, or because the manager does not want to create an uncomfortable situation or be seen as being hurtful. The end result is that the employee does not get the essential information about his or her performance and continues to perform or behave in a manner that is not consistent with organizational standards or objectives. The longer the manager withholds the negative information, the more dysfunctional the behavior becomes and the more difficult it becomes for the manager to intervene. This usually results in calling in a third party to help the employee correct the dysfunctional behavior or the employee being unfairly disciplined or terminated.

There *are* two types of feedback, and both are positive:

- *Supportive feedback* is critical in reinforcing appropriate behavior so that it is repeated.

- *Corrective feedback* indicates that the behavior needs to be changed.

Both are positive! Although supportive feedback is much easier to give and to receive, corrective feedback can also be given in a way that the recipient is willing to hear, consider, and make the related changes. Both methods also make it easier for the giver to be clear and willing to share the information.

2. Effective Feedback Is Essential for Motivation and Development

Almost all current theories of human motivation (e.g., Maslow's Need-Hierarchy Theory or Herzberg's Motivator-Hygiene Theory) stress the point that all people strive toward growth, increased competence, and self-actualization. Feedback is as critical for psychological growth as food is for physical growth. Feedback provides a standard by which behavior or performance can be measured and criteria on which to base decisions on whether one needs to continue with a specific behavior or to modify it.

3. Feedback Is the Only Tool to Constantly Control Behavior

This assumption is a "blinding glimpse of the obvious" yet very few managers are fully aware of its significance. All other tools available for reinforcing or modifying behavior are formalized and occur at specific times or within specific contexts. Annual performance reviews, promotions, service awards, reprimands, raises, disciplinary procedures, and the like all require some kind of organizational procedure and timeline to occur. For example, the time elapsing between an event and a resultant merit pay increase could be months. This is a formal recognition of something and is a good thing, but it provides no increase in awareness of the event. Without the use of constant and consistent feedback, managers have little ability to affect the behavior of their direct reports and are usually left in the position of either blaming or hoping that things will improve.

The Guidelines

Providing effective feedback is a very simple process and is easier to do correctly than not doing it at all, once you are aware of the things to include or avoid. As a matter of fact, it is as simple as the following three-step process:

Supportive Feedback

1.	*Point out the specific behavior:*	"Excellent analysis on the Digby proposal."
2.	*Show the effects of that behavior:*	"We got the account based on your suggestions."
3.	*Explore possible applications:*	"Could any of that apply to the Ogden proposal?"

Corrective Feedback

1. *Point out the specific behavior:*	"I think you were overly harsh in criticizing Jenny in the meeting today."
2. *Show the effects of the behavior:*	"She totally withdrew for the balance of the meeting and we lost her input."
3. *Suggest what might have worked better:*	"It might have been more appropriate to have shared your view with her privately after the meeting."

Guideline 1: Deal in Specifics

Although often producing good feelings for the recipient, generalities in *supportive* feedback have no impact on performance. For example, you say to a direct report, "Charlie, your work is really improving." How does he feel when he hears this? *Great!* What has he learned? *Nothing at all.* However, if you were to say, "Charlie, you have made every deadline since the beginning of the quarter." Now he feels great *and* knows what he has done to produce the result. In short, generalities in supportive feedback render the feedback useless.

In giving *corrective* feedback, you have to say more than, "Charlie, you had better start doing better work around here." The likely result of such feedback is to produce confusion and maybe even some anger. On the other hand, suppose I say, "Charlie, the last three units were off specs by 8 percent. You need to check the readings a little more closely before you start milling." What has happened and what needs to be changed are clear. In short, generalities in corrective feedback produce defensiveness, confusion, and hostility.

Guideline 2: Focus on Actions, Never on Attitudes

There is no such thing as an attitude problem! An attitude is a feeling and the only way any feeling can be expressed is through behavior. Ask people how they know another person has an "attitude problem," and invariably they describe a set of observable actions. Any attack on a person's attitude is an attack on the person's beliefs or values. It is taken very personally and invariably produces a defensive or hostile response.

Calling attention to a person's inappropriate behavior does not imply anything negative about the person as a person. The observation is a shared experience of which both people are aware, and it can be dealt with supportively. Note the differences in the following examples:

Attitude:	"You're not a team player."
Behavior:	"You seem unwilling to share the relevant data with Sally."
Attitude:	"You have a sloppy attitude about your work."
Behavior:	"Your error rate has been increasing over the past few weeks."

Attitude:	"You really are arrogant."
Behavior:	"You state your own positions clearly and strongly and you need to listen to what others have to say, as well.

Guideline 3: Depersonalize the Process

Your personal approval, or lack of it, is of little or no importance. The more you use your personal approval or disapproval as a reinforcer of subordinate behavior, the more you reinforce the "parent-child" role in the work setting. I suppose, when someone has accomplished something extraordinary, there is little harm in adding, "By the way, I am really pleased with how that turned out." It does not help, but it really does not hurt that much either.

On the other hand, suppose you tell a direct report, "I am really, really disappointed in your behavior at the meeting." That kind of statement is patronizing and implies that the employee's primary obligation is to please you, rather than to be appropriate. Any statement of personal disapproval in a corrective feedback situation automatically produces resentment and distancing.

Guideline 4: The Longer You Wait to Give Feedback, the Less Impact It Has

The rule of thumb is to provide feedback as soon possible after an event. The longer one waits to give feedback, the more new events occur that may be as important or more so. After a certain amount of time, the feedback has little or no impact on the employee's behavior. As a matter of fact, if you wait too long in giving supportive feedback, you risk having the opposite effect of what you intended. After a period of time, any supportive feedback is seen for what it is, an afterthought at best and a manipulating human relation's SOP at worst. The best this produces is a healthy dose of resentment and a loss of your credibility.

Guideline 5: Delivery of the Feedback Should Match Its Importance

Back in the 1960s, Marshall McLuhan said it best, "The medium is the message." When giving supportive feedback, particularly for a notable accomplishment, the surroundings need to support the message. For example, time has been allotted, no interruptions are allowed, the setting is away from the work area, and so forth. The same holds true for giving corrective feedback in that the surroundings also convey the message: "This is important."

Guideline 6: Praise in Public, Censure in Private?

This old bromide, like most old bromides, is only partially true. The true part is that unless you have really extreme circumstances, *never* deliver corrective feedback publicly. This only produces embarrassment at being corrected in front of colleagues and an entrenched desire for retribution. Be aware that, although the majority of people might bask in public recognition, a sizable number find it embarrassing. This usually applies to all male groups and the related group norms. Praising an employee in front of his co-workers could result in his also being playfully derided by them for being a "good little worker" and the boss's pet. If you think public recognition would be painful for someone, take him in private and give it to him. He might turn red, twist his big toe in the sand, and mumble something like, "Ah shucks, t'warnt nuthin'." Do it anyway because learning to accept supportive feedback is an important step in personal growth. Just do not do it publicly.

Guideline 7: Use And *Rather Than* But

When giving both supportive and corrective feedback is appropriate, the connector you use can have impact.

Example:

- "You did an excellent job on the Digby proposal *but* you forgot to include the extra copy."

- "You did an excellent job on the Digby proposal *and* you forgot to include the extra copy."

The term *but* has a tendency to discount whatever came in front of it. Thus the second part of the message is what gets emphasized and clearly heard. Using the term *and* increases the probability that both parts of the message get through clearly.

Guideline 8: Alternate Supportive and Corrective Feedback

Some situations call for a great deal of feedback, such as at the end of a major project or a quarterly performance review. Most people wallow in supportive feedback and attempt to block or avoid hearing corrective feedback. At best, they want to get through it as quickly as possible. The challenge to the manager is to keep the employee in an open and receptive position for *all* the feedback. An excellent way to do this is to alternate the feedback as you are giving it. A good strategy is to start and end with supportive feedback, and alternate the supportive with the corrective feedback. There is less chance of employees "shutting down" when they know that there is still supportive feedback on the way.

Guideline 9: When Feasible, Use Supportive Feedback to Cushion Corrective Feedback

In most cases, employees do a lot more right than wrong. Were that not the case, the employee's behavior would be an area of concern. One way to keep the employee open to hearing corrective feedback is to cushion it with *honest* supportive feedback. For example, "Jack, I'd like you to have the same commitment to getting here on time that you have to the excellent work you turn out." How hard is that to hear?

Guideline 10: Use Time to Your Advantage

When giving supportive feedback, use all the time you can without letting the process drag. Encouraging the employee to re-experience success does a lot to drive it home. Get the employee to brag about it. This can be easily accomplished by asking questions like, how did you come up with that? What obstacles did you encounter? How did you overcome them?

Hearing your supportive feedback is critical but not nearly as effective as employees hearing *themselves* say how important the accomplishment was.

In giving corrective feedback, use the minimum amount of time necessary to ensure that the employee is aware of the behavior, its effects, and the options—without rushing it. No matter how good you are at giving corrective feedback, it still is not pleasant. Once the feedback has been delivered and acknowledged, move on to something else, if possible. For example, "By the way, as long as you're here, I need your input on the Wallace project."

Guideline 11: End on a Positive Note

Feedback, regardless of its nature, is an interruption in the work flow. Transition the employee back into the work routine as seamlessly and as positively as possible. In the case of supportive feedback, a brief statement of congratulations is appropriate. In this case, being a bit general is not distracting because you have already been specific about the nature of the accomplishment. For example, "In wrapping it up, I just want to say again that your work was really outstanding."

Ending positively is even more important when concluding corrective feedback. Sometimes, regardless of how effective you are in providing the feedback, the employee still feels somewhat shaken or less self-confident. A word of encouragement goes a long way in helping the employee re-enter the work setting. Close with statements like, "I am confident that you will get on top of this" or "Let me know if I can assist." Such statements let the employee know that you are there to provide support.

A CLOSING NOTE

The most important and most obvious element in providing feedback is this: The necessary but not sufficient condition for providing effective feedback is that you are *authentic* at all times. The moment your credibility is questioned, your feedback becomes suspect, if not totally useless. With the best of intentions, some managers go overboard in providing feedback and in doing so discount everything that they are saying. A few precautions to keep in mind are:

1. Do not provide feedback on something the worker already knows. A simple acknowledgment suffices.

2. Do not provide supportive feedback for trivial accomplishments: "Way to get back from lunch on time!"

3. Do not withhold corrective feedback for trivial infractions: "I noticed you were late reporting in today. Anything wrong?"

4. Ask employees if they are getting the level of feedback they need from you.

5. It would not hurt periodically to ask your direct reports for feedback to make sure you are providing them with what they need from you. This also shows that you buy what you sell.

6. Keep it simple and direct, especially when providing corrective feedback.

7. *Never* apologize for giving corrective feedback. It is a gift!

REFERENCES

Karp, H. B. "The Last Act of Feedback." In J. William Pfeiffer, ed., *The 1987 Annual: Developing Human Resources*. San Francisco: Pfeiffer, 1987.

HELPFUL HANDOUTS

In this section of *The 2006 ASTD Organization Development and Leadership*, you will find seven helpful handouts. These handouts cover topics such as:

✓ Mentoring

✓ Hiring and managing breakthrough thinkers

✓ Working with resistance

✓ Managing programs

✓ Planning and strategic thinking

✓ Building trust

✓ Creating a healthy work organization

These handouts can be used as:

✓ Participant materials in training programs

✓ Discussion documents during meetings

✓ Coaching tools or job aids

✓ Information to be read by you or shared with a colleague

All the handouts are designed as succinct descriptions of an important issue or skill in performance management and development. They are formatted for quick, easily understood reading. (You may want to keep these handouts handy as memory joggers or checklists by posting them in your work area.) Most important of all, they contain nuggets of practical advice!

Preceding each handout is a brief overview of its contents and uses. The handout itself is on a separate page(s) to make reproduction convenient.

It is helpful to read these handouts actively. Highlight points that are important to you or push you to do further thinking. Identify content that needs further clarification. Challenge yourself to come up with examples that illustrate the key points. Urge others to be active consumers of these handouts, as well.

FOUR METHODS AND FOUR STEPS TO FAST-TRACK MENTORING

Beverly Kaye

Beverly Kaye, EdD, *is the founder and CEO of Career Systems International and one of the nation's leading authorities on career issues in the workplace. A dynamic and committed keynote speaker, Beverly's presentations engage participants, stimulate learning, and inspire action. Her career development, talent retention, and mentoring programs have been implemented by her training and consulting team at such leading corporations as American Express, AT&T, Citigroup, DaimlerChrysler, Hartford Life, Lockheed Martin, Marriott International, Microsoft, Sears, Sprint, Starbucks, Wells Fargo, and Xerox. Beverly's books include* **Love 'Em or Lose 'Em: Getting Good People to Stay***, now in its third edition (Berrett-Koehler, 2005), coauthored with Sharon Jordan-Evans;* **Love It, Don't Leave It: 26 Ways to Get What You Want at Work** *(Berrett-Koehler, 2003);* **Learning Journeys** *(Davies-Black, 2001), edited by Beverly, a collection of essays from top management experts; and the now classic book* **Up Is NOT the Only Way** *(revised, Davies-Black, 1997). Beverly is also a frequent contributor to the* **Sourcebooks***.*

Contact Information:
Career Systems International
3545 Alana Drive
Sherman Oaks, CA 91403
818.995.6454
Beverly.kaye@csibka.com
www.careersystemsintl.com
www.keepem.com
www.loveitdontleaveit.com

Overview The case for mentoring in organizations is now more compelling than ever. It is clear that mentoring supports the retention, development, and engagement of today's workforce. It is a direct link to an organization's productivity and, ultimately, profitability. No one really needs to be convinced as to what a powerful and dynamic process mentoring can be for both employees and organizations. It has the potential to elevate corporate dialogue from the mundane to the truly transformational. But the key concern has always been how do managers learn the skills, find the time, and build the relationships necessary to make it successful.

Many mentoring programs begin with high energy and good intentions, but end up with little impact and less long-term follow-through. In our current organizational climate, there is a pressing need for a practical way to educate managers and leaders quickly so that they see mentoring as a positive experience rather than a burden. The task is to integrate a simple and effective method to give managers, team leaders, and individual contributors the basic skills and practical how-to's of mentoring others that makes it part of their ongoing responsibilities and not an add-on.

It is a rare organization today that can afford to take mentoring partners offsite for extended training. The alternative is to provide an easy self-study process or brief facilitated program that highlights the most important aspects of the mentoring process and gets mentors started immediately. This handout outlines four methods and four steps to fast-track mentoring.

FOUR METHODS AND FOUR STEPS TO FAST-TRACK MENTORING
Beverly Kaye

WHAT MENTORS DO

Everyone brings unique experiences and expertise to the mentoring relationship. Allowing mentors to begin with their strengths gives them confidence and comfort with the process. Here are four different ways mentors can work with their partners. Mentors can try on each of these to see which works best for them.

Guide

- ✓ Helps partners in their learning by showing them different paths and warning of potential pitfalls.
- ✓ Shares strategic views of the organization.
- ✓ Helps partners reflect on their attitudes, skills, and patterns of behaviors and whether they help or hinder their success.
- ✓ Asks questions that challenge partners to think, analyze, and probe for meaning.

Ally

- ✓ Provides a risk-free environment in which partners can vent frustrations, share difficulties, and seek other perspectives.
- ✓ Appraises behaviors and helps partners see how others perceive them.
- ✓ Talks straight, not as a critic or judge, but as a candid and honest partner.
- ✓ Provides specific feedback and impressions—favorable and unfavorable—to support partners' personal growth.

Catalyst

- ✓ Motivates partners' enthusiasm and initiative.
- ✓ Helps partners see their future in the organization with a new insight and vision.
- ✓ Sees unanticipated possibilities that partners might make happen.
- ✓ Focuses on encouraging partners to discuss ideas, visions, and creative concepts that might not find a forum elsewhere.

Advocate

- ✓ Champions the ideas and interests of partners so that visibility and exposure is gained.
- ✓ Helps partners by opening opportunities for specific learning experiences.
- ✓ Captures the attention of significant others to help effectively connect partners.
- ✓ Uses a powerful voice to bring partners' ideas to the people in the organization who have the authority to implement them.

You can download this handout to your hard drive from the accompanying CD-ROM. The document can then be opened and printed.

FOUR METHODS AND FOUR STEPS TO FAST-TRACK MENTORING (CONT.)

HOW MENTORS DO WHAT THEY DO

A practical and direct process for use by new or seasoned mentors can be mastered in four simple steps.

STEP 1: EXTEND YOUR REACH

Managers often report that one of the most satisfying parts of their job is when they have the opportunity to share their knowledge, experiences, and insight with others. Reaching beyond the daily responsibilities of their job and profoundly affecting the growth and development of others brings the manager immediate rewards and the organization long-lasting benefits. Fast-track mentoring education begins with "where and how" to offer help to learning partners.

STEP 2: LISTEN, DON'T PREACH

The mentor's job does not start with giving advice—it begins with listening. A mentor needs to hear what their partners want from the process. It is also critical to learn about development needs and expectations. A good mentor must learn to explore the focus and understand the goals of their partners.

STEP 3: DO MORE THAN TEACH

The traditional mentor was a teacher—but today it takes much more to be a successful mentor. Four different conversation styles, which have been proven to promote learning and transmit knowledge quickly, can be used. Mentors need to learn how to share their stories, encourage dialog, debrief their partner's experiences, and help build network connections for their partners. As stated in step 2, the mentor's job does not start with giving advice—it begins with listening. You need to hear what your partner wants from the process and from you. It is critical to learn about development needs and expectations.

STEP 4: DEFINE ACTIONS FOR EACH

Mentoring partners have equal responsibilities in making the process work. They need specific action plans so that both mentor and partner can measure the progress of their work together. The mentoring process can be a great source of personal learning and satisfaction for everyone. But much of its success depends on finding the right balance between doing too much and doing too little.

HOW EVERYONE BENEFITS

Though the time-honored practice of mentoring has always been with us, it is now more than ever a dynamic tool for building collaborative relationships. Organizations need a simple but elegant way to demystify the mentoring journey. It also should work to develop the mentor as he or she works to develop others.

A successful process should provide mentors and their partners with specifics on what to do, what to talk about, and how to take action. Mentoring in the fast-track format might well be one of the most powerful ways to engage and retain both employees and managers. It should also provide a payback for the organization so that talent can be recognized and grown.

You can download this handout to your hard drive from the accompanying CD-ROM. The document can then be opened and printed.

TIPS FOR HIRING AND MANAGING BREAKTHROUGH THINKERS

Jeanne Baer

Since founding Creative Training Solutions in 1990, **Jeanne Baer** *has served clients as diverse as Chrysler, Duke Energy, Cliffs Notes, DuPont Pharma, Global Internet, Ameritas, and Omaha Steaks. Jeanne's work appears in 18 books by publishers such as McGraw-Hill, Harvard Business School Press, Pfeiffer, and ASTD. She is a frequent contributor to the* **Sourcebooks** *and has written more than 140 "Managing Smart" columns for* **Strictly Business** *and other magazines. She's also been quoted in* **Investor's Business Daily** *and other newspapers. Jeanne is featured in the frequently broadcast Speaking with Confidence course produced by Great Plains National Instructional Television, and she hosts the biweekly TrainingNow! television program on cable channel 13 in Lincoln, Nebraska. She has been active in ASTD since 1987 and has received several local and national leadership awards from the society.*

Contact Information:
Creative Training Solutions
1649 South 21st Street
Lincoln, NE 68502
402.475.1127 or 800.410.3178
jbaer@cts-online.net
www.cts-online.net

Overview You would like your organization to be more innovative. And you plan to do some hiring in the near future. Is it possible to hire people who are especially creative? If so, how do you identify them? Are they the ones wearing the wild and crazy clothes, bouncing off the walls? Can you administer a "creativity test" so that you can be sure you are hiring the best person?

And once you have hired them, how can you encourage these "wild ducks" to fly in formation while still being creative?

In short, whether your organization needs new processes, products, services, or markets, creative thinkers can take you there. Your challenge is to establish an environment in which they can flourish and also create profitable innovation for your company. These tips help you do that.

HIRING BREAKTHROUGH THINKERS
Jeanne Baer

Hiring for creative talent is not simple. However, seven factors can help you make a wise choice:

1. *Does the candidate have a prior history of creative work?* What can she tell or show you as examples? Look for examples of great ideas that also fulfilled a need, not simply interesting sounding ideas that were too outré to be ultimately successful. Ask experienced-based questions, such as, "Tell me about a time when you had to think out of the box. How about a time when a solution you proposed didn't work? Was there a time when you worked with a team to improve a process, product, or service?"

2. *Does the candidate think of himself as creative?* It may sound positively Pygmalion-esque, but the power of positive expectation is strong. People who expect themselves to have great ideas are off and running in pursuit of them, while people who are uncertain of their abilities waste hours whining.

3. *How does the candidate react to others' ideas?* Does she seem flexible and nonjudgmental when presented with potential solutions to a problem? You can sometimes observe this behavior by asking several candidates to solve a problem *together*.

4. *What is the candidate's attitude about problems?* Does he look at situations as problems (to be solved) or as conditions (to be tolerated or, worse, complained about)? Does he seem to perceive problems as threats or as exciting challenges? You might be able to discern the person's attitude by presenting him with a scenario and asking for a reaction.

5. *Does she have a sense of humor?* Usually people who do are also capable of seeing a situation from several perspectives and of approaching it with flexibility.

6. *Does the candidate have breadth and depth of experience?* Though creative insight seems to come from "nowhere," it actually depends on detailed past experience with similar problems. That does not necessarily mean that the candidate with the longest work history has the advantage; has the person been doing the same-old same-old work for 20 years? The *broader* the base of a person's experience is, the greater his variety of behavior and problem-solving skills will be.

7. *Will the candidate thrive in your culture?* Ask, "What kind of environment helps you be creative?" Possible answers include, "I usually get my best ideas working alone. I love bouncing ideas off of other people. I like to express my creativity with props, toys, and other items to stimulate my thinking. I need a lot of flexibility, no supervision." Whatever the answer, you can decide whether it fits your situation!

But before you dash off to go "shopping" for a breakthrough-thinking genius, consider one more thing: You might not need to. You are probably *already* surrounded by employees whose ideas can make a tremendous difference in your organization.

Use their creativity in small, incremental ways: For example, accountants figure out how to eliminate steps in a billing process, production workers suggest ways to avoid costly errors on the line, and truck drivers load their trucks so that the freight can be off-loaded faster. At American Airlines, a flight attendant pointed out a way to save eight cents per flight on unneeded disposable coffee pot lids. It might seem trivial, but it saved the airline US $62,000 per year.

You can download this handout to your hard drive from the accompanying CD-ROM. The document can then be opened and printed.

MANAGING BREAKTHROUGH THINKERS

So encourage every employee to generate at least one idea every week, to solve a problem, or to seize an opportunity. Implement the best ideas, but praise *all* of them. After all, the only way to get *super* ideas is to get a *lot* of them!

Credit Tom Watson Jr., former chairman of IBM, for inventing the term *wild ducks* to describe his creative R&D people. Watson used to tell a parable about wild ducks that went something like this:

> There was once a magnificent flock of ducks, which was heading south for the winter. One day they flew to the ground to rest for a bit and were delighted when a bird lover saw them and threw a bucket load of tasty treats out to them. The next day, he returned with another lavish smorgasbord, persuading the ducks to just hang out and vacation for a while! Naturally, the longer the feathered squatters camped in this Garden of Eden, the tamer (and fatter) they got, until they could only waddle and belch from place to place. Unable to fly, they became lazy, mooching pets.

The moral of the tale? You can tame wild ducks, but you cannot make tamed ducks wild again. What about your own wild ducks? Yes, they rock the boat, march to the beat of a different drummer, and annoy those who follow all the rules. They are sometimes more interested in realizing their own vision than in meeting deadlines or budgets.

FIVE WAYS TO HELP YOUR MAGNIFICENT WILD DUCKS FLY HAPPILY AND PRODUCTIVELY IN FORMATION

1. *Make the environment safe for creativity:* Give people prompt feedback on their ideas; make them feel safe to take risks; and, when they have a terrific idea, make it possible for them to implement it. When a seemingly good idea fails, do not sweep it under the rug. Discuss how it *advanced knowledge* on the topic, and talk about what might be done next time to get better results.

2. *Encourage a little creative chaos and conflict:* When everyone is orderly and in agreement, solutions are same-old same-old. When people actively brainstorm and respectfully argue, innovative solutions are discovered.

3. *Provide plenty of recognition:* Wild ducks throw their hearts and souls—their whole identities—into their work. Recognize them within your organization; maybe you can even start a "hall of fame" for the creative people who have made significant contributions. If possible, extend recognition beyond your company. Encourage them to enter their work in a regional or national competition run by their professional association, or see if you can wangle recognition on the association's Website.

4. *Control the ends, but not the means to the ends:* Freedom is a very strong need among creative people; it gives them a sense of control over their work and ideas. But even if micromanagement is the worst nightmare for wild ducks, they cannot be allowed to fly around aimlessly. Legendary entrepreneur John Kao advises managers to "Practice empathy. Don't kowtow to the rhythm of creative work, but always respect it." In other words, give people responsibility for coming up with the process *and* responsibility for meeting deadlines.

You can download this handout to your hard drive from the accompanying CD-ROM. The document can then be opened and printed.

5. *Help wild ducks see how their contribution fits into the big picture and the company's goals:* You can give them well-deserved praise, and you can steer them away from being creative *just* to be creative. After all, if their creation does not address the needs of your customers— if the solution is merely "elegant" or "fascinating"—it is not enough.

Managing wild ducks is an exasperating and exhilarating challenge. But take a page from the wild ducks' playbook: Be entrepreneurial yourself and take a few risks. Whenever possible, give creative people stimulating, useful, and worthwhile projects to work on. After all, the opportunity to solve an interesting problem is what gets many of us out of bed every day!

If you create a conducive environment, your breakthrough thinkers will not only drag themselves out of bed, they will take to the skies and fly with the eagles. You and they will be pleased with the results.

You can download this handout to your hard drive from the accompanying CD-ROM. The document can then be opened and printed.

SIX METHODS FOR WORKING WITH RESISTANCE

Robyn Wagner Skarbek

Robyn Wagner Skarbek *has more than 10 years of experience in organization development and performance consulting. She is employed by Deloitte Consulting, LLP as a senior consultant. Robyn is committed to helping her clients achieve their goals and has been recognized for her ability to build strong client partnerships. She has presented at international conferences, is an ISPI Awards of Excellence recipient for work with financial services call centers, and is a frequent contributor to the* **Sourcebooks***.*

Contact Information:
Deloitte Consulting, LLP
Two Braxton Way
Glen Mills, PA 19346
610.390.9337
rlws@hotmail.com

Overview This handout is designed to help people who engage in consultative relationships work with the resistance that is an inevitable component of such engagements.

Used as a training tool with new or veteran consultants, it can be included as part of training programs on consulting, industry workshops, or as a one-on-one coaching tool. Although the primary audience is human resource practitioners, sales representatives who utilize a consultative sales approach will also find the handout useful. Sales coaches can use it to coach sales reps on working with objections received during the sales process or as a tool during sales training.

SIX METHODS FOR WORKING WITH RESISTANCE
Robyn Wagner Skarbek

Webster's dictionary defines resistance as "(1) The act or capacity of resisting (2) A force that opposes or retards." However one chooses to define resistance, a visceral reaction is associated with the term. It can foster feelings of anxiety, fear, anger, or confusion. Working with resistance is a challenge that practitioners (trainers, performance consultants, organization development consultants, sales consultants, or other helping professions) deal with regularly. Working with resistance can occur effectively with the right skills and competencies.

Resistance develops in response to an unwillingness to give something up, a sense of comfort with stability rather than with change, a belief that the change does not make sense, or fear of the unknown. Given all that is known about adult learning, it is rational to acknowledge that adults have anxiety about trying something new and find comfort in known structures and processes. Another significant source of resistance is a lack of understanding regarding the reasons behind the change. Once resistance is generated, it can manifest itself through defense mechanisms, including repression and denial.

Working with resistance challenges practitioners to be grounded in the theory of their intervention or solution and to utilize strong consulting skills. Here are six methods for coping with resistance.

1. *Inclusion:* Including the client in planning and designing the change process is critical to surfacing resistance early and to promoting client ownership of the solution. Partnering with the client through any consulting engagement creates an environment in which clients feel safe enough to voice their concerns and enables the practitioner to effectively address the client's concerns.

2. *Recognize that resistance is a natural reaction:* With our knowledge of adult learning, we recognize that adults find comfort in what they know and that anxiety can be generated when something new is introduced. If an atmosphere of trust and openness has been created, then clients feel comfortable expressing their concerns. The time for the practitioner to be concerned is when resistance is not being expressed at all. This could indicate that the client does not feel safe enough to share concerns, thoughts, or feelings and the practitioner will not have the opportunity to address them. Recognize that resistance is natural and, if it is being expressed, the practitioner is making a genuine connection with the client

3. *Recognize resistance is a "buying signal":* Expressing resistance is a sign that the client is seriously considering adopting the options presented. The client is mentally walking through the process and identifying points of concern or question. This is why it is important to shift the paradigm from "overcoming" resistance to "working with" it. Overcoming resistance connotes "making it go away." A slight shift in words leads to a significant shift in thinking. In working with resistance, practitioners engage the client and generate a meaningful dialogue about the impending change, product purchase, and so forth.

You can download this handout to your hard drive from the accompanying CD-ROM. The document can then be opened and printed.

SIX METHODS FOR WORKING WITH RESISTANCE (CONT.)

4. *Listen empathetically:* Genuinely listening to the clients' concerns, expressing empathy, and comprehensively addressing their concerns all help practitioners work with resistance. This method includes remaining silent and not interrupting the client, maintaining eye contact, and/or providing verbal acknowledgment (especially if working virtually) and paraphrasing to ensure that their message was received in the manner intended. A natural reaction from the practitioner is to address clients' concerns and move quickly through the process. A key piece is to meet clients where they are and then move forward together. The more time you spend up front, working with concerns, the less likely there will be surprises further along in the process.

5. *Explain the reasoning behind the initiative:* Adults learn better when they understand the why behind a new initiative. Address this component in all communications and be willing to address it as many times as necessary. Just as everyone expresses resistance in a unique way, individuals vary in their adaptation processes. Adults can hear only what they are ready to hear as they adapt to the change. Therefore, communicating frequently throughout the process, using multiple communication mediums, and including the reasons behind the change all facilitate working with resistance.

6. *Analyze the audience:* Determine where the group is right now and engage them at that point. If you are at a feedback meeting and clients are expressing resistance, explore what is generating the resistance and where it focused. Then address it to let the audience know they have been heard. Make the process transparent so the clients are aware of the resistance and feel they are a part of addressing it.

Change stirs people's emotions at a deep level and it is critical not to underestimate the impact of emotions. By working with resistance rather than trying to overcome it, organizations and practitioners can learn to value resistance because people are seriously considering the new state. The questions generated and the resistance exhibited can help identify previously unseen leverage points and facilitate an engagement that is appreciated and valued by the client.

REFERENCES

Bettelheim, B. "Individual and Mass Behavior in Extreme Situations." *Journal of Abnormal and Social Psychology* 38 (1943): 417–452.

Bridges, W. *Transitions.* Cambridge, MA: Perseus Books Publishing, LLC, 1980.

Nevis, E. C. *Organizational Consulting: A Gestalt Approach.* Cambridge, MA: GIC Press, 1987.

Segal, M. *Points of Influence.* San Francisco: Jossey-Bass, Inc., 1987.

THE QUICK GUIDE TO PROGRAM MANAGEMENT IN FIVE SHORT STEPS

Mark Casey

Mark Casey *is a consultant with AARP, where he helps internal clients target performance solutions for their staff. He is an active presenter for both NASAGA and CBODN. Mark is developing a community of practice to discuss visual cues and interpretations in Web-based and virtual learning environments. He is a past contributor to both* **Sourcebooks***.*

Contact Information:
AARP
601 E Street NW
Washington, DC 20049
202.434.3395
mcasey@aarp.org

Overview   Somewhere along the line, the promise of simplifying program management through the integration of technology seemed to make a couple things more difficult. Many of the breakdowns in projects are usually attributed to team members who are unsure either of how they fit into the puzzle or of how they are contributing to the final product. Often team members feel alienated from a program because they have not been provided a basic idea of who they are, why they are important, and how they fit into the entire project team. This helpful handout outlines a five-step model for developing a healthy model of program or project management and for starting it off on the right foot.

THE QUICK GUIDE TO PROGRAM MANAGEMENT IN FIVE SHORT STEPS

Mark Casey

Step

Description

The overall program *description* is a cornerstone to any project, defining the client's needs and expectations. The description offers the entire team an idea of what the final product resembles, and answers basic questions like, *where are they/we now?* and *where do we need to be?*

While drafting the *description* for your program, ask and answer the following questions:

- What is the project?
- What problem will this product resolve?
- Why is the project important to the client?
- What challenges are immediately clear?
- What might the completed project resemble?
- Where are we right now?

Roles

Roles define each team member's identity on the project. They allow individual members to determine where they fit in the scope of the project and in the hierarchal structure of the team. Defining how each role touches the end product demonstrates the importance of each team member and stresses the necessity of a cohesive working unit—the project team.

While drafting the *role* descriptions for your program, ask and answer the following questions:

- What is the title of the role?
- What is the role's relationship to the final product?
- What is the role's relationship to the customer?
- What is the role's relationship to their teammates?
- Where does the role fit in the project schema?
- Where does the role fit in the project table of organization?

Expectations

Clear *expectations* allow staff to gauge their level of activity and the type of output required of them to ensure the success of the project. Communicating the expectations in a clear and concise manner helps team members understand how their contributions have a direct impact on their fellow members' deliverables and the overall success of the project.

While drafting *expectations* for each of your team members, ask and answer the following questions:

You can download this handout to your hard drive from the accompanying CD-ROM. The document can then be opened and printed.

THE QUICK GUIDE TO PROGRAM MANAGEMENT IN FIVE SHORT STEPS (CONT.)

- What will you deliver?
- Where does your deliverable fit in the sequence of events?
- Who are you working alongside?
- Who is counting on your deliverable? Whom are you counting on?
- How is the deliverable important to the project?

Feedback

Draft a plan that tells all members of your team how and when they will receive *feedback*. Providing team members with an idea of the type of feedback they can expect, as well as the channel through which they receive it, levels their expectations and ensures a smooth line of communication throughout the project—netting out to a positive impact on the final product.

While drafting a *feedback* schedule and plan for each of your team members, ask and answer the following questions:

- How often will you receive feedback?
- How will you hear about feedback?
- Who will provide you feedback?
- What should you do with the feedback?

Tools

Give your team members the *tools* they need to complete the job. Tools can encompass a variety of resources, ranging from skills training to software upgrades. Each team member should be consulted to determine what, if anything, is needed to accomplish his or her portion of the project. Remember that needs can change; keep that feedback mechanism working to ensure that your team members can get their hands on any tools they might need along the way.

When discussing what *tools* your team members might require, ask and get answers to the following questions:

- What information do you need to get your job done?
- Do you think you will need any additional support during the project?
- Should we consider purchasing any software or hardware?
- Are there books, courses, or otherwise that would better enable you to complete your deliverables?

A tool for each project should also include an informational diagram that identifies the points of intersection for each role throughout the project. The points could be related to specific deliverables or, as the software development project demonstrates in Figure 1, by contract phase.

You can download this handout to your hard drive from the accompanying CD-ROM. The document can then be opened and printed.

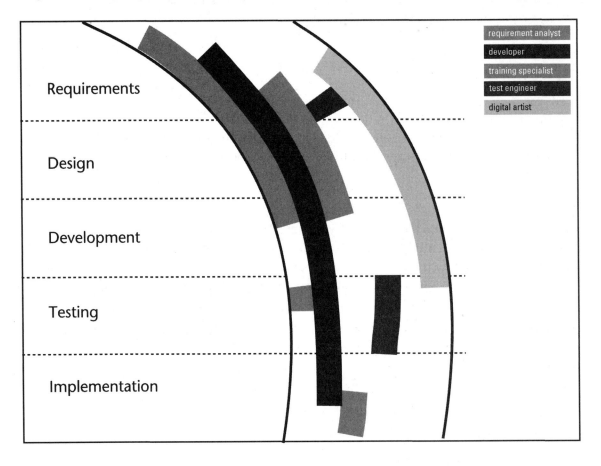

SEVEN STUPID THINGS PEOPLE DO WHEN THEY ATTEMPT STRATEGIC THINKING AND PLANNING

Roger Kaufman

Roger Kaufman, PhD, *is a professor emeritus, Department of Educational Psychology and Learning Systems, Florida State University, and director of Roger Kaufman & Associates. He is past president of the International Society for Performance Improvement (ISPI) and has been awarded that organization's highest honors: Member-for-Life and Thomas Gilbert Outstanding Achievement Award. He has published 36 books and more than 240 articles on strategic planning, performance improvement, quality management, continuous improvement, needs assessment, management, and evaluation. Roger is the recent recipient of ASTD's Distinguished Contribution to Workplace Learning & Development award. He is also a frequent contributor to the* **Sourcebooks***.*

Contact Information:
1123 Lasswade Drive
Tallahassee, FL 32312-2843
850.386.6621
rkaufman@nettally.com
www.megaplanning.com

Overview This handout outlines conventional and stupid (stupid because they are self-defeating and very avoidable) things most people do when they choose and use the strategic planning approaches that are advised in the literature and usual practice. It also provides a short overview of six critical success factors for developing a useful strategic plan and a decision checklist.

SEVEN STUPID THINGS PEOPLE DO WHEN THEY ATTEMPT STRATEGIC THINKING AND PLANNING

Roger Kaufman

STRATEGIC PLANNING STUPID THING #1—
CALL ALL LEVELS OF PLANNING "STRATEGIC" (WHILE NOT ALIGNING SOCIETAL VALUE ADDED, ORGANIZATIONAL CONTRIBUTIONS AND VALUE ADDED, AND INDIVIDUAL PERFORMANCE CONTRIBUTIONS AND VALUE ADDED VALUE).

"Strategic planning" is popular, even with some critics regarding the topic and methods employed. So to be in vogue, most people call any kind of planning "strategic"; that turns out to not be rational, realistic, or functional. In reality (and sensible practice,) there are three levels of planning: strategic, tactical, and operational. These three levels account for and align what any organization uses, does, produces, and delivers that adds measurable value to external clients.

Levels of Planning Table

Type of Planning (and Its Level of Planning)/Major Focus	Identifies External Value Added—Can Add New Organizational Purposes and Delete Existing Ones	Identifies Possible Ways and Means to Meet the Strategic Objectives in Order to Select the Most Effective and Efficient	Makes Sure the Selected Tactics and Tools Work Properly
Strategic (megalevel)	X		
Tactical (macrolevel)		X	
Operational (microlevel)			X

Subset of Strategic Planning Stupid Thing #1: Use a "system_s" approach. The commonly used (and abused) *system_s* perspective focuses on one area out of the whole, such as human performance technology (HPT), workplace learning, marketing, selling, manufacturing, organizational culture, or whatever. Then it intends to look at all the interactions among those immediate parts of the targeted system: thus a *system_s perspective*. A systems approach looks only at pieces, parts, isolated elements; it never looks at any organization as a whole, as it is nested in our shared society.

The basic, ethical, practical, and most useful *system approach* for any strategic thinking and planning perspective is society, now and in the future. I call this level of planning the *megalevel*, where the primary client and beneficiary is society. If you are not adding value to society, you are likely subtracting it.

You can download this handout to your hard drive from the accompanying CD-ROM. The document can then be opened and printed.

SEVEN STUPID THINGS PEOPLE DO WHEN THEY ATTEMPT STRATEGIC THINKING AND PLANNING (CONT.)

STRATEGIC PLANNING STUPID THING #2—
CONFUSE ENDS AND MEANS, AND BLUR STRATEGY, TACTICS, OPERATIONS, AND METHODS.

Many people think "strategy" is about means, or how to do it. That is not helpful. Strategy is about ends, consequences, and results. Strategic planning does not talk about means, resources, methods, or techniques. It only defines and justifies what value we are to add to external clients and society. *Tactical planning* is based on strategic planning results and identifies possible ways and means to meet strategic (mega) objectives. *Operations* are about using what you selected (based on previous plans) using appropriate methods. Strategic, tactical, and operational planning is about ends. Confusing and blurring strategy, tactics, operations, and methods is stupid.

Subset of Strategic Planning Stupid Thing #2: Prepare objectives that include the methods and resources in the statement. Objectives should never include how you are going to get the result accomplished. To do so is just plain destructive by selecting the solution before you have defined and justified the problem. Doing so is stupid indeed.

STRATEGIC PLANNING STUPID THING #3—
BASE YOUR STRATEGIC PLAN ONLY ON PERCEPTIONS, NOT ON PERFORMANCE RESULTS DATA.

If the strategic plan is not based on delivering required results and payoffs, it will not be useful. And just getting people's perceptions will likely deliver a weak or useless strategic plan. How does one get the valid performance data on which to base a useful plan? Not by just asking people. One gets it by doing a "needs assessment" (not a "wants assessment"), in which gaps in results for external clients and society are identified and selected.

Subset of Strategic Planning Stupid Thing #3: Assume that some things are just not measurable. Contrary to conventional (and uninformed) wisdom, if you can name it, you are measuring it. There are mathematical scales of measurement for purposes stated in nominal, ordinal, interval, and ratio scales.

STRATEGIC PLANNING STUPID THING #4—
DEFINE "NEEDS" AS GAPS IN RESOURCES OR METHODS (THUS CONFUSING ENDS AND MEANS).

Unfortunate for performance accomplishment professionals is the day that Maslow and his hierarchy of needs became the Holy Grail of performance improvement. If you want to follow this fine gentleman's advice and use "need" as a verb—a means or a resource—you will be in good but failing company.

You can download this handout to your hard drive from the accompanying CD-ROM. The document can then be opened and printed.

If you want to avoid the sin of not basing your strategic plan on hard performance data, never use "need" as a verb; use it only to define a gap in results. Any time you use "need" as a verb—such as "need to," "need for," "needing"—you are moving to select means and resources before defining and substantiating a problem as a gap in results that should be closed.

Subset of Strategic Planning Stupid Thing #4: Do a "training needs assessment." This usually places the focus on a means (training) and not ends (performance). If you believe Deming and Juran, starting with "training"—a means, not an end—you will be wrong 80 to 90 percent of the time. Why? They note that 80 to 90 percent of all performance breakdowns are not individual performance breakdowns but system (and, I suggest, also external) breakdowns. Why do an assessment before doing one at the mega-, macro-, and microlevels. No matter how well you fix a performance problem at the individual performance level, if the real problem is elsewhere, all you do is spend money and frustrate people. Choosing an approach that is so often wrong might be considered stupid. Or ill informed.

STRATEGIC PLANNING STUPID THING #5—
LET A FRIENDLY GROUP DEVELOP THE STRATEGIC PLAN.

Any plan, any initiative, any change (and strategic plans, by their nature, usually call for change) will predictably fail if people who are charged with implementing it feel they are not part of its development. So, even though it is a bit more challenging, get a representative group of stakeholders to develop the plan. To get what Peter Drucker terms "transfer of ownership," be sure that both internal and external clients and society are represented.

STRATEGIC PLANNING STUPID THING #6—
TARGET YOUR ORGANIZATION AS THE PRIMARY BENEFICIARY OF THE STRATEGIC PLAN.

If strategic planning stops at the organization's front door, you might be on your way to becoming another Enron, WorldCom, Tyco, or Andersen. They all took themselves on (as did a few executives) as the most important beneficiaries—as the primary client of the strategic plan. And if you really like failed strategic plans, go and benchmark theirs. If you were to read their published missions and visions and believed them, you are what you do and accomplish, not what you say alone.

STRATEGIC PLANNING STUPID THING #7—
DISMISS ALL OF THIS AS "NOT PRACTICAL, NOT REAL WORLD,"
OR "BECAUSE THIS IS NOT WHAT THE BIG PLAYERS DO."

You are right. What is suggested here is not the conventional wisdom. And it is not the way Enron, Tyco, Andersen, or the dot.coms did strategic planning. It is also not the way most people think about and do what they call strategic planning.

If you want to avoid disastrous mistakes, following is a brief of the approach I use (and I don't want to be accused of being stupid). It is a view from a higher altitude that will point you in the right direction. Is it magic? No. But it combines practicality and ethics. It could well put an end to the stupidity of doing strategic planning that fails. Here are six critical success factors for developing a useful strategic plan.

You can download this handout to your hard drive from the accompanying CD-ROM. The document can then be opened and printed.

SEVEN STUPID THINGS PEOPLE DO WHEN THEY ATTEMPT STRATEGIC THINKING AND PLANNING (CONT.)

SIX CRITICAL FACTORS OF STRATEGIC PLANNING

Strategic planning can and should be productive and useful. You can operate so that you ask and answer useful and important questions. You can choose to avoid the seven things that can derail any strategic planning effort. Here is a decision checklist for you to use.

• Move out of your comfort zone—today's paradigms—and use new and the widest boundaries for thinking, planning, doing, evaluating, and continuously improving.
• Differentiate between ends (what) and means (how).
• Prepare all objectives (including those for mega-, macro-, and microlevels) that rigorously state where you are headed and how to tell when you have arrived.
• Define "need" as a gap between current and desired results, not as insufficient levels of means or resources.
• Use and link all three levels of planning and results: mega/outcomes, macro/outputs, and micro/products.
• Use an ideal vision (the kind of world we want to create for tomorrow's child stated in measurable terms) as the basis for all thinking and planning: the megalevel.

You can download this handout to your hard drive from the accompanying CD-ROM. The document can then be opened and printed.

AVOIDING DOING STUPID THINGS WHEN DOING STRATEGIC PLANNING

Possible Stupid Thing to Do When Doing Strategic Planning	Now Do	Will Continue to Do	Will Change What I Do
1. Call all levels of planning "strategic" (while not aligning societal value added, organizational contributions and value added, and individual performance contributions and value added).			
1a. Use a "system*s*" approach.			
2. Confuse ends and means, and blur strategy, tactics, operations, and methods.			
3. Base your strategic plan only on perceptions, not on performance results data.			
3a. Assume that some things are just not measurable.			
4. Define "needs" as gaps in resources or methods (thus confusing ends and means).			
4a. Do a "training needs assessment."			
5. Let a friendly group develop the strategic plan.			
6. Target your organization as the primary beneficiary of the strategic plan.			
7. Dismiss all of this as "not practical, not real world," or "because this is not what the big players do."			

You can download this handout to your hard drive from the accompanying CD-ROM. The document can then be opened and printed.

For those who think this is bothersome, or irritating, I present a sign that I spotted on a construction site in Sydney, Australia:

> All Pearls Start with an Irritant

The purpose of this handout is to suggest a strategic planning and thinking pearl or two. And let anyone taking the advice avoid making stupid choices and harvest destructive consequences.

REFERENCES AND RELATED READING

Deming, W. E. *Out of the Crisis.* Cambridge: MIT Center for Advanced Engineering Technology, 1986.

Drucker, P. F. "Management's New Paradigm." *Forbes Magazine* (October 5, 1998): 152–168. http://www.forbes/98/1005/6207152a.htm.

Juran, J. M. *Juran on Planning for Quality.* New York: The Free Press, 1988.

Kaufman, R. *Strategic Thinking: A Guide to Identifying and Solving Problems. Revised.* Washington, DC and Arlington, VA: The International Society for Performance Improvement and the American Society for Training & Development, 1998.

Kaufman, R. *Mega Planning: Practical Tools for Organizational Success.* Thousand Oaks, CA: Sage Publications, 2000.

Kaufman, R. Seven Deadly Sins of Strategic Planning. *ASTD Links.* Arlington, VA: American Society for Training & Development, April 2004.

Kaufman, R, Watkins, R., and Leigh, D. *Useful Educational Results: Defining, Prioritizing, Accomplishing.* Lancaster, PA: Proactive Press, 2001.

Kaufman, R., Guerra, I., and Platt, W. A. *Practical Evaluation for Educators: Finding What Works and What Doesn't.* Thousand Oaks, CA: Corwin Press/Sage, in press.

Kaufman, R., Oakley-Browne, H., Watkins, R., and Leigh, D. *Practical Strategic Planning: Aligning People, Performance, and Payoffs.* San Francisco: Jossey-Bass/Pfeiffer, 2003.

Leigh, D., Watkins, R., Platt, W., and Kaufman, R. "Alternate Models of Needs Assessment: Selecting the Right One for Your Organization?" *Human Resource Development Quarterly* 11, no. 1 (2000): 87–93.

Mager, R. F. *Preparing Instructional Objectives: A Critical Tool in the Development of Effective Instruction,* 3rd ed. Atlanta: Center for Effective Performance, 1997.

Triner, D. Greenberry, A., and Watkins, R. "Training Needs Assessment: A Contradiction in Terms?" *Educational Technology* 36, no. 6 (1996): 51–55.

FIVE TIPS FOR BUILDING TRUST IN YOUR ORGANIZATION

Doug Leigh

Doug Leigh, PhD, *is an associate professor of education with Pepperdine University's Graduate School of Education and Psychology and presently serves as the director of its master of science in learning design and performance. He is coauthor of* **Strategic Planning for Success** *(Jossey-Bass, 2003) and* **Useful Educational Results** *(Proactive Publishing, 2001). Doug is two-time chair of the American Evaluation Association's Needs Assessment Topic Interest Group and past editor-in-chief of the International Society for Performance Improvement's journal,* **Performance Improvement***.*

Contact Information:
Pepperdine University
Graduate School of Education and Psychology
6100 Center Drive
Los Angeles, CA 90045
310.568.2389
dleigh@pepperdine.edu
www.dougleigh.com
http://gsep.pepperdine.edu/~dleigh

Overview The establishment of trust requires an understanding between the involved parties regarding the terms of a cooperative effort, followed by evidence suggesting that this agreement is being lived up to. Relationships of trust within and between organizations make it possible to engage in honest and reciprocal cooperation, fostering a stable and productive work environment (Fukuyama, 1995). However, workplace power differentials can create unequal partnerships (Hardin, 2002), in which employees may come to distrust their superiors and co-workers. This handout describes a process for building trust between individuals within workplace settings.

FIVE TIPS FOR BUILDING TRUST IN YOUR ORGANIZATION

Doug Leigh

Few things can help an individual more than to place responsibility on him, and to let him know that you trust him.

> —Booker T. Washington, reformer, educator, and author (1856–1915)

What is trust? Julian Rotter, who applied his Social Learning theory in various investigations of trust (1971, 1980a, 1980b), defined the concept as "an expectancy held by an individual or group that the word, promise, verbal or written statement of another individual or group can be counted on" (1967, p. 651). Trust exists within a context within which individuals do what they say they are going to do—a context of integrity (Carter, 1996). Whereas distrust serves the purpose of impeding cooperation when evidence comes to light that an individual has not been consistent with his or her word, trust can establish a ground for cooperation (Hardin, 2002). Specifically, Hardin (2002) points out that (a) trust is a relationship within which I trust you regarding a specific matter, (b) I trust you because I believe it is in your interest to attend to my interest regarding that matter, and (c) trust is a cognitive notion which, like belief, we do not choose but rather of which we are convinced or discover. But how does trust come about? The emergence of trust between individuals typically unfolds in situations with the following five features.

1. *Trust creates opportunities for cooperation.* Prior first-hand experience with another is not a necessary prerequisite for the establishment of relationships within which trust is possible. For example, you and I might have had a working relationship in the past; we might have been recommended to one another by a mutual associate; or we simply might have been assigned to work cooperatively on a given task. In any case, this opportunity provides an opening for dialogue regarding possible new cooperative efforts.

2. *Trust allows requests to be made and invitations to be extended.* Except for those cooperative efforts to which we are assigned, the opportunity to cooperate allows for either a request to perform a given task at one's behest (for example, asking me to input data into a spreadsheet) or an invitation to work collaboratively in an undertaking (for example, offering to share the task of interviewing job applicants). These actions might be one-time (such as photocopying an article from a trade journal), or they might involve protracted engagement (such as conducting an ongoing program evaluation). In all cases, the purpose of a request or invitation is to differentiate those actions that are desired from those that are not. Thus, it is important for requests and invitations to be both specific and time-based.

3. *Trust permits you to manage replies and negotiate terms.* On the basis of the request or invitation, you or I might choose to discuss the terms of the cooperative effort. This dialog can result in one of four replies: accept, decline, counteroffer, or promise to reply later (Krisko, 1997). First, you can *accept* or *decline* the stated terms of the cooperative effort without further negotiation. Alternately, should negotiation be pursued, you can make a *counteroffer* that amends the initial terms of the request or invitation, or promise to reply at a later date. Such secondary requests allow the party who forwarded the original request or invitation to accept or decline, to counteroffer, or to *promise to reply later*. For example, I might accept your request to develop an agenda for a meeting (or an invitation to do so with you), I might

---

You can download this handout to your hard drive from the accompanying CD-ROM. The document can then be opened and printed.

counter by requesting that we divide the effort, or I might promise to give you an answer by the end of the day. What should be avoided are responses that are not specific regarding the terms of both activities and the span of time over which they are to occur.

4. *Trust allows for agreement and satisfaction.* Consensual agreement is a decision that occurs when terms are agreed upon that are at least minimally acceptable to both parties. The agreement can be public or private, and to varying degrees it can be explicit or tacit (Kegan & Lahey, 2002). For example, I might explicitly agree to your invitation to manage a project, and we might make that agreement public by announcing our plans to colleagues. Alternately, we could form a tacit understanding, such as not disclosing details of a new product to competitors, and that agreement might exist privately. Each party can also have differing feelings about the terms of the agreement. For example, you might be very satisfied with our agreement that I lay off the director of human resources, while I might not be as satisfied. Although satisfaction is not a necessary prerequisite for trust, the lack of it can present difficulties in getting to agreement on terms that are satisfactory to both parties.

5. *Parties must become trustworthy.* Having agreed on the terms of cooperative effort, trust can develop unilaterally or mutually between cooperating parties, and it can come about at different rates. Typically, though, the development of trust takes place within an interaction among three mechanisms. The first, *cooperation,* occurs when we begin to engage in the agreed-upon undertaking; it is "doing what we said we would do." However, in and of itself, cooperation is not sufficient to build trust. *Evidence* of cooperation must also be apparent. Evidence provides feedback regarding whether the terms of the agreement are being met. *Renegotiation* is the third mechanism. If the evidence is perceived as suggesting that the terms of the original agreement are no longer agreeable, then the parties may choose to renegotiate the terms. Regardless of whether renegotiation takes place, further cooperation and evidence may be necessary to make the decision to trust (Hardin, 2002). To the extent that the perception exists that agreed-upon terms are not being lived up to, distrust becomes more likely, as does a reduction in cooperation between parties.

REFERENCES

Carter, S. L. *Integrity.* New York: HarperPerennial, 1996.

Fukuyama, F. *Trust: The Social Virtues and the Creation of Prosperity.* New York: Free Press, 1995.

Hardin, R. *Trust and Trustworthiness.* New York: Russell Sage Foundation, 2002.

Kegan, R. and Lahey, L. L. *How the Way We Talk Can Change the Way We Work: Seven Languages for Transformation.* Hoboken, NJ: John Wiley & Sons, 2002.

Krisco, K. H. *Leadership and the Art of Conversation.* Rocklin, CA: Prima, 1997.

Rotter, J. B. A "New Scale for the Measurement of Interpersonal Trust." *Journal of Personality,* 35 (1967): 651–665.

Rotter, J. B. "Generalized Expectancies for Interpersonal Trust." *American Psychologist,* 26 (1971): 443–452.

Rotter, J. B. "Trust and Gullibility." *Psychology Today,* 14 (1980a): 35–42.

Rotter, J. B. "Interpersonal Trust, Trustworthiness, and Gullibility." *American Psychologist,* 35 (1980b): 1–7.

SIX CORPORATE VALUES FOR CREATING A HEALTHY WORK ORGANIZATION

Shannon Griffin-Blake

Shannon Griffin-Blake, PhD, *is a worksite health promotion specialist for Northrop Grumman in Atlanta, Georgia. She has worked as a researcher, trainer, and consultant in the health and medical industries for 15 years. Her professional endeavors and multiple publications have focused on corporate programming, worksite intervention effectiveness and model development, multiculturalism, exercise adherence and motivation, and women's health issues. Shannon is also a past contributor to the* **Sourcebooks***.*

Contact Information:
Northrop Grumman Contractor
Division of Adult and Community Health
National Center for Chronic Disease
    Prevention & Health Promotion
Centers for Disease Control and Prevention
4770 Buford Highway, NE, Mailstop K-30
Atlanta, GA 30341-3717
770.488.5266
SGriffinBlake@cdc.gov
Dyu9@cdc.gov

Overview   Organizations that are "healthy" should be better able to attract and retain productive, satisfied workers, but they should also be more successful in managing costs and competing in the market. Yet achieving a healthy work organization is challenging because it often warrants individual and organizational change and requires a shift in the perceptions of organizational control and power. Creating a culture of empowerment is needed and can be difficult because it contests the traditional, hierarchical approach and behavior patterns that American businesses have used for decades. In its simplest form, empowerment can be viewed as offering employees the ability to make decisions, which is a foreign concept in most corporate cultures. Thus, the question can be raised about how employees and management can work together to create a healthy work organization.

The term "healthy work organization" derives from the idea that it should be possible to distinguish healthy from unhealthy work systems. Work organization generally refers to the way work processes are structured and managed (i.e., scheduling, workload, communication, compensation, and management style). Thus, when trying to examine if an organization is healthy, companies must go beyond the four structural walls of the company's building to probe other corporate elements, such as company policies, worker autonomy, job structure, and organizational support. When exploring the idea of a healthy work organization, analysts have examined work environments and company mission statements, consulted corporate leaders, and interviewed vast groups of employees trying to understand and define the concept of healthy work organization. As a result, several key values kept reappearing. This handout outlines these key values, which can be used as guiding principles for companies to explore their own culture and environment to determine how "healthy" their organization might be and to consider ways to move toward a more empowered workforce. Creating a healthy work organization is at the core of business success; in essence, establishing a supportive work environment and empowering your employees to work together can create the best product to be competitive in today's market.

SIX CORPORATE VALUES FOR CREATING A HEALTHY WORK ORGANIZATION

Shannon Griffin-Blake

Six key values can be used as guiding principles by your company to explore its own culture and environment to determine the "health" of the organization: (1) employee involvement, (2) open communication, (3) valuing diversity, (4) family/work life balance, (5) equitable rewards and recognition, and (6) meaningful work.

1. *Employee involvement:* In most traditional organizations, the old-style command and control approach is taken. Management defines tasks for employees at the lower levels, specifies the behaviors required to perform job tasks, defines performance goals for employees, and defines the priority of employee goals. In contrast, organizations with a culture of employee involvement operate differently because of a shift in the locus of responsibility. Employees monitor their own performance, while they collaborate with managers to create a shared company vision. Specifically, this work culture suggests that both employees and management care about the organization's performance and use their combined reasoning and dialog to determine how to achieve individual, team, and company success. Organizational change can be a daunting task; thus, creating a culture of involvement can entail starting small and adding leverage points to allow everyone to gradually grasp the purpose of empowerment, learn new attitudes, and develop new sets of skills. When sharing risks and responsibilities of the business, both employees and management define their own tasks in the context of the company's vision and objectives, determine the behaviors and action plan required to perform their tasks, define performance goals for individuals, and specify the priority of individual goals and how they relate to company goals. Change can be more successful when the concerns of employees are considered. Although management has viewpoints that must be addressed, how employees perceive change determines whether an innovation actually disseminates into the company. Involving employees allows them to be part of the concept creation and to feel more empowered by the collaborative process.

2. *Open communication:* The change needed to achieve a healthy work organization is not an event, but a process. Often, organizational change is desired by management but implemented poorly. For example, many people in management consider change as an action or specific event that occurs at a distinct time or on a particular date. Managers might announce an innovation at a staff meeting or training session and assume that employees will embrace it. Yet it might not be used appropriately or even at all. Continuous, open communication between managers and employees debunks misconceptions and allows the goal of a healthy work organization to become a shared vision. A shared vision is a mutually held image of a future that management and employees seek to realize together. Commitment to the vision is built collaboratively by talking about the desired goals and practices underlying the pursuit of the vision. Shared vision is most effective when it is connected to the purpose of the organization and the purposes of the individuals working in the organization. Building a shared vision challenges management because it requires avenues for input and an audible voice for all. In sum, continuous dialog between management and employees not only creates a clear purpose for the company but enhances its ability to remain productive and achieve business objectives.

You can download this handout to your hard drive from the accompanying CD-ROM. The document can then be opened and printed.

SIX CORPORATE VALUES FOR CREATING A HEALTHY WORK ORGANIZATION (CONT.)

3. *Valuing diversity:* The American workforce is becoming more diverse in terms of race, ethnicity, gender, and religion. With diversity as a corporate norm, the organization has to examine ways it can use such differences as a positive learning tool. A healthy work organization tries to embrace the diversity of its workforce and increase ingenuity through the exchange of unique experiences and different knowledge. With participation and input from a diverse source of employees, a set of ideas, a pool of data, and a list of options can be generated from the minds of many instead of just a select few. A healthy work organization embraces this notion of synergy—the idea that two brains are smarter than one. The company requires that workers use dialogical communication and collective thinking skills, so that managers and employees can reliably develop insight and ability greater than the sum of the individual members' talents. Diversity can be seen as an organizational tool that requires a process of learning collectively that challenges individuals intellectually, emotionally, socially, and spiritually. For instance, people are not generally comfortable with ideas, customs, and others that are different from what they are used to; therefore, employees must openly communicate with each other and management to understand everyone's perspective or frame of mind. Tension created by diversity can be constructive because it can lead to questions in a variety of voices that share new viewpoints. Improved communication and employee involvement can be liberating for many who feel their opinions are not heard or do not matter to the organization. As a result, managers and employees alike can feel empowered by the dialog and, together, develop shared alignment around organizational goals and purposes.

4. *Family/work life balance:* Trying to balance family and work life is a struggle for most working men and women. Both sexes are taking on the daunting responsibilities of family care as the number of dual-income and single-parent homes continues to rise. Today, the responsibilities of home life have expanded to include not only domestic household duties but also self-care management, child care obligations, and issues of aging parents and their health. With workers spending more than half their waking time at the workplace, designing the work schedule so that employees can meet personal needs is an important factor. Thus, companies need to examine their work policies concerning flexible work arrangements. Flexible work arrangements allow employees to manage their time and work tasks so as to meet job requirements while fulfilling their nonwork obligations and activities (i.e., attending health care appointments, responding to the needs of a child or family member). Such provisions can generate positive changes for organizations that are concerned with employee productivity because absenteeism has been found to be largely related to family issues. For example, an employee who has no control over the job schedule might take a full day off from work to make a child's doctor visit. If flexible work arrangements were available, the employee might take only a two-hour lunch and work an hour longer at the end of the day. In sum, by allowing employees more latitude in managing their job and personal schedules, productivity at work can improve because of lowered absentee rates.

---

5. *Equitable rewards and recognition:* Perhaps the looming issue facing most businesses and managers is that of equity, that is, the perceived fairness by employees concerning work compensation. Equity can come in two forms: (1) *distributive* equity representing the perceived fairness attached to the amount of money or rewards (e.g., merit pay increases) and their allotment across some performance criterion, and (2) *procedural* equity that entails the perceived fairness as to how the rules governing the reward system are applied across the workforce. First, an employee concern surrounding equity is that employees want to be paid fairly for their work and have performance level and tenure accounted for in their job assessment. For example, employees who have worked for an organization for five years want their loyalty acknowledged, through either a pay raise or a corporate commendation. Especially when pay is perceived to be average to low for the industry, employees feel that more praise or recognition is needed for the hard work performed. This is consistent with the idea that both tangible and intangible benefits are important to employees when evaluating the fairness of their rewards. Second, the rewards and recognition must be consistent across the workforce to be considered impartial. Companies should consider setting benchmarks for recognizing or rewarding employees for years of services (e.g., five, 10, 15 years of service) or performance standards (e.g., reaching the quarterly or annual sales goal). Recognition can be as simple as a certificate presented to the employee at a staff meeting, a corporate email announcing the team's achievement, or the employee's picture posted in the break room for a special accomplishment. When organizations are trying to cut costs and remain competitive with their employee packages, creating outlets for worker recognition and team excellence can provide employees with a greater sense that they are valued, encouraged, and supported.

6. *Meaningful work:* Meaningful work refers to an employee's perception that her or his job is valuable and worthwhile; however, not all jobs are created equal. Some workers have restricted control over their work; may complete repetitive, monotonous actions or physically demanding work; and even have exposure to loud noise or extreme temperatures. This chronic exposure to job strain has been associated with a number of negative health outcomes, including musculoskeletal disorders, psychological distress, injuries, and cardiovascular disease, which can drain a company's resources. In addition, a second financial loss occurs due to employee absenteeism resulting from the illness or injury and even turnover if employees become greatly dissatisfied with their jobs. Thus, providing opportunity for these workers to have a voice concerning job design and company resources is important. A company should allow employees to provide feedback about work issues, such as whether specific protective eyewear is needed in factories, lifting restrictions or stretching programs that may be warranted for physical positions, or rotations being available for jobs that have short cycle, repetitious work. By providing staff comment boxes on company floors, feedback boards in staff break rooms, or weekly team meetings that provide opportunity for employee remarks, workers feel that problems can be appropriately identified and adequately addressed, and management cares about their job safety and satisfaction—not just their productivity.

PRACTICAL GUIDES

In this section of *The 2006 ASTD Organization Development and Leadership Sourcebook*, you will find 13 practical guides. These "how to" guides are short articles containing useful ideas and guidelines for implementing training and performance support initiatives.

You will find advice about such topics as:

✓ Creating a request for a proposal

✓ Getting the most out of a meeting

✓ Navigating the complexities of transformation

✓ Planning for a negotiation

✓ Using the Organizational Savvy Model

✓ Designing and implementing reward and recognition programs

✓ Building a team for success

✓ Succeeding in the coaching process

✓ Understanding and benefiting from planning for the future

✓ Dismantling a culture of information hoarding

✓ Creating true team building

✓ Leading enterprise-wide change

✓ Taking things apart

Each guide contains step-by-step advice. Several have examples, illustrations, charts, and tables to enhance your understanding of the content. You will find that these guides are clearly organized and easy to read.

Here are four possible uses for the practical guides:

1. Guidelines for your own consulting, facilitating, and training interventions.

2. Implementation advice to be shared with peers and people who report to you.

3. Recommendations to senior management.

4. Reading assignments in team-building and organizational consultations and training programs.

HOW TO CREATE A REQUEST FOR PROPOSAL (RFP)

Teri Lund

*Since founding BLS in 1992, **Teri Lund** has provided consulting service in evaluation, competency-based performance management and needs assessment to such clients as Allstate Insurance, IBM, Intel, Microsoft, Nike, US Bancorp, Hewlett-Packard, and many others. She has coauthored a series of **Learning and Performance Workbooks** with ASTD. She frequently contributes to industry publications and has been a contributor to the **Training and Performance Sourcebooks** since 1997. BLS's corporate mission is to assist performance improvement professionals in providing services and products that will link to the organization's business drivers and needs, resulting in improved performance and a return on investment.*

Contact Information:
Teri Lund
5015 SW Lodi Lane
Portland, OR 97221
503.245.9020
tlund_bls@msn.com

When the recovery in the economy is slow, companies initiate new projects with care—and with an eye on cost and quality. Rather than adding to staff and overhead, many organizations "get the job done" by requesting contracts with suppliers by means of a request for proposal (RFP). Ensuring that this process has adequate controls and is time efficient is important because a well-organized and controlled RFP process:

✓ *Reduces the possibility of false starts and unforeseen risk to a project.*

✓ *Establishes an understanding among all parties that the organization endorses a workplace that is fair, where results are understandable and the selection processes are defensible.*

✓ *Provides to the organization the workforce or skills necessary to meet business objectives without incurring unnecessary overhead expenditures.*

✓ *Alerts vendors, suppliers, and/or consultants that a project is being outsourced, resulting in immediate proposals that are usually of high quality.*

✓ *Forces the organization to be clear about what is actually needed and the business impact expected, with more discussion about "what" and "how" before the project is implemented.*

✓ *Creates a contact between the organization and the RFP respondents in which the respondents demonstrate that they have the capabilities required by the RFP.*

✓ *Engenders an environment of competition with suppliers, vendors, and consultants, usually leading to competitive pricing.*

With all those advantages, why don't organizations routinely use the RFP process for most or all of their outsourcing needs? Crafting a request for proposal tends to take substantial time and effort, and responding to it can be an expensive and time-consuming task. But if the RFP contains well-documented requirements, both the organization and the winning respondent to the RFP come out ahead. An orientation to the project has already occurred, and both sides have created a foundation of mutual understanding that can speed the development or implementation of any type of project.

This guide is meant to increase the efficiency of the RFP process as well as add to the effectiveness of identifying the respondent that best meets the organization's need.

A SUGGESTED RFP PROCESS

An RFP is a request for proposal. This is often used when procuring outside resources for software development; technology implementation; courseware design and development; or any type of professional services that a vendor, supplier, or consultant outside the organization provides.

Typically there are three types of requests:

1. An *RFI* is a *request for information*: Perhaps your organization is building a database either of suppliers, vendors, and/or consultants in the area or of a particular skill strength that could be contacted for projects.

2. An *RFQ* is a *request for a quote or price*: This type of request is often made when you know exactly what you want, such as a piece of equipment, 250 leadership books, and so forth, and you wish to compare pricing.

3. *The RFP is a request for proposal and is the most complex of the three*: In this case you are asking for specific company information about the respondent; pricing; project details; specifications for

deliverables and references regarding the respondent's quality, timeliness, and value of the work provided.

When purchasing technology or professional services by means of an RFP, the organization has to put out products that are exceptional and that meet organizational objectives to support the business strategy. Often with this type of procurement, the desired product is complex and entails a high risk of problems or failure. The following RFP process provides the necessary information for vendors, suppliers, or consultants to respond with information that not only makes the selection process more efficient, but also ensures a higher likelihood of success in the final product.

In RFPs, the organization must clearly detail the requirements for the project. However, providing just the requirements is not enough information for an in-depth response. A detailed and comprehensive RFP makes certain that the parties responding have sufficient information to provide a complete proposal and, in the end, saves you and your organization time.

Tool 1 defines the schedule of events or tasks needed to ensure that the RFP is complete and builds or strengthens a relationship with the organization's vendors, suppliers, and/or consultants. In column 1, each event is listed, and, in column 2, the event is defined and the outcome for the event described.

TOOL 1: THE RFP SCHEDULE OF EVENTS

RFP Event	Event Description
Identify the need	In this step, gather all critical parties within the organization and outline what is expected of the project. Not only discuss the objectives of the project itself (such as install a new email system), but also identify the organizational need (for example, allow remote access to email to ensure traveling employees can access and respond to email to increase employee productivity). *Outcome:* A clear set of statements as to "why or what has created the need."
Quantify the success factors	With the same group, determine the measures of success for that project. In other words, what does the end result of the project need to be for it to be deemed a success? (Example: Provide an email system that allows secure access to email from remote locations, archives emails after 30 days, and allows scheduling and automatic email generation for meetings and conferences scheduled.) It is important to recognize that these are the project success factors, not business success factors. *Outcome:* Delineation of the need and the factors of success for the project.

RFP Event	Event Description
Determine the parameters	Agree on the constraints, issues, and limitations related to the project. (Example: Is there a time restraint? Perhaps a limited budget? A certain operating system that the product must interface?) *Outcome:* A list of the parameters the supplier must meet or work under for the project to be acceptable.
Identify the skill sets	This event is particularly important in procuring professional services because it identifies the actual key skill sets required. It is important to limit the skill sets to those that are critical to the success of the project. (Example: Previous work in a financial environment, or at least six years of instructional design experience, or the ability to formulate innovative business plans.) *Outcome:* A "job description" for the critical project skill sets.
Write the RFP	Identify the author of the RFP. (An outline of RFP contents is listed later in this guide.) *Outcome:* The RFP.
Screen the respondents	Prior to writing the RFP, the organization has to determine the process for screening the respondents. Perhaps it is a checklist and rating on the sections of the proposal you have requested within the RFP. (Example: On a scale of 1 to 10, how well does the respondent understand the need and respond to that need within the project plan provided in the proposal?) *Outcome:* Proposals are screened and the top proposals are chosen for further examination.
Develop the selection process	How will the organization determine which of the final candidates best meets the project needs? First, consider what is needed to ensure that the respondent can actually provide the best possible solution. Do you need a demonstration of what they can provide? Do you need to interview the team that would work with you? Will you interview previous clients for references? Often the final candidates are asked to provide a presentation that includes a little or all of the above. One important factor is that, if you have a project leader from the outside, you meet and interview that individual to ensure there is a match between that person and your organization. *Outcome:* A selection process for the final candidates.
Finalize the "deal"	Once you have chosen the successful final candidate, the organization has to process a contract. If your organization has a standard contract, process that, usually with the RFP and proposal as part of the attachments. The organization might also use the other party's contract. In either case, the legal department or advisor should review the contract to ensure that your organization is safeguarded. *Outcome:* A signed contract that is legal and binding.

RFP Event	Event Description
Conclude the RFP process	When a contract with the successful candidate is complete, a phone call should be made to the other presenters.
	For those who sent a proposal but did not go past the original screening process, a letter is all that is necessary, stating that they were unsuccessful.
	Outcome: Notify those who were unsuccessful and kick off the project with the successful party.

SETTING THE OBJECTIVES FOR THE PROJECT

The organization must be clear on its objectives, both internally before writing the proposal and within the RFP itself, so that respondents provide the correct information for consideration. Defining and gaining agreement to the objectives before asking for proposals and presentations ensures that everyone is on the same page about expectations and business outcomes. Specifically, what is expected of the project for it to be successful?

There are three types of project objectives. The first two objectives that should be defined are centered in the end results: "When the project is complete, what will be the effect or consequence on the business itself?" These objectives are:

- *Tangible objectives:* Tangible objectives have physical results that can be measured and quantified. Examples are a decrease in costs, an increase in sales, or a decrease in the cost of goods. The project itself has a direct correlation to the result.

- *Intangible objectives:* Like a tangible objective, this type of objective is an end result objective, but it cannot be as readily measured. It is more about impressions and subtleties that result from the project. Often these results are as important as tangible objectives. For example, the customer is more satisfied as a result of this project, or employee morale has improved. In the end, the bottom line might improve as a result of an intangible objective, but it is not as apparent as in the case of a tangible objective.

The third type of objective is the *project objective*, which describes the result of the project. This is not a business result, but rather an outcome directly related to the project, such as the installation of a new customer information system.

To clarify the relationships among the three types of objectives, **Tool 2** provides real-life examples.

TOOL 2: PROJECTS AND OBJECTIVES EXAMPLES

Project	Project Objective	Tangible Objective	Intangible Objective
Product training	To provide courseware to instruct new employees on the various types of products, benefits, and features for the products and on the consumers for these products and their characteristics	Sales will increase. Returns from customers will decrease. Customers will return to the store or will refer others because of their experience.	Customer satisfaction will increase. Employee knowledge about products will increase, and the learning curve on the job will decrease.
Account software installation	To install new accounting software that supports regulations and is easy to use	Posting time will decrease, and productivity will be raised. Regulation violations and penalties will decrease.	Employee morale will increase. Employee knowledge about accounting regulations will increase.
Manpower project. A consultant will steady the workflow and processes in the organization and make recommendations for efficiencies in a written report, identifying where efficiencies can occur.	To prepare a detailed report identifying specific workflow and business process improvements	Changes in workflows and improvement in business processes will increase productivity. The amount of waste will decline.	Employee morale will improve. The job will become less burdensome.

Tool 3 assists you in identifying the three types of objectives for your project. In the first column the type of project is identified. In the second column, questions are provided to support brainstorming of the specific objectives for the project.

TOOL 3: IDENTIFYING THE OBJECTIVES

Objectives	Questions to Consider
Tangible objectives	➤ What business-related outcomes should occur if this project is successful? How will you know? ➤ Will behavioral changes result in a cost savings or increase in revenue? If so, what are the changes?

Objectives	Questions to Consider
	➤ Will there be a change in a process that can be measured? If so, how?
	➤ Will there be an increase in safety? How will you know that this happens?
	➤ Will there be an increase in revenue, a decrease in costs, or any other measurable bottom-line impact or financial indicator change as a result of the project?
	➤ Will you have some type of market advantage as a result of the project?
Intangible objectives	➤ Will employee knowledge change or increase? What will be the change or increase?
	➤ Will there be some type of skill change or increase? What will it be?
	➤ Will employee or customer satisfaction increase? How and why?
	➤ Will information regarding the company, its products, or other necessary component be more readily available as a result of the project?
	➤ Will there be a behavioral change as a result of the project? By whom?
Project objectives	➤ How will you know when this project is complete? What will be different?
	➤ What are the end deliverables of this project?
	➤ What is the mission of the project? How do the project objectives support the mission?
	➤ If this project were not completed, how would you know?
	➤ What is the difference between the project objectives (what will be done) and the business objectives (what will be the outcome)? Can you delineate between the two? If so, how?

One of the most important functions of the RFP is to clearly delineate between the *project objectives* (as addressed in the RFP, such as design of a new customer information program by June 30 in seven of the organization's locations) and the *business objectives* (such as increasing market share through better product penetration or decreasing customer call time for product resolution). This distinction should be made for both tangible and intangible objectives.

Often the project objectives are easier for organizations to define. When the project is initiated, it is often clearly intended to fill a need. But by the time the RFP is written, the need has often been lost in the exercise of planning the project itself. Redefining the business objectives and linking them to the project refocuses the original need and makes sure that everyone is clear about the purpose of the project.

Stating the measures that would illustrate the success (or failure) of the project in the RFP is important. Potential measures include:

- Cycle time
- Manufacturing time effectiveness (MCE)
- Time to market
- Expense ratio
- Travel costs
- Cost per sale
- Rate of absenteeism
- Safety ratings
- Percentage of rework
- Time to proficiency
- Error rate

Various models can assist you in ensuring that measures include a balance of financial, business, and human measures, such as:

- Copano's Event and Decision Tree (a binomial model)
- The Balanced Scorecard (Kaplan/Norton)
- Accenture's Performance Prism
- Skandia's Intellectual Capital Navigator

The key to all these models, however, is to dig deeper than skin deep and to analyze potential links between the project deliverables and the business outcomes and success indicators. Such an effort demonstrates its own worth when your respondents clearly understand the outcomes of the project for which they are providing a proposal.

THE CONTENTS

Once the project objectives and measures are defined, it is relatively easy to create the RFP. The specific content, if provided in your RFP, actually improves the quality of the proposals and makes the selection job easier. A content worksheet is provided in **Tool 4**. In this worksheet, column 1 identifies the content category and describes what should be included. Column 2 is a place to make notes regarding the content that is specific to the project. Column 3 is a place to note the individual assigned either to gain information for the content and/or to draft the content for that category for the RFP.

TOOL 4: CONTENT WORKSHEET

Content	Your Notes	Individual Assigned
Company background: ❏ Company name ❏ Industry ❏ Number of employees ❏ Offices and locations ❏ Business entities ❏ Mission ❏ Products ❏ Senior management names and roles or an organization chart ❏ Board of directors		
Business model: ❏ Vision ❏ Future business models ❏ Business results of the project and the importance of those to the business ❏ Overall business strategy		
Project overview: ❏ Project summary (nature of work) ❏ The need the project meets ❏ Technology (current infrastructure, systems) related to the project ❏ Vision of project ❏ Expected timeline and expectations and deliverables ❏ Project milestones ❏ Desired skill sets of project team member ❏ Any certifications or licenses ❏ The reason for the RFP ❏ Project budget ❏ Conditions of contract and/or acceptance of project		

Content	Your Notes	Individual Assigned
Vendor information: ❏ Vendor qualifications ❏ Vendor's ability to meet project needs ❏ Examples of quality of work ❏ Pricing by deliverable ❏ Project plan and timeline ❏ References ❏ Confidentiality disclosure		
Evaluation criteria: ❏ Project criteria ❏ Method(s) of evaluation ❏ Who will be the evaluators		
Contact and response information: ❏ Process for questions ❏ Whom to contact ❏ Format for response		

In writing the RFP, consider how to respond to suppliers' questions (Section Contact and Response Information). Do you want questions addressed via email and, if so, to which address? Do you want responders to telephone a certain person? To reduce the number of repeat questions and time that it takes to respond, many companies hold an informational meeting. Local suppliers may attend on site, while others may attend via a telephone conference. **Tool 5** provides a mock agenda for this type of meeting. (Note: All questions are held to the end, so this meeting is at first a presentation.)

TOOL 5: AGENDA FOR AN RFP INFORMATIONAL MEETING

Topic	Contents
Objectives *(10 minutes)*	A discussion of the objectives and how the project objectives support the business objectives occurs during this time period. Critical objectives (those that must be met to fill the need that initiated the project) and supporting objectives (adjunct objectives that resulted as the project is discussed internally) are called out. Project objectives are delineated in this discussion as well as what must occur for the respondent contract to be seen as completed.
Company background	This short presentation focuses on the project activities, the customer, and a brief outline of the business strategy and organization chart.

Topic	Contents
Project background (20 minutes)	The nature of work, specific requirements, such as licenses or certifications, and skill sets should be outlined.
Project criteria (10 minutes)	Discuss the standards and conditions crucial to the project success, as well as the factors most important to your organization or what your organization will emphasize the most during the project.
Proposal evaluation criteria (15 minutes)	Spell out how the proposals or responses will be evaluated. Outline the process that will be used. If weighting will occur, discuss it.
Internal project personnel (if appropriate) (5–10 minutes)	The individuals who will be working on the project are presented. Their positions, skills, and roles in the current project are summarized. The project manager (if not the presenter) is introduced and provides a brief presentation of his of her skills and background. The working relationship that is expected (status meetings, reports, etc.) is also discussed.
Question period (30 minutes)	Set the ground rules (usually, "Please state your name and your company and then the question, and please do not repeat questions"). Questions are limited to a specific period of time. If there are multiple suppliers, you may limit each to a maximum number of questions.

PROPOSAL EVALUATION CRITERIA

Once the proposals are received, you need a process (as outlined in the RFP) to screen them. Try to pare the responses down to a final three.

First, compare the responses to the RFP and determine whether each is complete and has responded to all the requirements listed in the Vendor Information section in **Tool 4**.

Once you eliminate incomplete responses, the next screening criterion is often how well the respondent understands the project. Review each proposal for the project plan and how well it demonstrates understanding and response to the project need.

After you weed out responses that do not demonstrate either an understanding of the project or high quality, rank the remaining proposals on their merits. Judge them against the specific evaluation criteria already mapped out in the proposal. An example of typical evaluation criteria is found in **Tool 6**.

TOOL 6: EVALUATION CRITERIA

Criterion	Definition
Project criteria	Compare the proposals to pick out those that best meet the project criteria (what qualifications are best met by certain proposals), which vendors have worked on similar projects before (successfully), and the like. Typical project criteria are price, reliability of vendor, security, capacity, and capability.
Quality and timeliness of submitted proposals	Although you do not have to count every typo, compare the quality of proposals. Which proposals are bonded? Which proposals are well written? When was the proposal received?
Ability	Which of the proposals demonstrate the respondents' actual ability to meet the requirements and provide the stated deliverables in a timely, cost-effective, and efficient manner with a high level of quality?
Financial stability	How long has the respondent been in business? What is the credit rating of the respondent? Did the respondent provide financial statements and, if so, do they demonstrate stability?
Proven methods and tools	When the proposal states how the respondent would approach the project, does it present proven tools and methods? Does the respondent have a methodology often used for this type of project? What is the track record of the tools, methods, and methodology of the respondent?
Experience	What type of experience does the respondent have with this type of project? Has the respondent done this only once before or many times? Is the respondent considered an expert by the industry with this type of project?
Qualifications	What qualifications does the respondent bring to the table? How does one respondent's qualifications compare to others'? Are they higher, lower, about the same? Which of the respondents seems to be the most qualified?
References	Who are the references for the respondent? Does the proposal list the company name of the reference and when the respondent last worked with the reference?
Total cost of engagement	What is the total cost of the engagement? How do the respondents' costs compare? Is one substantially higher or lower than the others and, if so, why? Are there hidden costs not called out in the proposals, such as travel and living, shipping, material production, etc.?
Willingness to use contract of company	Will the respondent use your organization's contract, sign a confidential disclosure, and use the required project tracking software?

Regardless of the criterion selected, it must be:

- Fair
- Understandable
- Defensible

What if, after reviewing the proposals against the criterion, you still have more than three qualified respondents?

One way to reach the goal of three or fewer candidates is to check their references. Ask specific questions related to your project requirements (such as previous projects, qualifications, and past performance). **Tool 7** also lists five important questions to ask a reference.

TOOL 7: FIVE IMPORTANT REFERENCE CHECK QUESTIONS

Questions
1. Please discuss the project that you and the respondent worked on together, its outcomes, any problems that arose, how they were handled, and your working relationship with the respondent.
2. How likely would you hire this respondent again in similar circumstances? Why or why not?
3. Give me an example of a moment during the project where you were unsatisfied with the respondent's work. What happened? Was it resolved? If so, how?
4. If you were to do the project over, what is the one thing you would do differently and why?
5. What do you think is the most important thing we should know about the respondent and why?

Another helpful screening device is to call the respondent's project lead and conduct a telephone interview. **Tool 8** provides five key screening questions, although you will have others directly related to your project.

TOOL 8: FIVE IMPORTANT SCREENING QUESTIONS

Question
1. Explain how you will ensure that your deliverables meet our requirements.
2. Tell me about a time in the past when a project fell behind schedule. What did you do to ensure the deliverables still met the contracting organization's needs?
3. Give me an example of when you had a client unsatisfied with a product. Please be specific as to the issue and how you dealt with it.
4. What do you think is the most important thing about this project, and why do you think it is important?
5. What do you think is the most important thing we should know about the project we are going to initiate shortly and why?

With the number of candidates down to three, schedule a time for each to come to your organization and make a presentation (at their cost). Typically the presentation includes:

- How the supplier will approach the project.
- An example of what the firm has done in the past that is similar.
- The personnel of the project—most important, the project manager.
- The methods and tools used.
- How project risk will be minimized.
- The means of communication with you.
- Their understanding of and response to the deliverables.
- Pricing, what is included or excluded.

When you notify the respondent of the presentation, make sure that the contact person understands what is at their cost. Also make clear what you expect during the presentation.

Once the proposal is selected, begin to build the relationship with the successful respondent. There is, however, a remaining task. Contact those who were unsuccessful. Usually those who made it as far as a presentation are telephoned; others may be notified by letter. A typical letter is demonstrated in **Tool 9**.

TOOL 9: NOTIFICATION LETTER

Date

Address

Dear Ms. Robin:

After reviewing the many proposals for the XYZ Project, we have chosen another respondent who better meets our needs.

We would like to thank you for your response to our RFP and will keep your information on file should we have a need for someone with your qualifications in the future.

Thank you.

Trevor Lee

Project Manager

ADDITIONAL RESOURCES

It is often helpful to have additional resources when preparing to develop an RFP. The following tool, **Tool 10**, assists in the research or brainstorming that may be necessary while developing an RFP.

TOOL 10: OTHER RESOURCES FOR RFP DEVELOPMENT

1. ASTD: www.astd.org.
2. Barksdale, S., and Lund, T. *Rapid Needs Assessment.* Alexandria, VA: ASTD, 2002.
3. ———. *Rapid Evaluation.* Alexandria, VA: ASTD, 2001.
4. Darden Graduate School of Business Administration: http://www.darden.virginia.edu/olsson.
5. Mauck, R., and Abraham, R. *Recycling RFP Process Yields Success.* San Francisco: Digital, 2003.
6. *Project Magazine:* http://www.projectmagazine.com.
7. Reed, M. *Developing Successful Internet Requests for Proposal.* AEA Conference Publication, 2004.

CONCLUSION

Generating RFPs might take time and effort, but the results outweigh the costs at the end of the selection process. By following the process outlined in this guide, you reduce the time for eliminating the proposals that do not match your requirements and criteria. You also reduce the time normally spent in orienting the successful candidate on the project and its requirements. The successful candidate comes armed with a great deal of knowledge and thought on your project before day one, thereby saving money and time in the long run.

HOW TO GET THE MOST OUT OF YOUR MEETINGS

Tyrone A. Holmes

Tyrone A. Holmes, EdD, *is the president of T.A.H. Performance Consultants, Inc., a full-service human resource development consulting firm specializing in the enhancement of individual and organizational performance. As a dynamic speaker, trainer, consultant, and author, Tyrone has helped countless individuals enhance their ability to communicate, resolve conflict, and solve problems in culturally diverse settings. He has created and copyrighted numerous training systems, and speaks on a variety of communication, diversity, and consulting topics, including connecting diversity to performance, improving communication in culturally diverse settings, and leading teams in the 21st century. Tyrone is also a frequent contributor to the* **Sourcebooks.**

Contact Information:
T.A.H. Performance Consultants, Inc.
30307 Sterling Drive
Novi, MI 48377
248.669.5294
248.669.5295 (fax)
tyrone@doctorholmes.net
www.doctorholmes.net

Most of us have to attend frequent meetings. Whether for work, school, church, social groups, or some other aspect of our lives, almost all of us attend meetings at one time or another. Unfortunately, many of us also participate in ineffective and unproductive meetings—meetings that waste our time and energy. When properly facilitated, meetings can be extremely productive and can benefit participants in a variety of ways, but to obtain the benefits of an effective meeting, we must take specific actions. This guide describes six steps to ensure that our meetings are both efficient and effective.

SIX STEPS TO EFFICIENT AND EFFECTIVE MEETINGS

There are six steps to make meetings efficient and effective:

1. Identify the purpose of the meeting.
2. Determine whether a meeting is needed to accomplish the purpose.

3. Select the appropriate type of meeting.
4. Prepare for the meeting.
5. Facilitate the meeting.
6. Follow up on the meeting.

1. Identify the Purpose of the Meeting

What is the purpose of the meeting? One of the biggest mistakes made by meeting planners is the failure to define the purpose of the meeting narrowly. This means two things: First, identify what you hope to accomplish during the meeting. Whether the goal is to disseminate information, to resolve a problem, or to make a decision, be clear about what you want to accomplish during the meeting. Second, make sure that you do not attempt to accomplish too much in one meeting. Another common mistake made by meeting planners is the inclusion of too many agenda items. For an hour-long meeting, accomplishing one or two tasks is sufficient. Anything beyond that will make the meeting run long or require a superficial discussion of the issues. Meeting participants respond better to getting one thing done well than to doing five things poorly!

2. Determine Whether a Meeting Is Needed

Another mistake made by meeting planners is having unnecessary meetings. Meetings should be a last resort. Schedule a meeting only when there is no other way to accomplish the identified task. One of the reasons that people respond negatively to a meeting is that they find it to be unnecessary. Most of us have been in a meeting at one time or another when we felt the task could have been accomplished by phone or email. To keep this from happening, think about alternate ways to accomplish the identified tasks. For example, if the main purpose of the proposed meeting is to disseminate information, think about other ways to deliver it. Schedule the meeting only if you determine it is an absolute requirement to accomplish the identified tasks effectively.

3. Select the Appropriate Type of Meeting

Once you have determined that a meeting is an absolute necessity, select the appropriate type. This is important because different types of meetings require different facilitation tactics. Generally speaking, there are four types of meetings:

1. *Working session:* A working session provides an opportunity for participants to work together toward the completion of a specific job task. In other words, the participants come together because a specific work task requires their talents, insights, and skills. For example, a group might meet so that they can identify and develop the three phases of a one-day training program on effective communication to be facilitated by the training specialist during next month's

employee education session. The primary purpose of such a meeting is to create an educational program to facilitate employee development. The group is meeting to ensure that specific areas of expertise are included in the development process, and their task is to create the three modules needed to facilitate the full-day program.

2. *Problem-solving session:* In problem-solving meetings, group members apply a variety of processes and/or tools to define problems or conflicts, identify potential solutions, and make effective decisions. This type of meeting is similar to a working session, but the primary task is to manage a specific work problem or conflict effectively. For example, if an organizational process is not operating efficiently or effectively, a select group of individuals can come together to define the causes of the problem and to identify potential solutions. Once again, the group is meeting to ensure that specific areas of expertise are brought together to facilitate the problem resolution process.

3. *Informational session:* Informational sessions are among the most common of meetings. They facilitate the exchange of information concerning a specific topic or matter of relevance to the participants. For example, to maximize the quality of organizational communication, a CEO might meet with various employee groups on a quarterly basis to tell them what is going on and to respond to employee concerns. Informational meetings can be extremely powerful communication tools because they provide a consistent channel for information dissemination. However, they are often the most poorly utilized type of meetings for two reasons. First, many informational sessions are unnecessary because they provide information that can be readily obtained by other means. Second, a common mistake is to incorporate informational sessions into other types of meetings. For example, meeting planners often use working sessions to disseminate information because they have a captive audience. This use of the meeting can create problems if the information is not related to the group's current work task.

4. *Training session:* A training session is typically the longest of all the meeting formats. It includes sessions in which group members focus on learning and self-development. Such development is typically geared toward affective, behavioral, and/or cognitive skills. For example, an organization might implement a training program on effective meetings so that managers and supervisors can learn how to effectively facilitate a task-oriented meeting.

4. Prepare for the Meeting

Once you have identified the type of meeting, prepare for it. Meeting preparation is a relatively simple process. You should answer five basic questions before implementing any meeting:

1. *What* data, materials, and tools are needed for this meeting?

2. *Who* should attend this meeting? You must be specific, and include only individuals who add value to the meeting and who help to accomplish the meeting's tasks.

3. *When* should the meeting take place? Make sure the meeting is timely, based on the issues that must be discussed.

4. *Where* should the meeting take place? Make sure the meeting room is appropriate given the type of meeting, the number of participants, and the activities to take place during the meeting.

5. *How* will the meeting be facilitated? For example, what will be included in the agenda, who will prepare the agenda, how will the meeting materials be disseminated, what are the roles of the various participants, how will the room be set up, and who will facilitate the meeting?

5. Facilitate the Meeting

If you have successfully prepared for the meeting, facilitation is relatively easy. To maximize the effectiveness of the meeting, keep these six guidelines in mind:

1. *Start on time:* Some organizations have many late arriving participants because "the meetings never start on time anyway." People know they can come late. Start the meetings on time and people will start arriving on time.

2. *Follow a specific agenda with time frames:* Keep the agenda short and well focused. Stick to the time frame laid out by the agenda. A frequent complaint of meeting participants is about meetings that run overtime.

3. *Utilize a facilitator and establish ground rules:* Even if you are the manager or person who planned the meeting, you do not have to facilitate it. Utilize someone with strong facilitation skills to run the session. Or, if you are the group leader, have your team members take turns at facilitating the meetings. Facilitating is a very empowering experience for them and will likely increase the quality of the meetings in the long run.

4. *Involve all the participants:* Use meeting techniques, such as brainstorming or the nominal group technique, to get everyone involved.

5. *Summarize key points and all action items:* At the end of the meeting, summarize the key points, and specify the action steps to be taken as a result of the meeting, including who carries out each step.

6. *Keep a written record of the meeting:* Make sure you take meeting notes that can be provided to the participants at the end of the meeting. These notes do not have to be detailed. They should simply cover any decisions made and the actions that will result from the meeting.

6. Follow Up on the Meeting

Once the meeting has concluded, you need to do three things. Keep in mind that failure to take these steps can greatly reduce the effectiveness of your meeting:

1. *Distribute meeting minutes as soon as possible:* Generally speaking, meeting participants should receive this information within 48 hours of the meeting, especially if items must be acted on in a timely fashion. The easiest way to distribute meeting minutes is via email (assuming everyone has access).

2. *Follow up with meeting participants regarding the status of action items:* Check back with people regarding their progress on accomplishing a specific action item.

3. *Evaluate the meeting's effectiveness:* Whether you do this formally or informally, you should identify the strengths and weaknesses of your meetings, and make adjustments as needed.

HOW TO NAVIGATE THE COMPLEXITIES OF YOUR ORGANIZATION'S TRANSFORMATIONS

Linda Ackerman Anderson and Dean Anderson

Linda Ackerman Anderson *and* **Dean Anderson** *are cofounders of Being First, Inc., a change leadership development and transformational change consulting firm. These founding leaders in the field are highly sought-after speakers and consultants. They specialize in helping organizations plan and execute transformational changes that deliver the business results they need while simultaneously affecting the people and culture of the organization. Together they coauthored two books in the field of change leadership:* **Beyond Change Management: Advanced Strategies for Today's Transformational Leaders** *(Jossey-Bass, 2001) and* **The Change Leader's Roadmap: How to Navigate Your Organization's Transformation** *(Jossey-Bass, 2001).*

Contact Information:
Being First, Inc.
1242 Oak Drive DW2
Durango, CO 81301
970.385.5100
deananderson@beingfirst.com

Transformation is complex and dynamic. Knowing what to do—and when and how to do it—is a major challenge. In this guide, you will discover how to use the nine-phase Change Leader's Roadmap to plan, design, and implement your major change efforts successfully.

INTRODUCTION

How do you design and implement major organization transformation? Is there a roadmap to follow? Will the roadmap accelerate achieving your outcome? Will it reduce the cost of change? Will it lessen stress on employees? Absolutely yes!

Venturing into the unknown without a roadmap usually leads to getting lost. Clearly, no successful executive would step into the marketplace without a well thought-out business strategy and a plan to guide the way. Neither should you embark on the journey of change without a clear change strategy and process plan. For over 25 years, we have been developing, testing, and refining the Change Leader's Roadmap to provide guidance for developing your change strategy and process plan.

In this guide, we provide a high-level overview of the nine phases of work outlined in the Change Leader's Roadmap. This guide helps you identify how to tailor the Roadmap to fit your organization's change needs, its people's needs, and the outcomes. It also helps you identify the major areas of work that you are doing well and neglecting.

WHAT IS THE CHANGE LEADER'S ROADMAP?

A comprehensive change strategy consists of three areas: (1) content (the organizational and technical areas you must change); (2) people (the mind-set, as well as the behavioral and cultural changes, required to deliver your content changes); and (3) process (the actions required to plan, design, and implement all your changes [content and people] in an integrated and unified manner).

The Change Leader's Roadmap is a nine-phase process model, built to help you plan, design, and implement your content and people changes. It organizes the process for moving your organization from where it is today to where it needs to be to ensure continued success in the marketplace. As a roadmap, the model does not tell you what to change. Instead, it provides guidance for how to change so that you get your intended business outcomes while simultaneously engaging your people in positive ways to bolster your culture, change readiness, and capability to succeed.

The Roadmap embeds the essential human dynamics of transformation in the concrete tasks of changing structures, systems, processes, or technology. Our research demonstrates that a certain guarantee of failure is to pay inadequate attention to the people dynamics of changes in engagement, commitment, behavior, and mind-set, as well as the relationships between leader teams, culture, and emotional reactions. These critical tasks are not "bolted on" as a nice-to-do afterthought in the Roadmap; they are integrated right into the tangible content work that the Roadmap specifies.

The Change Leader's Roadmap is the heart of Being First's Change Methodology. The resources we have built around it offer a full range of conceptual to detailed guidance. Consequently, the Roadmap is usable by leaders who fill the various change leadership roles—from the change sponsor who only needs to understand the picture from 30,000 feet up, to the change process leader, project team member, or change consultant who needs more detail to ensure tangible success.

For ease of use, the Roadmap is organized like a project management methodology. Each of the nine phases (see Figure 1) is made up of activities, which are further composed of tasks. The work happens at the task level; the activities and phases simply organize the tasks into a logical flow for better understanding and application. In our most detailed resources, each phase includes not only key activities and tasks, but also task deliverables, work steps, tools, assessments, and checklists.

Although designed for transformational change, the Change Leader's Roadmap can be tailored for all types of change, as well as for any magnitude of change effort. Smaller, less complex changes require selective tailoring of the phases, activities, and tasks in the model.

Figure 1: The Change Process Model for Leading Conscious Transformation

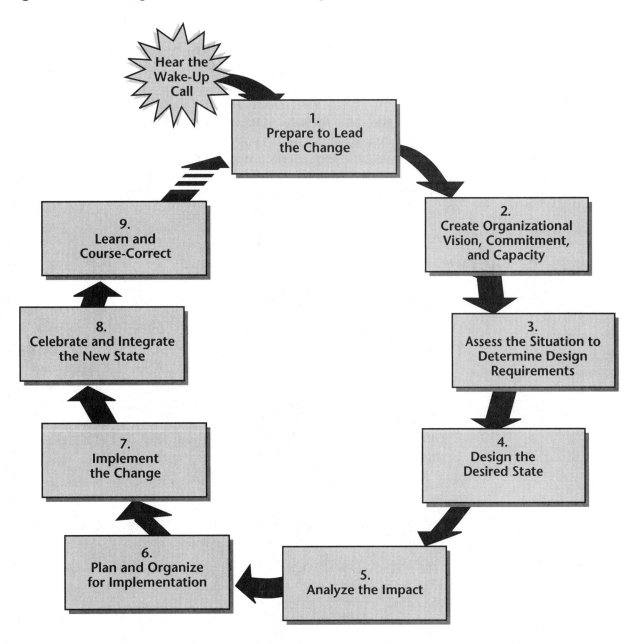

The nine phases of the Roadmap represent the inherent logic and flow of the activities of leading and achieving real change—the full terrain of content and people requirements. However, do not be fooled into interpreting the model's sequential nature to mean that you must complete one phase before you proceed to the next. Not so! In reality, you can be in two, three, or even four phases simultaneously. Furthermore, you can do the work of several phases in parallel!

The Roadmap is not a lockstep project management approach. Transformation is too dynamic for that, and requires constant course correction. Consequently, the Roadmap prescribes nothing. Instead, it is a navigation system, a thinking discipline that makes you aware of what change tasks you might need to engage in; then it helps you decide what to do and how to do it. We have built it to be comprehensive, leaving nothing out. You will never want to do everything described in the Roadmap. Instead, do as little as possible, yet enough to succeed. Select only the key tasks that your change requires.

Keep this in mind as you read through the phases. Due to the space limitations of this guide, this is a brief overview. For a more detailed version of the Roadmap, see our book *The Change Leader's Roadmap: How to Navigate Your Organization's Transformation*. And keep in mind that the detailed Toolkit that supports the Roadmap is over a thousand pages long. (Wow!) As you read the overview, think about a live change that you are currently engaged in, and identify the work you have successfully completed, what you may have missed that is causing you problems, and what you need to do from here.

OVERVIEW OF THE CHANGE LEADER'S ROADMAP PHASES

Phase 1: Prepare to Lead the Change

In Phase I, you set up the leaders of the change and your organization to succeed from the beginning. It is the most important phase, addressing the key people and process decisions you must make to get your change effort off to a strong start. Its purpose is to prepare your leaders to lead the change successfully by accomplishing six activities:

1. Start up and staff your change effort with the best change leaders and expertise.

2. Determine your case for change, the accurate scope of change, and the desired outcomes.

3. Assess your organization's level of readiness and capacity to take on and succeed in the change at this time.

4. Build your leaders' capacity to collectively commit to the change, lead it effectively as an aligned team through to fruition, and model the mind-set and behaviors required for it to succeed.

5. Establish the optimal conditions, change process, resources, and change infrastructure to achieve your change.

6. Clarify the overall change strategy, governance infrastructure, and project integration plans for achieving your results, and how you will engage your entire organization in ways that reflect your values and guiding principles.

With all these ducks in a row, your leaders:

- Have assured their ability to work as a unified team.

- Have established the conditions for the change to succeed (including identifying your employee engagement plan, communication plan, and training plan).

- Are capable of leading the organization through the thick and thin of your change as it unfolds.

Phase 2: Create Organizational Vision, Commitment, and Capacity

In this phase, you take your clarity, leadership alignment, and Phase 1 decisions out to the organization. You announce your case for change and the change strategy for how the overall effort and subinitiatives will be defined, integrated, and orchestrated over time. Your purpose is to build organizationwide understanding, commitment, momentum, and capacity so as to succeed in the transformation, especially among your key stakeholders. In your communications and engagement, you and the change leaders begin to model the behavior and thinking that you are asking of your organization, and you actively engage people in creating the new future.

Ideally, any part of the organization affected by the change participates in the creation of a compelling vision of the future that will bring the organization greater success. In organizations that have a history of doing well in their old state, the leaders create bold actions to wake the organization up to the need for transforming. Without understanding that the old way of operating is gone, your people cannot be motivated to change. So this phase mobilizes the necessary understanding, builds readiness, and prepares all stakeholders for aligned action.

Phase 3: Assess the Situation to Determine Design Requirements

Use the desired outcomes and vision you created in Phases 1 and 2 to generate design requirements for determining the actual future state. Assess the current reality in the organization for three key pieces of information:

1. What you already have that serves your desired outcomes
2. What you must stop doing or dismantle
3. What you need to create afresh to make your vision a reality

Also gather information from your customers, and surface important best practices in the industry that you want to embed in the desired state. These activities provide clear parameters for generating the best scenario for implementation. They also build the expectation for change within your organization. In all these tasks, use your engagement and communication plans to ensure employee involvement. The more you engage people in doing this work, the more they buy into the change.

Phase 4: Design the Desired State

Design the specific organizational and cultural solutions that will enable you to achieve your vision. The resources and vehicles to design your desired state can be critical drivers of momentum and excitement—or deterrents. If you use external experts to do your design work, you might get a sound solution, but you might also alienate your in-house resources and employees who have a greater understanding of the organization's strengths and weaknesses. If at all possible, engage key in-house stakeholders in your design process, with or without external experts. And fulfill the design requirements of Phase 3!

Phase 5: Analyze the Impact

Once you have your preferred future state design, assess its impact on your existing organization, its culture, and its people—all in preparation for planning a realistic implementation process. Impact analysis is an essential step in understanding just how much work is required to put your desired future in place. This is a great opportunity to engage resistors, if you have not already: You want to know why they think the change will *not* work! This informs you about further work needed to ensure a successful implementation. Or it might alert you to the need to redesign (i.e., go back to Phase 4) because the impacts of your current design are more than your organization, resources, or timing can tolerate.

Phase 6: Plan and Organize for Implementation

With lists of impacts and issues needing attention before implementation can occur, you can identify the actions required to officially implement the desired state. Integrate actions as much as possible to be efficient and to optimize your resource utilization, and develop your Implementation Master Plan. Only when you know the actual work required to put the future state in place can you realistically identify the timetable for implementation. Once this is clear, you also ensure that the organization is prepared for implementation and has the time and skill to see the changes through while effectively continuing the ongoing operation.

And, of course, a key part of your Implementation Master Plan includes human issues like training needs, emotional support, and continued communications and engagement.

Phase 7: Implement the Change

Carry out your Implementation Master Plan to achieve the desired state. Undoubtedly, your rollout will not go as planned. Rollouts never do, especially if the change is transformational. So you must build in ways to monitor legitimately what is happening and what is needed, and then correct the course of both the plan and your desired state design, as required. In implementation, people realize how real the change is, and, when they are required to actually behave differently, they can have a range of predictable emotional reactions that you have not yet seen. It is your job to support them through their reactions, so that they can let go of the past and continue on their path to the future.

Phase 8: Celebrate and Integrate the New State

Celebrate achieving your desired state. Let members of your organization know that they are now living in the new state, although the process has not ended and changes will continue. Reward your people's support for the changes to date and recognize all the hard work they have contributed to achieve the new state. Also support people's integration and mastery of the new behaviors and work practices required to make the change successful. Even when people have taken on new roles or new technology, they do not necessarily know how to succeed with them or how everyone fits into the larger picture of the change across the organization. So plan working sessions and communications to ensure that your people learn what works, iron out remaining operational kinks, and continue to refine the new state as they learn how to make it work most effectively. This occurs in intact work groups as well as across departments, functions, or processes, all in support of the organization as a whole.

Phase 9: Learn and Course-Correct

You have been learning and course-correcting your Roadmap and outcome all along. This phase focuses you on four important activities to conclude the round of change:

1. Create mechanisms to continuously improve your new state.
2. Evaluate and learn from how well you designed and implemented your change strategy and change process plan, for the continuous improvement of your change leadership.
3. Improve your organization's readiness and ability to lead future changes successfully.
4. Close down the existing change process by dismantling your temporary change infrastructures and conditions that no longer serve

the needs of the new organization. Frequently, leaders decide to maintain some of their change structures because they have discovered how useful they are to the resilience.

SUMMARY

The nine phases of the Change Leader's Roadmap take you from start-up through successful completion, and prepare you for the next round of changes inevitably knocking at your door. Tailor these phases and activities. When you consciously decide to skip key steps or decisions, be sure to first consider the impacts of doing so. Customize your process to each change effort you are leading, and encourage your stakeholders to identify the best change practices for your organization and its unique needs. Make the Change Leader's Roadmap your own so that it provides your organization and change efforts the greatest chance for success. Best of luck on your change journey!

HOW TO PLAN FOR A NEGOTIATION

Joan E. Cassidy-Huck

Joan E. Cassidy-Huck, EdD, *is a certified management consultant, educator, speaker, author, and president/CEO of Integrated Leadership Concepts, Inc. For more than 25 years, she has used whole-brain concepts to help managers and their employees learn the secrets of high performance. Her clients include national and international Fortune 100 and 500 companies and other private, public, and nonprofit organizations. In addition to writing dozens of articles, Joan is a past contributor to the* **Sourcebooks, Mission Possible, The Consultant's Big Book of Organization Development Tools, The Consultant's Toolkit, Break-Out Creativity: Bringing Creativity to the Workplace,** *and* **Celebrate Customer Service: Insider Secrets.** *She also is a collegiate professor at the University of Maryland University College, where she teaches online and face-to-face undergraduate courses in management and human resources management.*

Contact Information:
Integrated Leadership Concepts, Inc.
901 Nanticoke Run Way
Odenton, MD 21113
410.672.5467
drjoanc@aol.com
www.DrJoanCassidy.com

The very mention of the word negotiation *can strike fear or anxiety in the average person because for so long negotiation meant there were winners and losers, with the losers being destroyed. Some people still think negotiation means giving in to someone else's demands. Others think it is a contest of wills in which whoever is tougher and holds out longer wins. In reality, almost anyone can learn to negotiate relatively successfully. The secret lies in planning. Whether you are a salesperson, a customer, a manager, or an employee, it is in your best interest to learn how to negotiate better.*

The purpose of this guide is to provide you with strategies and tactics used by successful negotiators. At the end is a Negotiation Planning Worksheet (NPW; Figure 1) that you can use to plan your next negotiation.

An attorney friend of mine once told me that, when he prepares for a case, he prepares for the worst. In other words, he tries to identify everything that could cause him to lose the case. Then, he systematically addresses each one by developing strategies to help him win. In negotiating, the same principle applies. Good planning greatly increases your chance for success. One of the best ways to do that is to organize your data into four different areas:

- Information about you
- Information about the other side
- Information about the situation or the environment
- Information about the relationship

When you collect your information, you need to be as thorough as possible. Consider a number of different sources, such as:

- Your own personal knowledge and information about the negotiation situation.
- Information from friends, family, co-workers, or others familiar with the situation.
- Print media, such as newspapers, books, and magazines.
- Television, corporate Internet sites and reports, and other related Internet sites.

Information About You

One of the best places to start your planning process is with information about you. Answer the following types of questions:

1. What is your overall goal for the negotiation?
2. What are you specific wants, needs, and expectations (WNEs)?
3. Which are the most important?
4. What is your negotiation style?
5. What is your BATNA (best alternative to a negotiated agreement)?
6. At what point will you decide to walk away?

Let's look at each of these in more detail.

1. *Clarify your negotiation goal:* You have to be very clear about your overall goal. Some of the specific questions you must answer are:
   - Why are you going into this negotiation?
   - What is the purpose?
   - What do you want to accomplish?

You may need to use different strategies and tactics depending on your primary goal. For example, is it to win at any cost? Or is it more important to get the best deal possible without jeopardizing the relationship?

2. *List your WNEs:* Your WNEs are your wish list. Take some time to think about what you want, need, or expect to happen as result of the negotiation. Jot down everything that comes to mind. It is important to be thorough. It also is important to differentiate between what you *want* and what you really *need*. For example, you might *want* a job that pays $100,000 a year. On the other hand, you *need* to find a job in your current geographic locale. When you factor in the location variable, it might not be realistic to *expect* to find a job with that kind of salary. During the next step, you will prioritize your wish list.

3. *Prioritize your WNEs:* One of the easiest ways to do this is to sort your overall list into three separate categories:

   • *Must-have:* These items ultimately determine whether the negotiation is a success. For example, you may find the perfect job in Spokane, Washington, with the right salary, environment, training, and benefits. But you will not relocate to Spokane under any circumstances. Location is a must-have item and, therefore, a deal breaker.

   • *Nice-to-have:* These items add value to, or "sweeten," the end result. They are important, but not quite as important as the must-have group. For example, the company offers up to $2,000 a quarter for educational expenses. This would be nice to have and could sway you toward your final decision. On the other hand, if you do not get it, you would still consider the position.

   • *Would like to have, but can live without:* This final group is also important, but these items also are not deal breakers. In other words, if you have to make concessions, these are the items you put on the table first. Part of your strategy should be to give the impression you are trying to meet the other person halfway—that you are trying to be fair. For example, you would like to have four weeks' paid vacation, but you would settle for three. If it looks like they are holding firm on three weeks, you can agree to make a concession on that point, which could help you secure the job.

   Initially, this list is for your own use. It is necessary to reveal some of your must-have items in the beginning, but it is a good idea not to reveal all of them. Doing so makes you vulnerable. Always hold back some items, especially if you sense that revealing them will give the other side an advantage.

4. *Determine your negotiation style:* There are two basic approaches to negotiation:

   • *Win-win:* The emphasis is on collaborating and maintaining the relationship, while focusing on the "interests" of the participants.

- *Win-lose:* The focus is on competition and on identifying winners and losers.

We can make a further distinction by identifying specific negotiation styles. (See Table 1.) Some researchers suggest that negotiation styles can be directly correlated to personality, while others maintain that individuals choose a style depending on the context. Both positions have merit. You might have a natural or preferred style based on your predisposition. To be effective, however, you need to understand the context and then adjust your style accordingly. (We will discuss this topic further under "Information About the Relationship.")

Table 1: Five Styles of Negotiation

Style	Tendencies	Goal	Characteristics
1. Competing	High assertiveness/ low cooperation	To win	Will do whatever it takes to win; may use threats or insults, withhold information, or stretch the truth.
2. Avoiding	Low assertiveness and cooperation	To survive	Might resort to hiding, delaying, or stalling; might appear to be committed to nothing in particular.
3. Accommodating	Low assertiveness/ high cooperation	To be fair	Concerned about maintaining relationships; will tend to be courteous and to share information readily; will often make a concession with the expectation that the other side will do the same.
4. Collaborating	High assertiveness and cooperation	To understand and solve the problem	Will tend to be thoughtful; trust is not an issue—they rely instead on objective criteria and seek multiple options, even if there appears to be only one solution.
5. Compromising	Moderate in assertiveness and cooperation	To ensure that each party gets something	Will tend to be honest, sincere, and dedicated to the end result; very concerned about the "process" (i.e., are both sides happy with the result?).

5. *Identify your BATNA:* Your BATNA (best alternative to a negotiated agreement) is your backup plan in the event you fail to reach an agreement. In other words, suppose you reach an impasse? What if the other party will not budge? Have a backup plan in the event you are unsuccessful in the current negotiation. This is like "not putting all your eggs in one basket." For example, you really want a particular job, but your must-have terms are not met. You still have another one you might consider.

6. *Identify your resistance point:* Your resistance point is the deal breaker. If you have been thorough in the previous categories, it should be fairly easy to identify a specific point at which you must decide that the negotiation is not worth pursuing. In other words, at what point do you walk away? For example, you do not want to travel excessively. You try to negotiate the amount of travel, but the company insists that you must travel about 75 percent of the time. This is your resistance point—the deal breaker.

Information About the Other Side

Getting as much information as possible about the other side is critical. In some cases, you might need to make an educated guess. In others, you might be able to get fairly accurate information. For example, if you are applying for a job, find out as much as you can about the organization's culture, including dress standards and management style. Most job hunters tend to concentrate on anticipated salary, responsibilities, and the person to whom they will report. Although this information is important, you also should look at the potential employer's culture to see if there will be a good match. Failing to adjust to an organization's culture is one of the leading reasons for the failure of new hires. One of the best ways to find out about the culture is to ask these types of questions during an interview:

- Who are the company's top employees?
- What are they like?
- Do these employees manage the best units?
- Do they encourage teamwork?
- How are conflicts handled?
- How are decisions made?
- How does the boss communicate?

The answers to these questions reveal whether the company has a friendly, team-oriented atmosphere, or a competitive one in which rivalry dominates. If working in a friendly, team-oriented atmosphere is important to you, you might want to reconsider interviewing with a company whose employees are known for their competitiveness.

Another strategy is to imagine that you are in the other party's shoes. What would you do? Complete as much information as possible for the following types of questions:

1. What is their overall goal?

2. What are their WNEs?

3. How would you prioritize their WNEs?

4. What is their BATNA? What is their fallback position? What might they be willing to settle for? What else might they suggest?

5. What is their resistance point? At what point will they say "no deal"?

Some of this information might not be readily available; however, as the negotiation progresses, a lot is revealed. The key is to keep attuned to what is going on at all times and be ready to shift gears if necessary.

Information About the Situation or the Environment

This type of information is also critical. The more you know about what is going on in the environment, the better your advantage will be. For example, suppose you are getting ready to buy a car. Some questions you want to answer are:

1. Are there any deadlines for when you must have the car?

2. Are you buying a car based on an accident?

3. Will you get an insurance settlement? If so, how long will you have to wait? Are you willing to spend more than what you will get from the settlement?

4. What is the economy like?

5. What is the car market like? What kind of cars are people buying?

6. What is the going rate for a car like the one you are considering?

7. Has the cost of gas increased dramatically lately? How will that affect the type of car you are considering?

8. Is it the beginning or end of the month?

9. What kind of inventory does the dealer have?

10. Are there any special deals available from any dealers? Car manufacturers?

11. Where can you get the best financing rate?

These are just some examples of the type of information you should collect about the situation or the environment.

Information About the Relationship

Research has been conducted recently in an attempt to determine if there is a best way to negotiate. For example, is it more important for you to get the best deal or to maintain a long-term, ongoing relationship? If you are concerned about maintaining the relationship, then you should opt for a win-win approach. On the other hand, if maintaining the relationship is not important (i.e., you will not be involved with the individual in the future), focus your efforts on getting the best deal possible. Take a more aggressive approach. To help you decide, answer the following questions:

1. Will this negotiation be a one-time thing, or do you intend to come back in the future?

2. What is your negotiation style? Will it be an advantage or a disadvantage?

3. What are the potential consequences for any strategies, tactics, or actions you might be considering?

4. What is the other party's negotiation style?

5. What do you know about the other party's strategies, tactics, or actions?

6. Do you feel you can trust the other party?

7. Do you feel the other party trusts you?

8. How much authority do you have to negotiate? (Are others involved? Should they be?)

9. How much authority does the other person have to negotiate with you?

10. Have you prepared an agenda for the negotiation? Is the other party aware of it?

In summary, as the importance and/or complexity of the negotiation increases, thought and planning also should increase.

Figure 1: Negotiation Planning Worksheet (NPW)

Name: _____   Date: _____

Type of Negotiation: _____

What sources will you use to collect information?

_____Your own personal knowledge and information about the negotiation situation

_____Information from friends, family, co-workers, or others familiar with the situation

_____Print media such as newspapers, books, and magazines

_____Television, corporate Internet sites, reports, and other related Internet sites

What, if any, additional information should you identify?

_____

_____

A. Information About You

1. *What is your overall goal?* (Example: To buy a *new* car.)

_____

2. *List your wants, needs, expectations (WNEs).* What do you want, need, or expect to get out of the negotiation? (Example: A new, red Toyota Camry, with XX features, financed by dealer, target maximum cost of _____.)

3. *Prioritize your WNEs:*

Must Have	*Nice to Have*	*Would Like to Have, But Can Live Without*
a.	a.	a.
b.	b.	b.
c.	c.	c.
d.	d.	d.
e.	e.	e.
f.	f.	f.
g.	g.	g.

4. *What is your BATNA (best alternative to a negotiated agreement)?* (Example: If you cannot reach agreement for your primary choice of car at your maximum target level in dollars, what is your fallback position? What might you be willing to settle for? Where else might you go?)

_____

_____

_____

_____

5. *What is your resistance point (i.e., the deal breaker)?* At this point your WNEs are very important. You need to review your must-have list to help with this decision. In other words, if you must have "a new, red Toyota Camry, with *XX* features at *YY* price," and the dealer offers you "a black Toyota Camry with fewer features and the price is less than your maximum," do you take the deal? How important are the features, price, and other requirements? At what point do you walk away?

_____

_____

_____

_____

B. Information About the Other Side

Get as much information about the other side as possible. In some cases, you might need to make an educated guess; in others, you might be able to get fairly accurate information. One strategy is to imagine that you are in the other party's shoes. What would you do?

1. *What is their overall goal?* (Example: To sell you a car.)

_____

_____

2. *List the other side's wants, needs, expectations (WNEs).* (Example: To sell you a car already on the lot for the highest profit.)

   a.

   b.

   c.

   d.

   e.

   f.

   g.

   h.

   i.

   j.

3. *Prioritize their WNEs:*

Must Have	Nice to Have	Would Like to Have, But Can Live Without
a.	a.	a.
b.	b.	b.
c.	c.	c.
d.	d.	d.
e.	e.	e.

4. *What is their BATNA (best alternative to a negotiated agreement)?* (Example: If they cannot reach agreement to sell you a car that is already on the lot at maximum profit, what is their fallback position? What might they be willing to settle for? What else might they suggest?)

_____

_____

5. *What is their resistance point (i.e., the deal breaker)?* At what point will they say "no deal"?

_____

_____

_____

_____

C. Information About the Environment/Situation

This information is critical. The more you know about what is going on the environment, the better advantage you will have. These are the types of questions to answer. Choose the appropriate ones and write your answers below. Add any additional ones that you think are necessary.

    a. Do you have any deadlines?
    b. Are you buying a car based on an accident, insurance settlement, or other reason?
    c. What is the economy like?
    d. Are people buying cars? What kind?
    e. What is the going rate for a car like the one you are interested in?
    f. Has the cost of gas jumped dramatically lately?
    g. Is it the beginning or end of the month?
    h. What kind of inventory does the dealer have?
    i. Are their any special deals going on from dealers? From car manufacturers?
    j. Where can you get the best financing rate?

_____

_____

_____

_____

_____

D. Information About the Relationship Between the Parties

Is it more important for you to get the best deal or to maintain a long-term, ongoing relationship? Answer the following types of questions. Add any others that you think are necessary.

a. Will this negotiation be a one-time thing? Or do you intend to come back in the future?
b. What is your negotiation style?
c. What are the potential consequences for any strategies, tactics, or actions you might be considering?
d. What is the other party's negotiation style?
e. What do you know about the other party's strategies, tactics, or actions?
f. Do you feel you can trust the other party?
g. Do you feel the other party trusts you?
h. How much authority do you have to negotiate? (Are others involved? Do they need to be?)
i. How much authority does the other person have to negotiate with you?
j. Have you prepared an agenda for the negotiation? Is the other party aware of it?

_____

_____

_____

_____

_____

_____

_____

_____

_____

_____

HOW TO USE THE ORGANIZATIONAL SAVVY MODEL

Martin Seldman and Edward Betof

Martin Seldman *is one of the country's most experienced executive coaches, with over 1,300 worldwide assignments since 1986. The Organizational Savvy Model is the focus of his most recent book with coauthor Rick Brandon, **Survival of the Savvy** (Free Press, 2004).*

Edward Betof *is vice president, talent management, and CLO at Bector, Dickinson and Company, where he has responsibility for BD University, human resource planning/leadership development, and integrating worldwide performance and development processes. He is the lead author of **Just Promoted!** (McGraw-Hill, 1992) and has contributed to numerous journals and professional publications. Ed is also a frequent contributor to the **Sourcebooks**. He began a three-year term in January 2004 as a member of ASTD's board of directors.*

Contact Information:
Martin Seldman
support@seldman.com
www.seldman.com

Edward Betof
1 Becton Drive
Franklin Lakes, NJ 07417
201.847.4502
edward_betof@bd.com
www.bd.com

The Organizational Savvy Model was originally developed by applying Kelly Reineke's research on power dynamics to executive coaching. In coaching assignments, an approach was needed to help executives who were smart, functionally competent, and had the right values, but who were at risk of derailing their careers.

The second stage in the development of the model was the creation of seminars that taught practical, proactive ways to use the skills, strategies, and signals of organizational savvy. Using case studies, skill practices, and awareness exercises, Martin Seldman's business colleague, Rick Brandon, helped expand the model and created training that equipped participants to advance their careers while maintaining their moral compass.

Organizational savvy equips a leader to identify people with the right values, figure out how to get ideas implemented, and detect types of deceptive practices and behaviors, including unethical and illegal activity, as well as patterns of behavior such as:

- Overpromising.
- Exaggerating.
- Lying.
- Providing partial or misleading information.
- Hiding bad news.
- Giving superficial explanations.
- Taking undeserved credit.
- Scapegoating or blaming others.
- Refusing to admit mistakes.
- Unfairly tarnishing the reputation of others.
- Sabotaging the efforts of colleagues.
- Giving insincere flattery.
- Telling people what they want to hear.
- Punishing people who criticize or challenge ideas.
- Overcontrolling information.

Even if leaders have excellent personal values and good intentions, the absence of the ability to detect deception leaves them vulnerable in three ways:

1. *Unable to be an effective steward of the organization's resources and reputation:* In addition to internal decisions, the success of many companies depends on the choices leaders make regarding key external relationships, including partnerships, joint ventures, licensing intellectual property, franchising, and key vendors and suppliers.

2. *Unable to anticipate:* A leader might not anticipate power plays, political maneuvers, and potential sabotage, which in turn undermines his or her leadership position. That is a classic form of leadership derailment.

3. *Unable to recruit the right people:* Creating and maintaining a high-integrity organization involves establishing a critical mass of people with the right values and skills. If an overly political person—someone who is guided only by self-interest—attains power, he or she can do significant damage to an organization's fiscal and human resources.

Experience with these issues indicates that, in fact, bad things happen to good leaders in good companies. That is why organizational savvy training as a crucial aspect of the development of ethical leaders is advocated. Fortunately, the skills, strategies, and signals that make up the model can be learned and applied fairly quickly.

This guide provides a basic understanding of the Organizational Savvy Model so that you can apply its principles to your own organization.

POLITICS

Politics is one of the most negative words in the English language because it is almost always used in a negative context. Commonly heard phrases include, "She's so political," "He's only doing that for political reasons," "It's all politics."

In other words, in our effort to avoid appearing political, we prevent ourselves from acquiring essential awareness and skills. That is why we offer this alternative definition of politics:

> *Organizational politics: informal, unofficial, and sometimes behind-the-scenes efforts to sell ideas, influence an organization, increase power, or achieve other targeted objectives.*

Notice that this definition is value-free and ethically neutral. It does not tell you if the person practicing organizational politics is acting out of pure self-interest or a sincere desire to help the team.

To determine whether someone is using political skill in a way that will help or hurt the company, we need to look at the person's goals and values. We refer to this as the *ends* (self-interest versus company interest) and the *means* (what can I get away with, rather than what is the right thing to do?) of political behavior.

Therefore, a person can protect and add value to the company if he or she uses political awareness and skill (as we have defined it) and is guided ethically by the two questions: (1) What is best for the company? (2) What is the right thing to do?

The Organizational Savvy Continuum (Figure 1) shows us that people come to the workplace with different levels of political skill and value sets. People display a varied range of behaviors, and it can be useful to notice patterns, both in ourselves and in others.

THE LESS POLITICAL (LP) LEADER

People on the LP side of the continuum ask, what is the right thing to do? They place a high value on staying within an ethical framework. Often, they disdain politics and prefer situations in which facts, logic, or analysis point in a straightforward way to what is best for the organization.

Figure 1: The Organizational Savvy Continuum

← Less Political (LP)		Overly Political (OP) →
Less Political What's the right thing to do?	**Savvy Leader** What is right for the shareholders, the company, and the customers?	**Overly Political** What can I get away with?
High integrity	High integrity	Low integrity
Low level of political skill	High level of political skill	High level of political skill

These people believe that business should be a meritocracy. Skin color, gender, percentage of body fat, where you went to school, with whom you associate on weekends, and so forth, should not matter. The best ideas and the most deserving people should advance.

Consequently, this type of person often relies on the old saying, the results will speak for themselves. Doing good work will eventually be noticed and rewarded; so they feel little need for self-promotion.

Assuming this less political person is competent, the described qualities make him or her an asset to an organization. We recommend that such people hold onto their values and focus on these questions:

- What is best for the organization?

- What is the right thing to do?

However, we have found that the LP leader is vulnerable to certain career and company risks.

LP Career Risks

1. *Being underestimated:* Letting the results speak for themselves can be a good approach if you are certain that key decision makers know what you did and how you did it. Senior management may be so busy, however, that they might not know.

2. *Becoming pigeonholed:* Sometimes the LP leader is unaware that he or she has a positive, but limiting, reputation. Others at the company might describe the LP leader as "a functional expert" or "tactical." Others might advise, "Point him or her in the right direction and he or she will get the job done." As the saying goes, "The difference between perception and reality is that people make decisions based on perception." The LP leader might ignore how perception drives career decisions.

3. *Not getting credit for contributions:* LP leaders dramatically increase risks to both their careers and their companies when they deal with overly political (OP) people. OP leaders are willing to

take credit, assign blame, and sabotage colleagues if they think they can get away with it. LP leaders are often slow to anticipate those actions and to protect themselves properly against them. By not getting their names associated with their contributions, they leave themselves vulnerable to OP tactics.

4. *Speaking truth to power:* Ask an LP leader for his or her honest feedback, and you will often get it. Unfortunately, not everyone in power who asks for feedback really wants to be criticized or challenged. Many LP leaders have hurt their careers by misjudging the risk of criticizing an OP person with power or powerful friends.

LP Company Risks

1. *Not expecting or detecting deception:* The LP leader might naively trust that others within the company also want what is best for it. That might leave the LP leader unprepared to anticipate and detect the practices of an overly political colleague. Unfortunately, an honest, sincere person is often easier to mislead.

2. *Allowing an overly political person to gain or maintain power:* If an OP person attains any power, it is only a matter of time until he or she hurts the organization. The longer this person continues at the company, the more its resources and reputation are at risk. The LP leader may not understand how the OP leader maintains power and may not have the political skill or will to remove the OP leader.

THE SAVVY LEADER

Often, savvy leaders operate with the same core values and have the same goals as less political colleagues. They would like the corporate world to be a meritocracy in which results and integrity are all that is needed. In fact, they use their influence, skills, and decision-making abilities to move their teams in that direction.

However, savvy leaders' experience and training have taught them to deal with the realities of human nature and corporate politics. As a result, they operate differently from LP leaders in ways that both reduce their vulnerabilities and increase organizational impact.

The savvy leader:

- Studies power dynamics—how decisions get made, who has access to and influence on power.

- Builds and maintains key networks.

- Knows cultural norms and core values.

- Understands how to implement ideas.

- Promotes himself or herself with integrity.

- Challenges ideas and addresses difficult issues without embarrassing others.
- Creates an accurate perception of his or her ideas, talents, and potentials.
- Factors in timing, setting, conflicting agendas, allies, and advocates in deciding which "battles" can be won.
- Detects patterns of deception, personal and hidden agendas, and self-serving information.
- Uses verbal discipline with people he or she does not trust.
- Holds firm on integrity issues and is willing to take a stand.

Using those skills, signals, and strategies, the savvy leader, like the LP leader, asks these two questions:

- What is best for the team?
- What is the right thing to do?

Career and Company Risks

Savvy skills reduce most of the career and company risks for an LP leader. However, savvy leaders may need to be especially vigilant and skillful in three potentially risky situations:

- An overly political person with power or access to power joins the company.
- The company merges with another organization whose culture is more political.
- The savvy leader is asked to work in a culture in which the level of deceptive practices is greater than what he or she is used to.

THE OVERLY POLITICAL LEADER

The OP leader has a deep understanding of human nature and political behavior. Unfortunately, that knowledge is used to advance self-interests, even if the behavior might damage the company, its employees, and its shareholders.

The OP leader does not operate in an ethical framework, but instead asks the question, what can I get away with?

It is important to understand how an OP leader operates and how power can be gained and maintained.

1. *Deferential dismissive:* If an OP leader thinks you have power or access to power, you are probably not as smart, funny, or good-looking as he or she is saying you are. An OP leader can be charming to select people. On the other hand, if you do not have power or powerful friends, or if the OP leader thinks you are a nice person

who will not use your power, he or she can be quite dismissive. That behavior includes not returning phone calls, coming late to meetings, interrupting, teasing and sarcastic comments, and lack of cooperation.

2. *Access to power:* The overarching objective of the OP leader is to stay on the right side of power. The OP leader is aware that senior managers have complex, busy lives and that a limited number of people gain access and exposure to them.

3. *Managing the airwaves:* OP leaders use their access to power and skill by managing the airwaves—sending messages early and often to achieve their objectives.

4. *Loyalty versus competence:* The OP leader places a higher value on loyalty than on competence. Inside a team run by an OP leader, you will see many decisions based on relationships, bonds, and favoritism. People who deserve to be promoted, but who do not manage up correctly, might not advance. The OP leader might protect team members who perform under par or who demonstrate inappropriate behavior.

5. *High concern for image:* Although everyone is somewhat concerned about image and sensitive to criticism, the OP leader takes those issues to the extreme. He or she may excessively self-promote and be acutely conscious of status issues. The OP leader is often unwilling to admit mistakes and too ready to punish people who criticize him or her.

OP Career Risks

1. *Too obvious:* The OP leader's behavior can be blatantly manipulative and self-serving. The OP leader's corporate "buzz" can become negative, diminishing his or her credibility.

2. *Key supporter leaves:* If the person who is the main source of the OP leader's access to power leaves the company, the OP becomes vulnerable. Anyone who has been mistreated now has no reason not to retaliate.

3. *Scrutiny of deceptive practices increases.* A combination of regulatory agencies, industry watchdogs, keen observers, and others are all helping to ensure that questionable business practices do not go undetected.

OP Company Risks

The OP leader diverts a company's resources to advance his or her personal agenda. The company, therefore, cannot use the assets optimally and goals are not met. The human resource costs are equally severe.

The OP leader has a negative impact on the company's employees, including the individuals he or she has attacked. People with integrity feel trapped on the OP leader's team.

An OP leader may cost a company millions. However, if the media discover and publicize the OP leader's transgressions, the impact on the company's market value can be in the billions. In 1997, when Cendant revealed unethical behavior, the stock dropped 50 percent in one day.

CREATING A HIGH-INTEGRITY ORGANIZATION

Savvy leaders who are not at the highest level of power in an organization can still use awareness and skill to protect themselves and their team. Their ability to shape the company's culture, however, is limited.

If the savvy executive is the CEO or can influence senior management, he or she is capable of using organizational savvy to diminish destructive political behavior.

A primary goal of the HR planning process is to identify and elevate competent leaders who are able to achieve results, build strong organizational capability, and demonstrate the organization's values and ethical behavior. It is equally important to identify and remove OP team members if their behavior cannot be improved through feedback and coaching.

HOW TO SUCCESSFULLY DESIGN AND IMPLEMENT REWARD AND RECOGNITION PROGRAMS

Dean Spitzer

Dean Spitzer, PhD, *is a senior researcher and consultant with IBM Corporation. He has over 30 years' experience in helping individuals and organizations achieve superior performance. Prior to joining IBM, Dean led his own consulting firm. In that capacity, he directed over a hundred successful training and performance improvement projects. Prior to leading his consulting firm, Dean was a training/HRD manager and internal consultant with several Fortune 100 companies, assistant director of a U.S. government education center, and a professor at five universities. He has also lectured in and traveled to 96 countries. Dean is an internationally renowned expert on organizational motivation. His book **SuperMotivation: A Blueprint for Energizing Your Organization from Top to Bottom** (AMACOM, 1995) is widely recognized as the pioneering work in this area, received the Outstanding Communication Award from the International Society for Performance Improvement (ISPI), was honored as "one of the thirty best business books of 1995," and was translated into several languages, including Japanese. He also coauthored **The 1001 Rewards & Recognition Fieldbook**. Dean is the author of 130 articles and several other books.*

Contact Information:
Almaden Services Research
IBM Corporation
3685 Emerald Lane
Mulberry, FL 33860
863.425.9641
spitzer@us.ibm.com

Organizations are increasingly looking for new and better ways to motivate employees. As a result, rewards and recognition programs are gaining increased visibility and importance. Unfortunately, organizations are also increasingly discovering that traditional rewards are limited in their capacity to motivate today's workforce. Even more disturbing, they are frequently prone to dysfunctional effects. It is not unusual for organizations to spend millions of dollars on rewards and find that unintended negative behaviors actually occurred.

In his book, *The Greatest Management Principle in the World* (1985), author Michael LeBoeuf presents the case that the world's greatest management principle is, What gets rewarded gets done. He reached this conclusion after hearing the following parable:

A weekend fisherman looked over the side of his boat and saw a snake with a frog in his mouth. Feeling sorry for the frog, he reached down, gently removed the frog from the snake's mouth and let the frog go free. But now he felt sorry for the hungry snake. Having no food, he took out a flask of bourbon and poured a few drops into the snake's mouth. The snake swam away happy and the man was happy for having performed such good deeds. He thought all was well until a few minutes passed and he heard something knock against the side of his boat and looked down. With stunned disbelief, the fisherman saw the snake was back—with two frogs!

Although a parable, this story is bound to ring true for too many readers. Many organizations are inadvertently conditioning their employees to be "coin-operated"—by offering them incentives to do whatever they want them to do, but find that these employees do exactly what they are being rewarded for, no more and no less—even if it is the wrong thing to do. Clearly that is not the kind of workforce that most organizations want today.

If you want to appreciate the problem with reward programs, consider whether they really tend to make your organization better overall, how long a typical reward program lasts before it is junked (soon to be followed by the next program du jour), how unhappy they make most people (especially those who do not get a reward), and what the reward programs do to intrinsic motivation. (Incidentally, research evidence is clear that the expectation of a tangible reward in connection with a task is strongly associated with less voluntary time spent on the task later as compared with a no-reward condition.)

Fortunately, these kinds of problems with reward and recognition programs are not inevitable. Despite the obvious challenges, well-designed rewards and recognition can have a powerful positive impact on employees' morale and organizational performance. However, designing and implementing an effective reward and recognition program is not intuitive. It requires considerable knowledge. This knowledge is very similar to what it takes to be successful with any significant organizational change program. The rest of this guide provides a clear roadmap for successful organizational reward and recognition program design and implementation.

STEPS TO SUCCESS

1. *Determine the need for the recognition program:* Make sure that there is a legitimate need for the program. Do not just implement a recognition program because it seems like a good idea or because it might be fun for employees. Rewards and recognition are serious

business and should be treated as such. One of the best reasons for a recognition program is that there is a need to get employees more focused on a particular aspect of the business performance (such as quality), but you might not want to do something as drastic as changing the compensation system. This is what happened at the Tennant Company, a Minneapolis, Minnesota-based manufacturer of industrial and commercial floor maintenance equipment. Like many traditional companies in the 1970s, Tennant struggled with quality problems. In 1979, it finally woke up and took heed of the "quality revolution," when customers started complaining about hydraulic oil leaks in Tennant's best machines. After inviting quality guru Philip Crosby to visit the company and being educated about the huge costs of poor quality, Tennant's president Roger Hale started taking personal leadership to find a solution. The development of this solution, of which recognition become a central component, is the case study that runs throughout this guide to demonstrate the steps to success.

2. *Define the goal and business alignment of the recognition program:* Once the business validity of the need has been established, the next step is to define the goal for the proposed program. Tennant did just that by determining that one of the keys to their quality strategy should be *recognizing superior quality performance.* Then, make sure the program goal is aligned with business objectives. Will the program advance an important organizational objective? If not, it would be advisable to make sure the program is aligned before implementing it. At Tennant, quality was one of the most important strategic drivers and a key objective for business survival, as well as improvement. The business alignment was clear to everyone!

3. *Establish program sponsorship:* It is vital to identify a senior manager who will be providing business leadership for the program. Sponsorship means more than having an executive say, "Go ahead!" It means that an executive owns the program and is willing to do whatever it takes to make the program successful. Sponsorship is crucial not only for getting organizational recognition launched, but also for sustaining it long enough to have the desired impact—from the tip-off to the final buzzer! Like any other change program, a recognition program will die an untimely death without such active leadership. At Tennant, the sponsor of the program was the company's president, Roger Hale, which certainly highlighted the importance of the program.

4. *Create the program vision:* The vision for the program relates to the high-level, big-picture view of the program, where the program fits with other initiatives in the organization. At Tennant, there was a realization that the recognition could not just be reserved for the few top performers; it needed to encourage employees on the road to quality. Consequently, while there was formal, annual recog-

nition for the company's top 2 percent, most employees felt unrecognized and relatively unengaged in the quality effort. There was clearly a need for a more personal, more responsive program that bridged the gap from the annual recognition for the celebrated few and the infrequent and sporadic supervisory kudos given on a day-to-day basis for isolated quality behaviors. The new Tennant vision was for a three-tiered recognition system: (1) annual recognition for the few top performers, (2) daily recognition by supervisors, and (3) a more just-in-time type of formal recognition that would be visible, fun, and employee driven. The third type of recognition was the focus of the current effort.

5. *Assess the organization's readiness for the program:* Based on the program design, it is important to objectively determine whether such a program will be successful. Is the timing for the program right? Are there circumstances in the internal or external environment that could undermine the program? If so, you might want to consider taking remedial actions before going forward with implementing the program. Another aspect of organizational readiness is to be on the lookout for demotivators that could sabotage the program. Other than not aiming at the right goals, the second most common reason for motivation program failure is *de*motivation. Incongruously, many programs intended to motivate actually do the opposite. Reward and recognition programs are sometimes viewed as hypocritical (If quality is so important, why are we producing so much scrap?) or examples of tokenism (Why are executives getting big bonuses for quality, but this is all we're getting?). Be aware of, and take action to remove, these often hidden factors that can undermine your program, even before it starts. The close engagement of senior leadership and management's involvement on the program's coordinating team minimized any threat of demotivation in the Tennant program, and a thorough assessment revealed that the organizational climate was truly friendly to the program!

6. *Design the program:* The design of the program operationalizes the vision. It defines the what, who, when, where, and how to the program.

   What kind of recognition will be given? The most effective recognition is symbolic, because the meaningfulness of the recognition to the employee is more important than its monetary value. At Tennant, the design team conceived of an innovative form of recognition based on Koala T. Bear [as in quality bear], a stuffed teddy bear dressed in a Tennant quality improvement t-shirt and a Tennant hard hat. Although of little financial value, this recognition item has become a highly coveted award in the company. The employee also receives a certificate.

   Who receives it? Koala T. Bear can be earned by any employee when the employee meets specific criteria: demonstrating extra effort to meet or exceed customer needs, going above and beyond job standards, exhibiting a commitment to quality.

When is it received? It is given as soon as the employee achieves the criteria, as determined by a committee composed of employees from throughout the company. It is not given on a competitive basis, and, therefore, the recognition does not engender any internal competition, which would be contrary to Tennant's quality philosophy.

Where is it given? It is given at the employee's work area.

How is it given? It is given with appropriate pomp and ceremony by a committee member dressed in a Koala T. Bear costume, which makes it fun, personal, and visible. Tennant realized that how recognition is delivered to recipients can be as important as the recognition itself.

7. *Develop the program:* The next step is to actually develop the program based on the program design. During the development process, consider some of the key success factors of effective reward and recognition programs, including involvement, responsibility, flexibility, closure, and measurability. It is strongly recommended that you include the *involvement* of some employees in the development of the program to increase the likelihood that the program will be well received. This involvement can take the form of just asking employees what they think or enlisting a more formal team or committee. Also, make sure that someone is assigned the *responsibility* for administering the program. No recognition program runs by itself. Although the sponsor confers legitimacy to a program, someone else needs to be responsible for running the program on a day-to-day basis.

At Tennant, involvement and responsibility were one and the same. As already mentioned, a volunteer committee of employees at all levels across the company was assigned responsibility for developing and administering the program. This responsibility was considered to be a part of their job, and they were given sufficient "comp time" to perform their program-related duties. Rarely do we get things perfect the first time. In the real world, most improvements are fine-tuned continuously until we get them right. Therefore, develop the program with sufficient *flexibility*, so that, in the likely event that it might have to be modified, the program can be changed quickly and relatively painlessly.

It is also advisable to "time-bound" the program to provide *closure* for the program when it has served its purpose. Reward and recognition programs rarely are meant to last forever. Unfortunately, too many recognition programs are left to fizzle out, which is not very motivating. The best recognition programs are instituted to get attention and change behavior, not necessarily as a permanent fixture. By time-bounding the program, you can keep excitement high, rather than leaving the program to die. Of course, if you want to extend the program, you can always do so. It is much better to extend it by declaring victory than end it prematurely and having to declare defeat! Surprisingly, Tennant's Koala T. Bear program has had unusual longevity; it has lasted over 20 years and is still going strong! However, this is more the exception than the rule.

8. *Plan the project:* Whatever you do when developing a reward and recognition program, be careful not to shortchange planning. A recognition program can be a complex endeavor (although it might sometimes appear deceptively simple), and it must be managed like one. Remember the Five Ps: *Proactive planning prevents poor performance.* Do you have a project plan that can instill confidence that it can be successfully implemented from beginning to end? Make sure the plan includes a schedule, a budget, and a contingency plan. At Tennant, the Koala T. Bear program was planned meticulously before it was implemented. Of course, such good planning does not guarantee that the program will be glitch-free. That is why the next step is also important.

9. *Implement a pilot:* Too often reward and recognition programs are implemented organizationwide from the start. Then, when something goes awry—and it inevitably will—the organization regrets it. Although optional, a pilot, with a subset of the total population (such as a department, location, or store), allows you to try out the program on a small scale with minimal risk. It also encourages experimentation, creativity, and something that might be out of the ordinary. Then, based on the pilot, the program can be fully implemented with even more confidence and support. At Tennant, the Koala T. Bear program was piloted before it was implemented organizationwide. This allowed the coordinating team to work out the wrinkles before the full-scale launch to the entire organization.

10. *Measure it:* Unfortunately, measurement is rarely done for improvement efforts, except as an afterthought. Even when people have the best intentions about measurement, they rarely follow through on those intentions. Sometimes there is a business case to gain funding, but the loop is rarely closed. Measurement should be built into your program for several reasons. Measurement makes things happen; it can actually drive success. What you measure is what you tend to get! In addition, without measurement, it is impossible to know if the recognition is working. By collecting data on how well the program is working in driving toward the goal, you can manage it to success, rather than just wishing and hoping. It also can reinforce management commitment. This is what happened at Tennant. The pilot of the Koala T. Bear program was measured, which showed how successful it was. It also revealed some minor glitches that were easy to fix.

11. *Modify it:* Based on the feedback from measuring the pilot, the program can usually be easily modified. This typically involves fine tuning, or occasionally a major program redesign. At Tennant, the quality culture had embraced Deming's plan-do-check-act improvement cycle, and realized that any major change requires an iterative effort. Fortunately, there were only a few minor modifications to make in the program before it would be "ready for prime time." But, if the changes had not been made, the impact of the program might have been far less positive than it was.

12. *Launch it:* Now, with the program tested and enhanced, you can launch the program to the organization as a whole with confidence. At Tennant, the Koala T. Bear program was now ready for organizationwide implementation.

13. *Terminate or reenergize it:* When the time comes to reassess the program, you can terminate it if it has achieved its purpose or reenergize it if it looks like its lifetime should be extended. As explained above, although the program was not intended to last forever, the Koala T. Bear program has become one of the most enduring and important programs the Tennant Company has ever had.

14. *Learn from it:* No matter what happens, make sure you learn from the program. Have a formal debriefing with the sponsor, with the advisory team (if applicable), with participants, with managers, and with any others who can provide a useful perspective. This learning might be the most valuable outcome of the program. There have been enormous learning and growth at Tennant as a result of the Koala T. Bear quality program, and that learning has been used to further enhance the program and provide best practices for the design of other recognition efforts and other company programs. In fact, Roger Hale and a colleague, Rita Maehling, learned so much from their lessons-learned sessions that they published a book on the subject!

15. *Do it even better next time:* The purpose of an iterative process, such as the one described in this guide, is to keep doing things better. As Bob Nelson and I advocate in *The 1001 Rewards & Recognition Fieldbook* (2003), it is important that our recognition *not* become routine or rote. The challenge is to keep doing it better each time. We advocate *recognition breakthroughs*, through which we can contribute to energizing our organizations to higher levels of performance and motivation. As we say in the book, "A [recognition] breakthrough need not involve a long drawn-out process. A breakthrough improvement decision can result from the realization that 'I am not satisfied with giving the same old recognition ... I want to go to the next level, and an *aha* about what to do next'" (Nelson & Spitzer, 2003, p. 690). These kinds of *ahas* are likely to come from using the approach described in this chapter.

You will find that using this process (in part or in full) enables you to design more successful reward and recognition programs. In addition, most of the steps can be used to design *any* successful organizational improvement program. It worked for the Tennant Company and with many clients of mine, and it will work for your organization as well.

Use the following Reward and Recognition Program Roadmap (Figure 1) for Success to guide the design and implementation of your organization's next recognition program.

Figure 1: Reward and Recognition Program Roadmap for Success

Program Need
Program Goal and Business Alignment
Program Sponsor
Program Vision
Organizational Readiness
Program Design
Who? What? When? Where? How?
Program Development
Involvement: Responsibility: Flexibility: Closure: Measurability: Other:
Project Plan
Schedule: Budget: Contingency Plan:
Pilot
Measurement

Modifications
Launch
Terminate or Reenergize
Lessons Learned
Do It Better

REFERENCES

Hale, R., and Maehling, R. *Recognition Redefined: Building Self-Esteem at Work.* Minneapolis, MN: Tennant Company, 1992.

LeBoeuf, M. *GMP: The Greatest Management Principle in the World.* New York: Berkley Books, 1985.

Nelson, B., and Spitzer, D. *The 1001 Rewards & Recognition Fieldbook.* New York: Workman, 2003.

HOW TO BUILD A TEAM FOR SUCCESS

Catherine Mercer Bing

Catherine Mercer Bing *has served Lockheed, NY Times Company, and Chase Manhattan Bank in the HR/OD function and has external experience as an HR/OD consultant. She has coauthored **"Beyond Translation: Globalization of Training"** (Training and Development, 2000), **"Helping Global Teams Compete"** (Training and Development, 2001), and **"Communications Technologies for Virtual Teams"** (OD Practitioner, Vol. 34, No. 2, Spring 2002). Her conference presentation topics include repositioning global team development from operational tactics to corporate strategy, what makes it global and why does that matter? As former vice president of new business development and now president of ITAP, she focuses on the challenges facing global, virtual, and multicultural teams. Her other specialties include cross-cultural training, global competency development, and offshoring/outsourcing.*

Contact Information:
ITAP International
The Atrium at Newtown
4 Terry Drive, Suite 5
Newtown, PA 18940
215.860.5640
cass@itapintl.com
www.itapintl.com

Clients often call HR professionals and ask for team-building training when there is something "wrong" in the team (or with the team leader). They might express their desired outcomes as:

- *Better relationships among team members.*
- *Improved communications to avoid confusion and rework.*
- *Higher performance and quicker outcomes.*
- *Stronger commitment to the work of the team.*

Conducting team-building training often focuses on:

- *Building relationships between team members and getting to know each other better using outdoor games or problem-solving simulations.*

- *Defining which stage the team has achieved (forming, norming, storming, or performing) to show them that their difficulties are "normal."*

- *Identifying the personality style of the team members and using that to "define" the "culture of the team" or to improve understanding and explain behaviors between team members.*

Too many teams struggle and need outside support such as team-building interventions. Although these approaches can make a significant difference to teams in trouble, sometimes team leaders or members view such approaches as a waste of time—as just "having a little fun" together. The more task-focused the team leader is, the more likely members are to ask, what does team-building fun have to do with the work of the team?

Building teams becomes more complex with multicultural teams and even more so with virtual teams. How one builds relationships and trust differs across cultures. Saehi Han, president of ITAP Asia-Pacific, points out, "The phrase 'team building' sounds like the participants do not know how to work as a team; Asians have a difficult time understanding why 'team building' is necessary." Note: Most Asian cultures are group-oriented.

It is very difficult to build relationships virtually. So to build really successful team foundations, start getting to know each other better (personally and professionally) at the outset—before there are problems, issues, or challenges. Even have a little fun before the work of the team actually begins, but be careful when working across cultures.

This guide describes how to build any team for success from the beginning.

STEPS TO TEAM SUCCESS

To build a team for success, work with it over time with a focus that starts and stays focused on the work of the team. To build a strong foundation for the team:

- Make sure the team's work can be accomplished (i.e., the right people are on the team and the right people are supporting and championing the work of the team).

- Understand and strategize how to handle the struggle of team members to balance team and functional work.

- Define protocols to help team members work together (across functions or cultures).

- Establish appropriate ways for team members to communicate (who needs to know what?).

1. Setting the Stage for Team Success

Someone always is charged with putting the team together. Often human resource professionals are called in to help decide who can be "given" the assignment: Who needs the development opportunity? Who can afford to spend the time on this?

A. Before choosing team members, start with the stakeholders. Someone almost always stands to benefit from the work of the team (often more than one person). Ask:

- Who (which departments or people) will benefit from the team's work? Who are all the stakeholders in the process/project?
  - ❑ What departments are directly and indirectly affected by the work?
  - ❑ What departments own the process and which are supportive?
  - ❑ Which departments may not be supportive and need encouragement to change their approach?
  - ❑ Which senior managers can intervene with groups that create barriers or are not supportive?
- What are the reasons (the business case) for chartering the team?
- What are the expected/desired outcomes?
- What is the time frame for completion of the team's work?
- Which departments need representation on the team to achieve the outcomes?
- Who in the departments needs such a development opportunity? Is this the best resource, given the timing for this project? If not, who is a better resource?

B. Create your short list of team members and define your communication plan. Ask:

- Who needs to define the team (member and leader) selection process?
- Who needs to approve those selected?
- How should the selection for this team be handled? By invitation (you have been selected ...)? By functional manager assignment? Other?
- How should the invitation or information be disseminated and from whom should it originate? (Please do not say, "You have some free time. Would you ... ?")

C. Look at each stakeholder group. Ask:

- Does this stakeholder group need representation at all stages of the team's work?
- If so, who should represent the stakeholder on the team, and in what capacity are they serving (support, decision making, review of decisions made, reporting to the real stakeholder, etc.)?

- If not, when do they need representation in the team? How much communication should they receive about the team's work prior to the stage at which their representative joins the team? When they do need representation on the team, who should represent the stakeholder on the team, and in what capacity are they serving (support, decision making, review of decisions made, reporting to the real stakeholder, etc.)?

- Do those chosen to participate in the team's activities have the full support of their functional head to do the team's work?

D. Choose the team members and invite them to a kickoff meeting for the purpose of chartering the team. (See the preceding questions that also relate to communications to team members.)

- If the team members cannot meet in person (as in the case of a global or virtual team), what would be helpful for them to know about each other prior to the first meeting? (Collect and share information that is both personal and work-related—relationship-based and task-focused. Add pictures if they cannot meet in person. Face-books with pictures and personal information, plus some professional background, work very well.)

- Arrange for the stakeholder to attend and present the overview and purpose (business case) for the team's work to the team.

- Have the team leader run the meeting. (Do the background work to support the team leader, such as outlining the meeting content.)

2. Build the Team Foundation

Chartering the team well means making sure that team members and leaders have an opportunity to establish communication protocols, discuss how success is going to be measured, create timelines, think through project plans, and start to know each other's cultural preferences and work styles.

The following list can help the team leader frame what he or she needs to accomplish during the chartering meeting. HR professionals can create the interactions (exercises/discussions, etc.) to support the team leader.

- Do the team members know each other and have an opportunity to get to know every members' background, experience, strength, and responsibilities toward the team's work?

- Is the team's success clearly defined? For example, in drug development, killing a compound early should be seen as a success.

- Are the milestones clear, and is some formal transition activity planned to move the team through the new phases beyond each milestone?

- Have communication protocols been established so that all team members know the following:
  - Who gets which information and who gets copied?
  - How records will be kept and by whom?
  - What responsibility each team member has to keeping and sharing records?
  - What responsibilities each team member has to educate those outside the team of the team's work?
  - How quickly team members agree to respond to requests from other team members?
  - What medium is preferred by each team member (e.g., voicemail, email, etc.)?
  - When does the team leader want to be involved or called upon (e.g., when barriers are identified, when snags occur, when things go faster than planned, etc.)? What else should be included in the role of the team leader?
- Do team members know where they can go for information (e.g., the team leader, an electronic bulletin board, etc.) on meeting schedules, to track progress of the work of other team members, to access past reports, to access work schedules, and so on?
- Has the team leader described his or her style of leadership and given examples?
- Have team members been given the opportunity to ask the leader questions about the leadership style, background, and personal life?
- Do the team members have the opportunity to discuss with the team leader what he or she expects of the team members?
- Has there been a technology audit to find out what kinds of technology challenges face each team member
- Do the team members know the preferred communication style for reaching the team leader and other team members (voicemail, email, etc.)?

3. Track Team Success

After the kickoff to charter the team, measure human process interactions over time. Usually, measurements should take place at least quarterly, although the short life of some teams means measurement needs to happen more often.

- Do those chosen to participate in the team's activities understand the nature and breadth of the team's work?
- Do the team members understand the team's charter (objectives) and know the team's champion?

- Is the team clear about its objectives—the expected outcomes and time tables for completion?

- Does the team understand how the team's work aligns with the company's strategic direction?

- Do those chosen to participate in the team's activities communicate about the work of the team to others (outside the team)?

- How well do team members communicate about the work of the team to others on the team?

- How evenly or fairly is the work distributed across the team?

- How is the leader perceived?

- How are issues resolved and are they resolved to everyone's satisfaction?

- What are the barriers to team success internal to the team?

- What are the barriers to team success external to the team?

- Are new members appropriately introduced to the team?

- Are successes celebrated at milestones?

- Are all team members given credit for the work of the team?

Provide the team members with the results of the assessment, and compare their progress since previous assessments.

- Use feedback sessions to identify what team members agree is going well.

- Focus on areas where they agree things are not going well.

- Use areas where the team members disagree (some think things are going well and others do not) as the intervention to get them to talk to each other about their perceptions and the impact of the situation.

- Use their discussion as a springboard for action planning on how to work better together.

If analysis of the results indicates a need for team interventions, ask:

- What does the data tell me about what is going well with the team and what needs improvement?

- What does the data tell me about the level of agreement or disagreement on the team on what causes the team's problems?

- Am I providing exactly what this team needs, or something too generic?

- On which areas will this team get the maximum benefit from my intervention?

A team's needs vary from simple clarifications to major overhauls. Data can provide you and the team leader with the information to focus interventions to root out the problems.

What if your problem is the team leader? Measurement can identify this as well. Savvy HR professionals can use the data collected, present the data to the leader, and define areas for support and improvement/ development for the team leader. Working behind the scenes to coach and develop the leadership capabilities can go a long way to improving team interactions.

Often team leaders make the best deliverers of the good news/bad news (results of the assessment) because the delivery by the team leader helps members realize that the leader knows what is going on, cares about what is and is not working, and expects to work with the team to resolve team issues.

HOW TO SUCCEED IN THE COACHING PROCESS

Steve Albrecht

Steve Albrecht, DBA, *is a trainer and consultant in San Diego, California. He specializes in high-risk human resource training topics and corrective coaching. His 14 books include **Ticking Bombs**, which was one of the first business books published on workplace violence, and **Tough Training Topics: A Presenter's Survival Guide** (Pfeiffer, 2006).*

Contact Information:
9528 Miramar Road #270
San Diego, CA 92126
619.445.4735
drsteve@drstevealbrecht.com

Change, in most areas of our lives, is driven by events. We change our eating, smoking, or exercise habits only after a significant health scare. We put an alarm system in our homes or cars only after a burglary or a break-in. We became focused on air travel safety and passenger/luggage screening only after the tragic events of 9-11. Products get recalled after an injury or death; grates or safety railings go up after someone has fallen; and organizations make changes through training, new policies, or updated procedures only after a problem erupts, including the threat of litigation, bad publicity, or a class action settlement.

And so it goes with the coaching process. Internal, external, or organizational development coaches can get called to help when someone has sexually harassed a co-worker or subordinate, victimized others with yet another angry outburst, harmed a vendor or client relationship yet again, or somehow violated the boundaries or policies of the organization for the umpteenth time. The work in these events could be called "career rescue," because the organization has had it with the employee in question, and he or she is close to termination.

Yet senior management (often driven by complaints or suggestions from the HR office) holds out hope that, if the coach can succeed in changing the employee's behavior, the relationship, the position, and the quality of the employee's work product or performance might be salvaged.

In such circumstances, the irony is that the quality of the employees' work is often good. They are often excellent salespeople, programmers, engineers, and so forth. but are plagued with either a terrible personality, a complete lack of social intelligence, or both.

This guide looks at:

- *The common dimensions for a coaching intervention.*
- *Coaching styles and a four-square model that can help assess an employee's potential contribution.*
- *Coaching suggestions for the four different coaching candidates.*

DIMENSIONS OF A COACHING INTERVENTION

Here are four common dimensions for a coaching intervention:

1. *Category 1—Strategic* (typically for senior executives): The focus is on the long-term direction of their business, department, or career goals.

2. *Category 2—Developmental* (for managers and supervisors): The focus is on problem solving, managing their "What Bugs Me" list, employee supervision issues, team or individual conflicts, delegation, time management, stress management, and career enhancement.

3. *Category 3—Corrective, aka Career Rescue* (for managers, supervisors, and employees who "don't get it"): The focus is on helping them understand the negative impact of certain behaviors on their jobs and on others, then getting them to comply, change, or stop the behaviors. Issues include anger management, sexual harassment, micromanaging, or aggression.

4. *Category 4—Special-Purpose* (for high-risk HR cases involving on- or off-the-job threats by or to employees or the organization): Coaching interventions are almost always *driven by events*, such as:

   - A sharp downturn in the business success of the department or the organization.
   - The failing "mental health" of the executive level or departmental management teams.
   - Topped-out career advancement problems with certain apathetic employees.
   - Departmental conflicts between work groups and related team performance problems.
   - Employee behavioral issues related to their compliance problems (sexual harassment, anger management, off-the-job concerns spilling over to work, suspicion of drugs and alcohol use).
   - Angry or threatening employees.

It helps to look at the four coaching styles as part of a bell curve. The Strategic and Special interventions are on either end (since they are rarer, statistically and operationally). The other two (Developmental and Corrective) are in the middle.

Because the majority of coaching time tends to be spent with people needing these midrange services, the four-square model shown in Figure 1 uses archetypal labels to describe four possible coaching candidates. To better understand it, you generalize it a bit and describe certain coaches in terms of their stereotypical behavior. (This is not a subtle approach; after reviewing these four types, you might instantly recognize colleagues or subordinates from your own organizational history.)

The modalities described in the four-square model are:

1. *The Smart Slacker:* This employee has been around a long time, has "retired on duty," and no longer wants to break a sweat. He or she knows *how* to do the work but does not really *want* to. These employees can *appear* to work hard when the boss is around. They have lots of knowledge (and could make a real and valuable contribution because of their history with the company, their collected and stored knowledge, their "institutional memories," and all their training and experience).

   Upside: They could be helped by coaching if we can just find the "on" button.

   Downside: The "on" button is often hidden by lots of protective layers or emotional baggage. These employees are at the top step and often overpaid (two new employees could be paid to do the work of this one). Generally, they cannot be promoted, do not want to move or change jobs, and feel they cannot be fired as long as they just show up every day. Their potential contribution to the success of the department or firm is high; their actual or real contribution is low.

2. *The Problem Child:* There are two types: acute problems (a good worker suddenly develops serious off-the-job problems) or chronic problems (a problem child since day one). Acute cases should be offered support, access to counseling, and an individual development and/or performance improvement plan. Chronic cases should be given progressive discipline, last warnings, and then termination. Their potential and actual contributions are usually quite low.

3. *The Plow Horse:* This is a good worker who does the job but without much imagination.

   Upside: These folks are reliable; they get to work at 8 a.m. and leave at 5 p.m.

   Downside: They do not cause problems, but they have a marked tendency to sit on the plow whenever they hit a rock, waiting for a supervisor to tell them how to solve the problem. They lack either the ability or the desire to use option thinking or creative problem solving. They get working at standard evaluations and are largely happy doing what they were hired to do. Maybe they are fearful of the stress and responsibility of advancement, so they do not look for career help. They are often happy at their level and do not want too much on their plates. Their actual contribution is high, but their potential contribution is unknown or untapped by supervisors who will not or do not want to take the time to delve into the range of their possibilities.

4. *The Rising Star:*

   Upside: They are easy to delegate to, usually love more responsibility, and work hard without being asked or reminded. They go the extra mile to get and earn above-standard evaluations.

   Downside: They can be perceived as teacher's pets by the other employees, they may treat others badly when the boss is not around, and they can act imperially and self-satisfied if not monitored. It is possible and likely that supervisors can burn these people out with too much work, too much autonomy, and not enough reward. Good coaches get these people onto a career path that plays to their strengths and improves their weaknesses.

The chart in Figure 1 can help you assess an employee's potential contribution to the team, department, or organization, and compare it to his or her actual contribution. The goal of coaching is to see where an employee might appear on this chart. The function of coaching is to move the candidate to the top right position, as rapidly, as effectively, and as economically as possible.

Figure 1: Developmental or Corrective Coaching Candidates: The Big Four

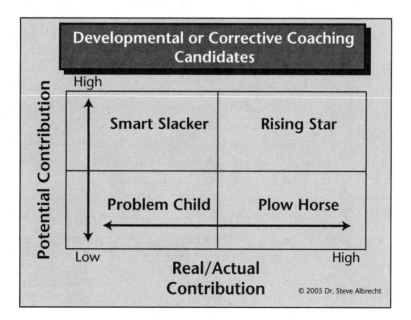

The following points can help accelerate your process with each of the Big Four:

- Do not wait until the performance review process to request performance or behavioral changes.
- Hold personal accountability meetings with all employees on a regular basis, not just during performance reviews.
- Script your main points and refer to your notes during the meeting. These discussions can be stressful; prepare yourself with notes and talking points in advance.

Smart Slackers

Confront their behavior, attitude, or performance. Remind them of their "legacy employee" status. Ask for their help in creating solutions you both can live with.

Write a *performance improvement plan*.

Problem Children

Use the progressive discipline process. Ask them to make a stay or go choice, as in, "You seem unhappy here and I'm not happy with your performance. Is this a job you really want?"

Write a progressive *discipline* or *termination plan*.

Plow Horses

Encourage them to use option thinking to problem solve. Reward their progress in this area, no matter how small it seems at first. They will grow with more praise for their efforts in thinking outside the box.

Write a *skill improvement* plan to help the Plow Horse with option-thinking and problem-solving skills. Include required performance goals, giving more immediate feedback to the supervisor, and boundary setting for the employee.

Rising Stars

Give them challenges but watch for job burnout. Create a career path that offers them opportunities for advancement.

Write a *career path plan*. Include the training course needed, the new skills you may need to teach, and the timeline for the employee's promotability in your organization.

It bears repeating:

- The *goal* of coaching is to determine an employee's potential contribution to the organization.
- The *function* of coaching is to get that employee working at that level rapidly, effectively, and economically.

HOW TO UNDERSTAND AND BENEFIT FROM PLANNING FOR THE FUTURE

Brian Pomeroy

Brian Pomeroy *is a senior solutions consultant with the Information Services Department at The Children's Hospital of Philadelphia. Since 1995 Brian has been involved with Web and technology development, as well as adult education. A member of the American Society for Training & Development (ASTD), the American Medical Informatics Association (AMIA), the World Future Society, and the IEEE Computer Society, Brian writes and speaks frequently on futures and technology-related topics. He is a Certified Internet Webmaster and the author of* **BeginnerNet: A Beginner's Guide to the Internet and the World Wide Web** *(Slack, 1997). Brian is also a frequent contributor to the* **Sourcebooks**.

Contact Information:
The Children's Hospital of Philadelphia
34th Street and Civic Center Boulevard
Philadelphia, PA 19104
267.426.0826
pomeroy@email.chop.edu or
info@futurewire.net
www.chop.edu/
www.futurewire.net

The better equipped an organization is to face change, the sooner it can "get ahead of the curve" and respond to events when they transpire. If the change is good, organizations can prepare themselves to benefit and profit from it. If the change is bad, they can make adjustments to minimize threats. Fortunately, organizations can use a number of techniques to envision the future, how it fosters innovation, how it will affect the world around them, and how to best respond. This guide explains strategies for thinking about change and the future, tools for data gathering, and ways to determine how changes will affect your organization.

How does your organization plan to meet the future? It does plan to meet the future, right?

Sure, you have long-range plans and strategies. But are you really thinking about the trends that will affect your business one, five, or 10 years from now? If so, are you ready to meet them?

We cannot stop the future. We cannot know for sure what it will bring either, because so many conflicting factors influence it. Yet future events will have an enormous impact on your customers, your employees, and your competitors. Even trends and changes that do not appear relevant to your organization can affect it, presenting you with unexpected challenges.

One thing we can do, though, is envision one or more possible futures so that we might have starting points for our strategic planning. This guide gives you an introduction to thinking about emerging trends, technologies, and events, and how your organization can prepare for and even benefit from them by developing or adopting innovative products, services, and processes that address the changes.

WHY FUTURE INNOVATIONS MATTER TO *YOUR* ORGANIZATION

When people think about the future, they tend to think about science or technology. It is easy, therefore, for a business not engaged in those fields not to worry about how the world around them could change drastically. Or they assume that their industry is "stable" and that introducing change into it would simply cause problems.

This is wrongheaded thinking on many levels. For one, just think of the changes that have occurred in the world over the past 10 years. Spend a few minutes (you might need more than a few) and write down all the things existing now that didn't exist then ... or existing then that are no longer around. Technological changes are the first to come to mind. Fashion styles, new construction, and new businesses are also obvious. But think of the subtle things that maybe you have not noticed appearing or disappearing. These changes, while minute, have almost certainly affected you or your organization on some level.

For instance, did you ever notice how few knobs are on public washroom sinks anymore? These days, you just put your hand under a sensor in the sink without touching anything, and water comes out. What does that mean to manufacturers of plumbing products and sensors? Is that changing people's behavior? If so, how?

Cell phones have changed a lot over the past 10 years. Technological aspects aside, what have they done to how we interact with one another? How have they changed the public space? When you hear someone talking and no one's around, do you think that person has lost his or her mind? Or do you just assume the person is being rude by talking on a cell phone loudly? And if you are a cell phone user, when was the last time you used a pay phone or a calling card? When was the last time you saw a pay phone or a calling card?

When was the last time you saw a cigarette machine? A paper-based card catalog at a library? Carbon paper? When was the last time smoking was allowed in your workplace? What do you suppose the past few years have done to businesses whose revenues depended on cigarette machine servicing or carbon paper sales?

When was the first time you saw a PDA or sent an email? Can you remember a time when "yahoo" and "google" were just funny words, not the names of multimillion-dollar businesses—or, in the case of "Google," a verb?

Has a big box discount retail store moved into your neighborhood? If so, what was the impact on traffic in the area? How did it affect other businesses? Who benefited, and who got hurt?

Whatever you consider in this exercise, you realize the effects that these changes have had on you and others. Businesses and careers have been created or destroyed by these changes. Perhaps yours is one of them.

Activity:
Write down 10 new things that have appeared over the past decade, along with 10 things that are not around anymore or have become very rare. These can be technologies, trends, fashions, laws, products, or behaviors. Next, discuss the factors that prompted these things to either appear or disappear.

SYSTEMS THINKING ... OR WHY EVERYTHING RELATES TO EVERYTHING ELSE

Changes do not just emerge by themselves. And when they do appear, they affect the environment around them, causing unintended effects—both good and bad.

Think of changes as rocks thrown into a pond: the bigger the rock, the bigger the splash and the more powerful the ripples. Yet forces created that rock and left it by the pond so that it could be thrown. Another way of looking at causes and consequences is the so-called Butterfly Effect, stated by Edward Lorenz in 1972: "Does the flap of a butterfly's wings in Brazil set off a tornado in Texas?"

The mass-produced automobile is a classic example of an innovative change that has had causes and consequences far beyond its anticipated scope. The assembly line technology pioneered by Henry Ford, combined with lower costs, abundant and inexpensive fuel, the need and desire to traverse long distances, and government support of road construction all combined to create the market for personal automobiles in the early 20th century. Trucks in particular led to a huge increase in productivity, allowing goods to be shipped more quickly and efficiently than ever before. Cars and trucks had a fringe (and largely forgotten) benefit of reducing the number of animals in cities; up to that time, manure and carcasses had been a major source of disease in crowded urban areas. The personal freedom provided by owning one's own car also has a profound psychological impact on individuals, providing many with the means to physically leave their immediate families and communities for the first time. In the early days, it seemed that the only people who wouldn't benefit from the automobile were the proverbial buggy whip manufacturers.

The construction of the interstate highway system that began after World War II drove up the demand for cars and trucks even further. With their ever increasing ability to compress distance, cars led to the advent of suburban communities and shopping malls outside city centers. The mass exodus from the cities to the suburbs, however, created a whole new set of problems. Inner cities, newly depopulated and bypassed by interstate highways, fell into decline. Meanwhile, smog from car emissions became a problem. Tetraethyl lead, a common gasoline additive until the 1980s, posed serious health hazards. And when the energy crisis of the early 1970s struck, we in America suddenly realized how dependent our economy had become on gasoline—much of which came from unreliable foreign sources. Our need to protect this source led directly to the 1991 Gulf War, which in turn had implications in the attacks of September 11, 2001, the War on Terror, and our current involvement in the Middle East.

Understanding the development and impact of an innovation in this way is called *systems thinking*. This helps us understand how an event came to be and visualize how it could evolve and impact other situations.

A key principle of systems thinking is that of *convergence*, which occurs when two discrete situations combine to form something new. One example is the convergence of computer technology and radiology to create CAT scans and magnetic resonance imaging (MRI) technology. Another, somewhat more obscure, example came with the arrival of air travel and air conditioning. The two technologies made possible resort communities on formerly uninviting tracts of desert (Las Vegas) and swampland (Orlando, Florida).

Systems thinking teaches us that all types of emerging trends and technologies can have an impact on our lives and organizations—even if the connections do not seem obvious at first. The trick is to determine which ones will have the greatest impact. If the impact is positive, the organization needs to understand how to leverage it to its advantage. If the impact is negative, the organization must avoid it, or at least be able to minimize the damage.

Activity:
1. Select an innovation. What factors led to its development? What consequences has it had on business or society (good, bad, or neutral)? What consequences could it have for your organization?
2. Select two separate innovations. Could they somehow be combined? If so, what might be the possible result?

SIGNALS OF CHANGE

Using systems thinking principles, the type of information you most want to scan and search for initially involves *signals of change*. This involves changes on a variety of levels; some are very broad and general, and others directly affect your organization. Signals of change encompass business, the environment, world events, society, politics, the economy, and science.

The broadest of all signals of change involve *gaia events*, long-term trends that have global implications. The aging of populations in the developed world is an example of a gaia event that will affect nearly all facets of society. Another gaia event is the theory of "peak oil," which states that the world's demand for petroleum will soon outstrip its supply.

The trick is to identify gaia events as early as possible, then link them to specific innovations, as well as to strategies your organization can take to either leverage or protect itself.

Activity:
1. What are some of the important gaia trends going on in the world?
2. How can these changes impact your organization?
3. What specific innovations are on the horizon as a result of these gaia trends?

ORDERS OF CONSEQUENCE

Once you have identified some signals of change, the next step is to try to anticipate the way they might play out. This provides us with a way to anticipate the greater impact of an event and to explore the benefits and drawbacks that it will have on a variety of situations.

Orders of consequence are simply cascading events that might occur as a result of an event. The first-order consequence is the event itself, followed by direct results of that event (second-order consequences), and so on. Orders of consequence can go on indefinitely and branch off from one another.

For instance, consider the impact that a new "big box" discount retail store might have on a vicinity: Granted, this is a highly simplistic scenario that does not take into account a lot of variables or conditions particular to a community. But it illustrates how orders of consequence can be used to think about future impacts of current events.

Consequence	Event
First-order	New retail store brings greater quantity and variety of consumer goods, as well as lower prices, to the community.
Second-order	More people shop at the store, causing traffic congestion in the vicinity.
Third-order	Traffic officials must find a way to reengineer the local roads.
Fourth-order	To pay for new roads, local taxes rise.
Fifth-order	Higher taxes cause many residents to move from the area.
Sixth-order	Property values fall.

> **Activity:**
> Choose a topic and see how many orders of consequence you can derive from it. How many can you think of? Did you discover multiple consequences that you hadn't thought of before?

SCENARIO PLANNING

Another tool used in developing future visions is building scenarios, or narratives that describe a future state. These scenarios might be constructed to answer a question, such as, what will the _____ industry look like in 10 years? You might develop multiple scenarios, some of which might be contradictory. A group of scenarios might include some that are either optimistic or pessimistic, envisioning industry growth or contraction, embracing new technologies or no technology at all.

The complex disciplines used by professional scenario planners are outside the scope of this paper. However, you can take steps toward building scenarios simply by brainstorming and discussing ideas with thought leaders within your organization. An excellent introduction to scenario planning is available on the *Wired* Website (http://www.wired.com/wired/scenarios/build.html) and on the Website of Drs. Linda Groff and Paul Smoker (http://www.csudh.edu/global_options/IntroFS.HTML). Useful books include *The Art of the Long View* by Peter Schwartz (1991) and *Scenario Planning* by Gill Ringland (1998).

SCANNING THE HORIZON

Now that you have some ideas of how to manage information about the future, how can you gather that information? Several strategies are available to help you understand emerging trends and innovations—in many cases, long before news of them shows up on your competitors' radar.

Solid *scanning* practices are fundamental to any emergence initiative. *Scanning*, for our purposes, is simply the practice of constantly monitoring news and information sources for the latest trends and technologies. Over time, you will likely assemble a collection of print and Internet resources that you will review regularly, making scanning second nature.

Scanning is a regular task, as opposed to *searching*, which is the act of looking for specific information. On the Internet, a comprehensive search engine such as Google (www.google.com) is one of the easiest ways to perform accurate searches by keyword. Professional researchers leverage research firms such as Gartner (www.gartner.com), Forrester (www.forrester.com), and Yankee Group (www.yankeegroup.com).

So where does all this great information come from? Indeed, it is more accessible than most people realize. Even better, it is mostly available either for free or at a very low cost.

Recently, *Weblogs*, or *blogs*, have appeared as a rich information resource. Most blogs allow the readers to subscribe through rich site summary or real simple syndication (RSS). The content is in the form of *feeds*, which are files encoded in extensible markup language (XML). Numerous applications are available to help users collect and manage blog feeds.

Although most blogs are available via the Web, RSS is a convenient way to aggregate a collection of resources in one handy place. Many users find feed readers to be faster and easier to use than Web browsers—a particular advantage when scanning resources.

Figure 1 shows a screen capture of a free RSS feed reader, called SharpReader (www.sharpreader.com), for Windows-based PCs. The left-hand frame shows a list of subscribed blog feeds, which can be organized in folders. The right top frame shows a list of feeds from a selected feed; the right bottom shows text and images from a single post.

Beyond the technical advantages of RSS feeds, blogs are often on the cutting edge of new ideas. Technologies and concepts are discussed on blogs sometimes weeks, even months before they appear in the mainstream media. Reading blogs regularly, therefore, can give you an edge when scanning and searching for the very latest information.

A comprehensive list of RSS feed readers, including readers for Macintosh and Linux computers, is available on the Hebig.org blog (http://www.hebig.org/blogs/archives/main/000877.php). Many readers are also completely Web-based, allowing you to create an account and access it from any Web-enabled computer. One of the most popular of these is Bloglines (www.bloglines.com).

Figure 1: Screen Capture of the SharpReader RSS Feed Reader

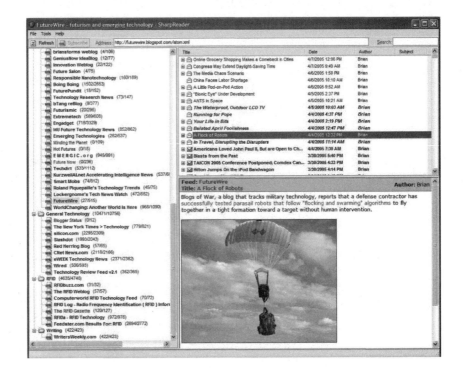

Another useful tool is participation in *futurist organizations*, most notably the World Future Society (www.wfs.org). Subscription to their monthly magazine, *The Futurist*, is by itself worth the price of membership. On a more local level, you might find informal innovation- and future-minded groups by using Meetup (www.meetup.com), LinkedIn (www.linkedin.com), or other *social networking Websites*. These tend to be small, and they usually meet at local restaurants and other public venues.

Finally, simply keeping up with *world, national, and even local news* gives you an cdgc in spotting signals of change. A solid understanding of news events provides context for seeing how discrete stories fit into larger, long-term trends.

A list of useful Websites, books, blogs, and other materials that cover emerging innovations is available at FutureWire (http://www.futurewire.net/resources.htm).

THE IMPACT OF CHANGE

Now that you have identified and analyzed some future trends, how might they affect your organization? How might you leverage them and even benefit from them?

One useful and easy way to evaluate innovative changes is to follow the Four Laws of Media, developed by the legendary media theorist Marshall McLuhan. For every innovation you are considering, ask yourself the following questions:

1. What will the innovation enhance?

2. What will the innovation make obsolete?

3. What unintended problems will the innovation cause? (This phenomenon is known as *reversing*; McLuhan also called it *over-extending* a technology. Plotting out orders of consequence will help you here.)

4. Will the innovation bring back any capabilities or conditions that were previously lost? (This phenomenon is known as *retrieval*.)

Asking and answering these questions gives you at least a general idea of the impact an innovation can have on your organization.

Another, more detailed method of thinking about changes is to divide them into sustaining and disruptive innovations. These terms, coined by Clayton Christensen (1997) in his landmark book *The Innovator's Dilemma*, describe how innovations develop and the impact they have on the marketplace.

- A *sustaining innovation* builds on trends and technologies that are already in place, offering incremental improvements and refinements. It offers the customer distinct benefits without changing the underlying approach to the way he or she works. A software upgrade is an example of a sustaining innovation.

- A *disruptive innovation*, however, represents a radical break with established trends and technologies. Often, it is so revolutionary that it takes years for people to understand how to use and benefit from it. Depending on one's perspective, a disruptive innovation can be either highly advantageous or extremely dangerous.

Christensen lists three main criteria for an innovation to be disruptive:

1. It must possess a unique functionality and meet a heretofore unmet customer need.
2. It must offer a level of performance that is at least comparable to existing products or services.
3. It must lower costs for customers in some way.

Christensen cites the telephone as a classic disruptive innovation. Nothing like it had ever been created before. When Alexander Graham Bell attempted to sell it to the major telecommunications firm of the time, telegraph giant Western Union, he was turned down flat. "What use could this company make of an electrical toy?" This was what Western Union president William Orton is supposed to have said of Bell's invention.

The electrical toy, however, met a unique customer need that Western Union did not foresee. Unlike the telegraph, which required skilled operators who could send and receive messages only at central stations, the telephone allowed individuals to contact each other directly and immediately. Aside from providing unique functionality, it also lowered costs and provided new opportunities for businesses.

The impact of the telephone was rapid and profound. Faced with a paradigm shift it could not counter, Western Union lost its ability to compete with Bell's phone company, AT&T, in the telecommunications market. Ironically, AT&T bought Western Union in 1915. Thirty years earlier, it could have been the other way around.

More recently, personal computers disrupted the computing and business worlds by bringing computing power to the individual. The Internet similarly offered an entirely new level of easily accessible information and communications. In both cases, the customer could perform tasks that before were impossible, and perform other tasks in a more cost-effective manner than ever before.

Though sustaining and disruptive innovations are important to organizations, understanding disruptive change is a crucial advantage. These innovations, after all, tend to come out of nowhere and blindside an industry. Adopting, or at least understanding, disruptive innovations early can give an organization a leg up on its competition.

Innovations of any type can produce losers as well as winners. Western Union is a case in point. Similarly, IBM could have become a computer-age dinosaur if it had not seen the potential in microcomputers early on and developed its PC ... with some help from a little-known software development shop called Microsoft.

SHOW THEM THE MONEY

One question you will ultimately be asked about a technology is, what is its potential in the marketplace? Many a brilliant idea has proven to be a business failure because the market for it does not exist, or it is too immature to succeed in the marketplace. This is clearly an important question to ask if your organization plans to turn an innovation into a product or service, but it is also important if the organization plans to make a substantial investment in the innovation.

To answer that question, we once again turn to Clayton Christensen. In another of his books, *Seeing What's Next*, Christensen (2004) identifies three consumer groups who determine an innovation's success in the marketplace:

- *Overshot customers* are wary of expensive technology but open to improved solutions as long as they are proven and reasonably priced.

- *Undershot customers*, for whom current solutions are not working, are open to innovative ideas.

- *Nonconsumers* do not currently have a need and must be sold on an innovation's benefits. Once sold, however, nonconsumers often become the best customers.

For an innovation to be commercially successful, it must appeal to at least one of these groups.

PUTTING IT ALL TOGETHER

Now that you have an awareness of emerging innovations—and maybe even have identified a few that could impact your organization—you need to put it in the context of your business.

What changes can you see in the world that can foster disruptive innovations? If you are a product manufacturer, are there innovations that you can incorporate into your product line? Are there disruptive innovations that threaten your position or that could be a competitive advantage? If yours is a service-related firm, are there opportunities to offer new services? Does your organization have internal processes that could be improved or retooled with innovations that improve customer service and lower costs?

Perhaps the trickiest part of evaluating emerging innovations is attaching a measure of success to their adoption. If an innovation leads to a profitable product or service for your organization, that is a fairly straightforward metric. But what if the benefits are intangible, such as improving employee safety? Linking the innovation to some kind of specific measurement (insurance dollars saved, for instance, or the cost of having an employee out on disability) provides you with an idea of the innovation's benefits, in addition to getting the attention of senior management.

Finally, understanding innovations gives you the ability to spot bad ideas early. You provide your organization an immeasurable service if you can steer it clear of innovations that, despite the hype, do not provide value or work as advertised.

REFERENCES AND RELATED READING

Christensen, C. *The Innovator's Dilemma.* New York: HarperBusiness, 2003.

Christensen, C. *Seeing What's Next.* Boston: HBS Press, 2004.

Cross, M. "The Butterfly Effect." Available at: http://www.cmp.caltech.edu/~mcc/chaos_new/Lorenz.html.

Day, G. S. and Schoemaker, P. J. *Wharton on Managing Emerging Technologies.* New York: Wiley, 2003.

Kappelman, T. "Marshall McLuhan: The Medium Is the Message." Leadership University Probe Ministries. Available at: http://www.leaderu.com/orgs/probe/docs/mcluhan.html.

Ringland, G. *Scenario Planning: Managing for the Future.* Chicester, NY: Wiley, 1998.

Schwartz, P. *The Art of the Long View; Planning for the Future in an Uncertain World.* New York: Currency Doubleday, 1991.

Schwartz, P. *Inevitable Surprises: Thinking Ahead in a Time of Turbulence.* Gotham Books, 2003.

HOW TO DISMANTLE A CULTURE OF KNOWLEDGE HOARDING

Jamie S. Walters

Jamie S. Walters *is the founder of Ivy Sea, Inc., a San Francisco-based conscious-enterprise and organizational-transformation consulting collaborative, and the author of* **Big Vision, Small Business,** *a handbook for visionary enterprise (Berrett-Koehler, 2002). Jamie is also the founder and producer of* **Ivy Sea Online,** *a highly acclaimed Web journal and skill-enhancing library praised by Harvard Business School, CEO Refresher, Edu-Leadership, About.com-Human Resources Guide, Inc.com, and many others. She contributed to the book* **Positively MAD: Making a Difference in Your Organizations, Communities, and the World** *(Berrett-Koehler, 2004). Jamie is also a past contributor to the Sourcebooks.*

Contact Information:
Ivy Sea, Inc.
3701 Sacramento Street, #199
San Francisco, CA 94118
415.778.3910
jwalters@ivysea.com
www.ivysea.com

Despite the many corporate initiatives launched to decrease information overload, increase teamwork, and facilitate knowledge sharing, many organizations still find themselves stymied by cultures in which knowledge hoarding and self-interest behaviors flourish. Although some of the programs designed to help turn out to be more costly than valuable, it is also true that hoarding, failing to share credit, and the lack of skillful communication and true teamwork also have high costs. What is a leader to do? This guide outlines steps that a leader can take to encourage information sharing.

A SNAPSHOT OF THE PROBLEM

Research has shown that poor communication and knowledge hoarding (and information hoarding, which are not necessarily identical concerns) are alive and well in corporate cultures, as well as in health care organizations, law firms, consulting firms, and the like. Not even nonprofits escape the problem, despite missions that some might guess would make them "kinder and gentler." Studies strongly suggest that poor communication and interpersonal or relational issues, such as knowledge hoarding and a failure to share credit, are directly related to staff morale and higher turnover rates.

To compound the issue, employees and managers alike have problems integrating information and knowledge that is shared or that they have access to—a reality that has vexed some knowledge management consultants, because their costly initiatives go the way of reengineering strategies in their failure to produce impressive results that justify the expense.

A key reason for such failures might be the same for both knowledge management and reengineering initiatives: Both are often designed with a reliance on rational, linear, numerical data—and expectations—and yet both have historically failed to take into account the degree of human and psychological influences inherent in organizational culture and its relationships. MBAs and others design programs using spreadsheets, data analysis, and project management software, and then are vexed when people fail to act like widgets or gears. (This is one of the reasons that current MBA programs have come under heavy criticism.) Even the language used by initiative creators is often more appropriate to an industrial engineering plan than one that involves large groups of people.

But people are, well, human beings ... who do not always act rationally or communicate skillfully! Human beings and human systems have much more in common with chaos and complexity theory than with the Newtonian, Darwinian biases of the professionals designing corporate "human capital" initiatives. Perhaps they would do better to understand what makes an environment in which knowledge sharing flourishes naturally, and foster such an environment if the organization's structure and mission would truly allow it, rather than to continue failing at the knowledge engineering programs.

WHY DO PEOPLE HOARD INFORMATION AND KNOWLEDGE?

The issue is both simple and complex. On one hand, it is simple because we know that hoarding information, being stingy with vital knowledge, and communicating and managing unskillfully are costly and not so productive behaviors. We know we are capable of better.

The issue is complex because most traditional work environments are still hierarchical—and might need to be to achieve their missions (the real, bottom-line missions rather than the ones wordsmithed for public relations purposes). In such environments, the traditionally rooted organizational cultures are hypercompetitive; people hoard knowledge because it makes them more valuable and thus more likely to be promoted (or less likely to be sacked). In such organizations, for better or worse, the emphasis on competition, individual achievement and reward, and financial opportunities has well fertilized these patterns of behavior.

Particularly in very large companies, the organizational system required to maintain order among the many parts ends up impeding true collaboration, knowledge sharing, or the chaos required for creativity—not to mention organic, creative exchanges. Smaller groups or organizations might have a greater likelihood of success in each of these areas, because the smaller size requires fewer control structures.

Compounding these traditional cultural issues are ones brought about by economic strains, when repeated rounds of layoffs heighten fears of joblessness and encourage some individuals to hoard information, to take individual credit for a team's accomplishments, and to tend more toward cover-their-rear behavior than to collaborative efforts. Through not optimal, such behaviors make sense; individuals who fear losing their jobs will act in ways that they believe will make them indispensable, no matter how many team-building rope courses they attend with colleagues.

In addition, hoarding knowledge or the inability to make use of it is magnified by problems of information overload and a basic problem of an individual's inability to manage his or her schedule and priorities. Those who feel chronically behind are more likely to lapse into security behaviors, such as hoarding information (or just failing to share it) or thinking only of their own job survival. Again, many corporate cultures, with their lust for longer-than-necessary meetings, perpetual change and layoffs, and the like, help to foster such problems.

What Might Encourage Knowledge Sharing and Discourage Hoarding?

There is no easy answer, for larger, more established companies or for the younger enterprises that emulate their elder brethren. Yet a leader—or an enterprising and courageous employee—might sample some things to create a group culture that is at least more balanced, if not completely successful at collaborative, more natural systems efforts.

- *Create subcultures or initiatives that focus on small group interactions.* The subcultures or initiatives can tolerate a greater degree of chaos or complexity in their way of functioning, and individuals/ groups can tap systemwide tools that act as information repositories. The dynamic nature of an individual's or a group's knowledge renders such complicated or systemwide tools or repositories chronically out of date. Still, technological tools that allow people to share information, knowledge, and experiences can be excellent resources.

- *Model from above.* Many employees act according to how they perceive their leaders and managers. Managers who share information, award credit where credit is due, and display collaborative, group-centered behavior are more likely to attract and encourage the same in their employees. Acting in a noncollaborative way can be deeply ingrained, stemming from a long, cultural devaluing of the gifts and talents associated with "feminine" ways of working or being. The latter attributes, however, are increasingly important to the sustainability of our traditional organizations and culture as a whole, and they often flourish more in a natural system, rather than the Newtonian, Darwinian engineered system of our marketplace and its organizations.

- *Integrate "teaching and sharing" into the group fabric.* Again, this is more likely accomplished in an autonomous small group—"grass-roots up," "top down." Some simple ways to do this include:

  —Asking people to share instances in which one of their colleagues shared knowledge or information to help them do their work more effectively.

  —Asking staff members to do "miniworkshops at staff meetings, in which they take 10 or 15 minutes to share a best practice story or tip for more effectively doing their work.

  —Asking staff members to contribute in a group-led dialogue—in the format of a miniworkshop at a staff meeting or retreat—in which everyone in the group teaches something about how knowledge hoarding and lack of credit sharing is harmful to work and its outcomes, and how sharing knowledge and credit improves work effectiveness, efficiency, and satisfaction.

  —Asking people to share best practice stories—or have one person collect such stories—for use in a group, department, or organization newsletter, and for sharing and collecting for use in a best practices and "peak performance" library (online or physical).

  —Ensuring that these performance issues are included in formal job descriptions and performance evaluations, and identifying and measuring them accordingly—with either reward for effectiveness or accountability for improvement.

  —Creating and emphasizing an organizational and group culture in which peak performance and relational skillfulness are most valued, rather than relying solely on one's educational degree and title or position with the organization.

  —Ensuring that the culture of the group and organization has been "made safe for change," that the culture makes it safe for people to demonstrate behavior different from the norm and makes people feel confident that, if they share examples, they won't be punished (formally or informally).

  —Creating a group blog (Weblog) that is searchable, in which group members include clear keywords for areas that are a priority to the group's peak performance, or having someone else routinely gather such stories and "blog them" (as well as put them into other sharable formats).

—Assigning a "story keeper" and ensuring that the person has the leeway to fulfill that function. (Many organizations vastly underestimate the importance of such communication- and relationship-oriented roles, while tribes and other groups that more easily operate in these areas routinely value such roles, including that of "knowledge keeper" or "story keeper.")

- *Deal with the "unnecessary meeting" problem, which most large companies have.* People who move rotely from one too-long meeting to the next unnecessary meeting—meetings characterized by lifeless agendas and "sleepy food snacks"—are not going to have the time or the motivation to share valuable knowledge or integrate it into their own activities.

- *Ensure that both the directors/leaders and the staff gain organizational and time-management skillfulness.* They will be more likely to well-manage their day and less likely to fall prey to less skillful habits because they are always feeling disorganized and behind. Again, the group culture has to be safe for people to decline meetings and prioritize their own projects and tasks.

Needless to say, this topic, along with its issues and solutions, is the subject of much research. Yet there is progress to be made if we can step away from traditional formats and cultivate pockets where chaos, creativity, and natural relationships can flourish. The sharing of knowledge is more likely to occur by default, more effectively than any current hyperquantitative, highly controlled, enterprise-wide engineering solution will tolerate.

HOW TO CREATE TRUE TEAM BUILDING

Kevin Eikenberry

Kevin Eikenberry *is an expert in developing organizational and individual potential and the chief potential officer of The Kevin Eikenberry Group, a learning consulting company based in Indianapolis, Indiana. The Kevin Eikenberry Group provides organizations, teams, and individuals with the tools to transform their potential into results. He speaks frequently to corporations and associations and has served as both chair (two terms) and president of the North American Simulation and Gaming Association. Kevin is a contributing author to* **Walking with the Wise** *(Mentors Publications, Inc., 2003) and a frequent contributor to the* **Sourcebooks.**

Contact Information:
The Kevin Eikenberry Group
7035 Bluffridge Way
Indianapolis, IN 46278
317.387.1424 or 1.888.LEARNER
Kevin@KevinEikenberry.com
http://KevinEikenberry.com

This guide helps consultants, trainers, and leaders consider what they really need when thinking about team building, and suggests several alternatives to the standard team-building session.

WHAT WE ASSUME ABOUT TEAM BUILDING

Teams are everywhere and everyone wants to build a better team. Consultants and trainers hear it all the time: Can you do a team-building session for us? The assumptions underlying that question include:

- Team building is about getting people to like each other.
- All team building is the same. A good consultant/facilitator can give me a solution that will work for any team.
- The right team-building event will solve many of a team's problems in an afternoon.

And, apparently, most trainers and consultants either:

a.   Agree with these assumptions.

b.   Or are willing to play along for a payday.

Most of the events that happen as a result of this process are fun in the eyes of most participants, and, while deemed "a waste of time and money" by the most cynical (or those who have been through many of these events in the past), they are viewed positively by most.

Some of the events even include time designed by the facilitator to help people translate the good feelings and laughter into learning—helping people bring value back to work for the time spent together in team building. (This is often a touted component in the consultant's plan, but is often missing in actual application.)

These facts lead to a vicious cycle in the team-building business. Budgets get built each year that include funds to be used for team building. The events do not necessarily provide any real return on investment. However, people like them, and managers get kudos for much the same reasons as cruise directors on ships are liked—they know how to put on a great event.

So team-building events continue.

And teams still struggle to be as effective as they could be.

This guide provides a look at team performance that puts traditional relationship-focused team building in its proper perspective: that improved relationships are only a part of a team's performance puzzle. It introduces new ideas and, more important, it puts many known facts into a comprehensive model that you can use, starting today, to create and maintain more highly effective teams.

THE CARB MODEL

Dr. Robert Atkins made a living and created a cultural phenomenon teaching people to reduce their intake of carbs (carbohydrates). In a strange way, team-building efforts have taken this advice unknowingly. CARB is an acronym representing the four major dimensions ultimately responsible for a team's effectiveness (see Figure 1):

Commitment to the team and each other

Alignment and goal agreement

Relationships among team members

Behaviors and skills

This guide could be described as the anti-Atkins diet for teams: It takes *more* CARBs (or more of each of the CARB components) for teams to be successful.

Relationships alone are not enough.

Figure 1: The CARB Model

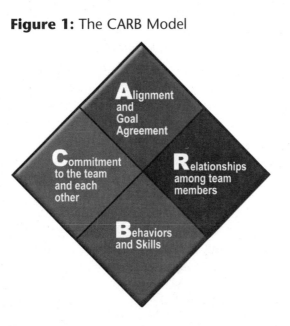

COMMITMENT TO THE TEAM AND EACH OTHER

Commitment is a very powerful thing, and, without it, the work of teams will not be as successful as possible.

Why?

People are busy. They have many tasks and priorities. The work of the team just falls into that long list of priorities unless people find a reason to be truly committed to the team itself and its goals. With only so much focus and energy to spread around, without commitment, they will not be fully participative and effective on the team.

There are two parts to this commitment. People must feel a commitment to the team and its purpose, and they must have some commitment to the individuals on the team, believing in them and in their contributions to the team.

Thinking about commitment in this dual way helps undermine the assumption we started this guide with: that people who know and like each other will make a great team. There is a difference between liking people and liking the team. And there is a huge difference between being committed to the people on a team and being committed to the work and purpose of the team.

Both are required. Ignore this fact at your own risk.

Of course, commitment can be (and often will need to be) built. It will not preexist when you put people on a team. Because team formation, development, and success are complex processes, several of our other CARB factors aid in the development of commitment. But recognizing its importance is a good first step.

How will you know when you have built a level of commitment, or what are the factors that will build that commitment? High levels of commitment correlate with several factors, including:

- *Belief:* People will believe in each other. Individual motivations are clear and generally understood. People are able to believe in the team, its individual members, and the work of the team.

- *Agreements:* People have a mutually agreed-to set of behaviors that are acceptable to the team. By building a set of agreements on performance, behavior, and "how things are done," productivity is greatly improved. Why? Effort and energy are not spent on distractions. Effort can be directed to the work at hand.

- *Trust:* A major underpinning for team performance is trust—trust in team members and trust in leadership. It is clearly necessary for the levels of commitment required for high-performing teams.

- *Support:* Support is a critical factor, but it is also a bellwether for the other factors. If people are supporting team decisions, commitment is likely present. If people are supporting each other through tough parts of a team's life, they are likely committed to each other.

Can a team get results with low commitment? Sure, you can get some results. But you will never approach the results possible with people who are committed to the team and each other.

ALIGNMENT AND GOAL AGREEMENT

Teams cannot succeed in a vacuum, but far too often that is what organizations expect them to do.

Sometimes the vacuum is created by omission: Leaders just are not thinking about the context for team success or are "too busy" to create it. Other times the reason is optimism: Leaders believe in their team members and their skills. After all, they hired bright people, and bright people will figure it all out. Assumptions like these can frustrate or burn out talented people and kill teams.

Sometimes the vacuum is caused by a far more pervasive problem: no clear organizational goals, objectives, or strategies. Leaders must create clear strategies, and they must create a clear line of sight throughout the organization, so that people and teams can connect their work to the important strategies of the organization.

It takes effort to get a team in alignment with the organization's goals and strategies. It is impossible when the goals and strategies do not exist.

Even when strategies and goals exist and even when they are communicated, this is a good start but not enough. Teams cannot gain the clear direction they need without conversation, and leadership has to provide the opportunity for it. Conversation brings the understanding that provides the team the context they need to clarify their goals and make the decisions in the course of their work.

If you want to build a stronger alignment between the team's work and the organization's goals, consider the following:

- *Start at the beginning:* Make sure the organization's goals and strategies are set. If not, the team does not have much of a chance of being highly successful. At a minimum, the team needs to understand, from the start, why their work product matters in the bigger picture and how they can make a positive impact.

- *Generate conversation:* Do not deliver the goals in the email when you ask people to join the team. Do not put it in the packet of materials people get when being hired. Make the time to have conversation. The required alignment needs to be deep—almost visceral. Help individuals and the team develop meaning and purpose. Help them understand how they can create work that matters.

- *Get the team's help:* Get their input. Remember that you are trying to create alignment and agreement. When people have the chance to shape the goals of the team, when they have the opportunity to have input into such decisions, they will have greater agreement with the goals.

- *Provide a connection:* Teams need someone in leadership "above" them who can provide support and resources, someone who can answer questions and keep them on track. Some people call this a team sponsor. Sponsors do not need to be on the team; rather they provide leadership, support, and connection. They keep the team from feeling all alone.

- *Make them accountable:* If the alignment is clear and the goals set, the team needs to be held accountable for results. If accountability has been lax in an organization in the past, this may seem like a jolt, but it will not be long before accountability not only drives results but improves team dynamics too.

It is easy to see how these steps will help a team succeed. But more than helping them deliver a desired result, the sense of clarity, meaning, and direction that these steps create helps teams get over many other hurdles.

Why? People want to belong to something that matters; they want things to believe in. When we give them those things, collectively they work through many personal issues and challenges, and they become more committed to the end product.

A nonaligned team could enjoy each other and their work, and they could accomplish much. And all of that could be completely counter to what the organization needs. Can you see this happening?

It is not just a fantasy. I have seen it.

And then a leader might look for some "team building," because "the team just isn't getting the results we need."

The Holy Grail of effective teams is relationships, right? "We need people to get to know each other better. Once we have done that, we will be fine."

As previously mentioned, this is a terrible and dangerously limiting view of teams.

This is not to say that the relationships between team members do not matter; they do. When teams with good relationships also have the other CARB factors in large amounts, look out—team performance can soar.

Traditional team-building events can be helpful. They can help people get to know each other, and they can help people find common ground. They also, at least in the short term, build a sense of camaraderie. And although all of these things are important, they are not the things that cause lasting improvement; they only set the stage for it.

The best designed relationship-focused, team-building events do more than create laughs; they create learning. These events help people do more than get to know each other; they provide opportunities for teams to:

- *Learn each other's strengths:* Strong teams not only like each other, they know each other's strengths. They are collectively able to tap into the strengths and experience of the members of the team.

- *Find ways to capitalize on those strengths:* The best team-building activities give people a chance to be themselves, without all the structure and trappings of the workplace. And when people are themselves, others see them in new and often flattering ways. This gives their strengths a chance to shine, and helps others see how the team can tap into those strengths.

- *Get comfortable with asking for help:* Highly effective team members are willing to ask for help, regardless of their role on the team. Team-building activities can help raise people's comfort with asking.

Other aspects of team relationships might not get addressed in traditional team building, but they are important. Again, these require effort and time to develop processes—and most likely support from leaders outside the team. These include:

- *Initiation processes:* How new team members are added to a team, as well as how they become oriented and acquainted with team members, norms, and expectations, is typically left to chance or a quick meet and greet. Organizations that develop processes and plans for this have greater success with teams that change membership frequently.

- *Role definition:* Team members need to understand where they fit in and what their roles are. When new teams are chartered or started, they need a format and plan for discussion of team member roles and expectations.

As you can see, even the relationship component of the CARB model is about more than just "liking one another." So why do people always feel that relationships are the key to more effective teams? Along with popular opinion and habit, sadly, the most prevalent reason is that a team-building "fix" is completely inwardly team focused. Leaders can invest money in a team-building session so that people get to know each other, but they do not have to invest themselves or look at the systems they have created as a part of the problem.

BEHAVIORS AND SKILLS

Being a successful member of a team requires different behaviors and skills than are required of an individual contributor. Therefore, when you put people together on teams, they perform more confidently and successfully if they have the right skills.

Although the list of skills and behaviors that support success on teams is long, here is a short version to get you thinking about the types of behaviors and skills to look for when creating a team or developing an existing team:

- *Strong technical skills and competence:* Having the subject matter knowledge, industry perspective, or specific skills the team needs is critical. Of course, not everyone should bring a cloned set of skills, but it is important to identify the subject matter needs of the team and make sure that each team member contributes to one or more of them.

- *Able and willing to collaborate and share credit:* Working alone allows for people to feel the spotlight and glory when things go well. It also means individuals will be held accountable when they are not so successful. Highly effective team members recognize that the team success reflects on them most when they focus on team success rather than on individual accolades. The best team members are willing to collaborate.

- *Able to trust others:* Trust is developed between people over time. In fact, as relationships are built, trust can blossom. The best team members, though, are willing to start from a position of basic trust in their teammates. Certainly this trust can deepen and grow, but the most effective team members are willing to assume the best and work together more effectively from the beginning. This behavior becomes more important as the makeup of individual teams changes more quickly.

- *Able to participate and lead effective meetings:* Meetings are an important component of team success. Whether the team meets every day or only quarterly, on remote conference calls or face to face, the ability and willingness to contribute ideas and insights, to help the team move toward the desired results, to provide feedback when needed, and to stay focused are critical skills for effective teams.

- *Comfortable and competent at group problem solving:* Some problems a team faces can be solved by individuals. Sometimes a subteam can tackle a problem, and sometimes it requires the entire team. In every case, effective team members know how to work together to solve problems; how to listen to the ideas of others; how to ask questions without being condescending, and how to make sure that the strengths, experiences, and insights of each team member are taken into account in the problem-solving process.

- *Willing to continuously learn:* The work of today is more complex and demanding than it has ever been. For teams to succeed, each individual on the team needs to continuously improve his or her skills.

The workings and success of a team are complex, and, as we tend to do in the face of many complexities in our world, we try to find easy answers. We try to isolate one factor that can make the difference. For most people the one factor in team building is getting people together to have some fun and giving them a common experience.

In the real world, this is just one way to improve team performance.

Before you call me (or any consultant) to ask for a team-building event, think more about the team, the organization it is a part of, and the team's makeup and goals. Then, when you make the call, encourage your consultant to give you options and approaches that will help your team where it really needs help the most.

Use the CARB model to remind you that highly effective team building requires more than a recreational retreat.

HOW TO LEAD ENTERPRISE-WIDE CHANGE

Stephen Haines

Stephen Haines *is a CEO, entrepreneur, and strategist. He is also a leader, facilitator, and systems thinker as president and founder of both the Centre for Strategic Management and Systems Thinking Press. He is a prolific author and internationally recognized leader in strategic leadership and management. He has 25 years of CEO experience leading over 200 planning and change efforts everywhere. Steve is a U.S. Naval Academy graduate and was president and part owner of University Associates. He was also executive vice president at ICA, senior vice president of Freddie Mac, and a leader with eight top management teams. Steve is also a frequent contributor to the **Sourcebooks**.*

Contact Information:
CENTRE *for* STRATEGIC MANAGEMENT®
Systems Thinking Press®
1420 Monitor Road
San Diego, CA 92110-1545
619.275.6528
619.275.0324 (fax)
stephen@csmintl.com
www.csmintl.com
www.SystemsThinkingPress.com

This guide details what enterprise-wide change (EWC) is, why 75 percent of all major change fails to achieve its goals, and why it is different from traditional organization development (OD). Some keys on how to lead an enterprise-wide change effort are also presented.

WHAT ENTERPRISE-WIDE CHANGE (EWC) IS

Enterprises of all types today have a need for enterprise-wide change, whether they are in the public, private, or not-for-profit sector. Why? Even high-performing enterprises are subject to the effects of a rapidly changing, highly competitive, global economy buffeted by technological changes.

Specific examples of enterprise-wide change initiatives and activities include:

- Enterprise resource planning system (ERPs) installations.
- Behavioral, process, and structural changes to create new cultures.
- Business and operational excellence initiatives.
- Mergers, acquisitions, joint ventures, and strategic alliances.
- Major new technologies installed.
- Difficult and complex strategic and business planning and execution.
- A customer-focused culture.
- Major customer service enhancements.
- Major growth and expansion.
- Major cutbacks, downsizing, and business process outsourcing.
- Organizational restructuring and redesign for enhanced efficiencies and effectiveness.
- Six Sigma and quality improvements.
- Supply chain management changes.
- Radical new product development and deployment.
- Transformation of an entire enterprise.
- Significant boosts in innovation.

Enterprise-wide change also incorporates many of the organization-wide changes in which OD and change consultants are typically involved, such as team building, visioning, leadership and executive succession, talent development, human resource (HR) planning, and change execution.

WHY EWC FAILS

An estimated 75 percent of all major change efforts fail and, so far, the author has identified 33 different reasons. However, the three big failure issues are:

1. An analytic, piecemeal approach to a systemwide problem (with multiple conflicting frameworks and mind-sets).

2. Focusing primarily on the economic alignment of delivery (an artificial "either/or" mind-set).

3. Focusing primarily on cultural attunement and people issues (another artificial "either/or" mind-set).

Enterprise-wide change requires a systems thinking approach because it is fundamentally different from other traditional change processes for many reasons. EWC:

- *Has a major structural/fundamental impact:* EWC has a major structural and fundamental impact on the entire organization or business unit in which change is to occur.

- *Is strategic in scope:* The change to be effected is strategic. It links to the business's unique positioning in the marketplace, even the public sector marketplace.

- *Is complex, chaotic, and/or radical:* The change is either complex and chaotic or constitutes a radical departure from the current state. The change is so complex that desired outcomes and approaches to achieve them can be unclear.

- *Is large-scale and transformational:* The scale of desired change is large and will result in a significantly different enterprise.

- *Has a long time frame:* The desired change requires years, with multiple phases and stages within major changes.

- *Entails cultural change:* The rules of the game change: the norms, guideposts, values, and guides to behavior.

To prevent the big three failures, a new set of players, structures, and roles for enterprise-wide change is needed (see Figure 1).

Figure 1: Players of Change

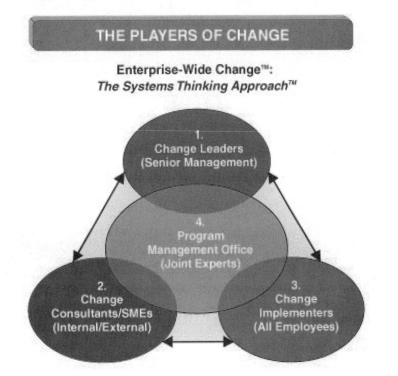

Players and Roles

Players and Role 1: Change Leaders

With change on the agenda, senior management must (1) take a pro-active leadership role on change and (2) run the business day to day. They *now* have two full-time jobs.

Success requires that change leaders think differently and have a deep understanding of enterprise-wide change and systems thinking. They need the discipline and courage to require tight integrity and focus of the entire enterprise to their strategic marketplace positioning—time after time.

They also require persistence and energy over the long term to ensure superior results.

Players and Role 2: Change Consultants and Subject Matter Experts (SMEs)

The CEO and line executives always require the support of internal and external cadres of competent support staff and subject matter experts in HR, finance, planning, communications, training, OD, and the like.

Players and Role 3: All Affected Employees

Participation and involvement are key to the buy-in and stay-in of employees to the desired changes: *People support what they help create.* Some excellent participation practices include the Whole Systems Approach, Search Conferences, Public Consultation, and the Centre's Parallel Involvement Process.

The fundamental agreement is that people today want to have input and involvement in the process of decision making on matters that affect them—before the final decision is made. Better decisions are the result, as is ownership for implementation.

Players and Role 4: Program Management Office (PMO)

A program management office is needed. It is led by a credible senior executive from the enterprise. It is co-led by an external master-level *systems consultant* and supported by internal staff and SMEs. The PMO needs to be a full-time leader in direct support of the CEO. Someone must be guiding the systemic nature of the change effort on a daily, full-time basis. Managing the many separate, yet parallel, change projects is a systems problem. And thus, it requires an integrated, coordinated, total systems solution to be successful.

The Systems Thinking Approach: How We Think ... Is How We Act ... Is How We Are

If it were not for the common characteristics of us as human (living) systems, we would not be able to move from organization to organization and from industry to industry as executives, employees, vendors, customers, or change consultants. However, the complexity of diverse people, interests, and personalities creates piecemeal thinking and often *unintended negative consequences* for others.

Systems thinking helps you sort out the complexities.

- In systems thinking, the whole is primary and the parts are secondary.
- In analytic thinking, the parts are primary and the whole is secondary.

Figure 2: Rubik's Cube

This is analogous to thinking of your organization as a dynamic Rubik's Cube, a complex set of parts in constant movement (see Figure 2). Enterprises and Rubik's Cubes each have over one trillion moves, many of them wrong.

To successfully lead an enterprise through wide-ranging, large-scale change in today's complex Rubik's Cube world, you need a higher view. Visualize getting into a helicopter and climbing to 5,000 feet for a better perspective (see Figure 3). This mental exercise and better view of the system can help enormously as you apply the concepts in this guide.

The helicopter view gives you a better, more comprehensive vantage point on life and work. It helps you to think in systems terms and get the "bigger picture," high above the Rubik's Cube.

Systems thinking is a new orientation to life, not just another set of tools.

Figure 3: Helicopter View

Overall Enterprise-Wide Change Flow: Outside-Inside-Outside Again

The rhythm of the enterprise-wide change is outside-inside-outside again. Although each enterprise-wide change process is customized and unique, this short systems thinking primer should give you an overall helicopter view of enterprise-wide change in operation.

Stage One: Work on the System (Outside First: Clarity of Purpose)

Systems thinking works first from the outside-in by looking at the whole system or enterprise with clarity of purpose (the complex Rubik's Cube) in its dynamic rapidly changing environment. This is the helicopter view that offers more simplicity of thought. Seeing not only the different and natural hierarchical levels of living systems (individuals, teams, departments, organizations, marketplaces, and societies), but also how they interact, collide, and/or collaborate with each other, is critical to success in a complex change effort.

Each living system has natural input-output phases and a circular flow that defines it as a system. The phases include an enterprise's:

- Inputs of today (Phase C).
- Business processes or throughputs (Phase D).
- Leading to multiple desired outputs (Phase A).
- In a rapidly changing environment (Phase E).

All living systems have a natural feedback loop (Phase B) that can be harnessed to measure the status of the outputs. Then feedback can be used to correct, adapt, or modify inputs to improve outputs. These phases allow us to see, and elegantly clarify, the main parts of each whole living system (enterprise) within its environment.

We have organized this systems thinking approach into a circular A-B-C-D-E framework for ease of understanding and use (see Figure 4).

STAGE ONE DETAILS: BUILD A SMART START

Stage One: Work on the system first. This first step is often missed in enterprise-wide change efforts, and the omission results in violating the old axiom: An ounce of prevention is worth a pound of cure. The preconditions for enterprise-wide change success include a number of items to clarify and simplify before beginning the journey. A two-day plan-to-implement retreat is an essential first activity. Some of the tasks include:

Educating

- Educating the executives on the principles of change
- Understanding the difference between content, process, structure, and the importance of each to success
- Developing the needed leadership skills and competencies of the collective management team to have the long-term capacity to create and sustain the change
- Educating and building innovative project teams to ensure they are competent as the *implementation vehicles* for the successful execution of each change initiative and project or process

Assessing

- Analyzing the waves of change as they apply to all levels of your entire enterprise (This analysis usually results in a host of issues and action plans required to cascade the waves of change desired to all levels and units in the enterprise.)

- Assessing and refining your performance accountability and management system (tying in rewards to support this EWC process with a special focus on frequent recognition)

Tailoring

- Clarifying your ideal future vision of what business excellence and superior results mean to your specific enterprise-wide change desired outcomes
- Selecting from a range of change structures and establishing those that are required (The number one criterion for success is the change leaders' forming a change leadership team to meet and focus only on the changes.)
- Establishing the program management office and selecting the master systems consultant and senior executive to jointly run it (the number two criterion for success)
- Tailoring the enterprise-wide change process to your specific needs

Organizing

- Building a communications plan with regular communications, follow-up, and booster shots to develop a critical mass in support of the change
- Having all executives develop personal leadership plans on what they are going to do *personally* to lead the change
- Building a yearly map of implementation, including the key annual strategic change review (and update) sessions
- Resourcing and budgeting for the extensive change process adequately (money, people, time, information, technology, equipment, spaces, etc.)

Finally, use all the preceding steps to build an actual enterprise-wide change game plan, which is typically composed of five elements:

1. Content of the Change (Clarity of Purpose)
2. Structures and Roles to Guide the Change Effort
3. Processes for the Change (the Flow and Sequence)
4. Capacity for Change (Competencies, Commitments, and Resources)
5. Yearly Map of Implementation (to tie it all together)

IN SUMMARY: ACHIEVE CLARITY OF PURPOSE

Goal 1: Develop an overall enterprise-wide clarity of purpose (along with the game plan for enterprise-wide change).

Using a systems model, focus on:

Figure 4: ABCs of Enterprise-Wide Change

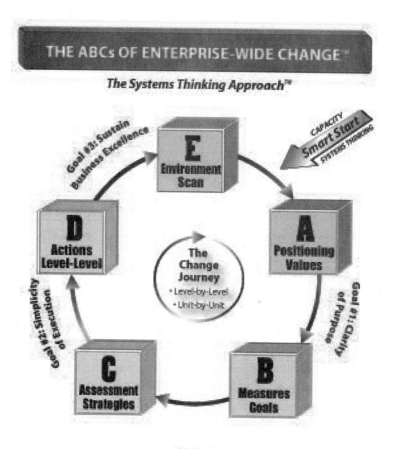

THE ABCs OF ENTERPRISE-WIDE CHANGE

The Systems Thinking Approach™

Result:
Business Excellence and Superior Results!

- Conducting a future environmental scan (Phase E).
- Defining your ideal future vision (Phase A).
- Defining your positioning in the marketplace (Phase A).
- Clarifying your core values (Phase A).
- Developing your key success measures or goals (Phase B) for the desired change.

Conduct an Enterprise-Wide Change Assessment

The last part of working *on* the system is conducting an enterprise-wide assessment and diagnosis. It should be based on one (*and only one*) mental map or model of an organization as one system. Structure the assessment around this mental map. Remember, this is one of the three most common reasons for failure. As a result of the assessment, define your core strategies and their key initiatives for achieving your change vision.

Only after working on the system should you work in it.

Stage Two: Work in the System (Inside: Core Strategies Are the Glue)

Now you are ready to spend time more effectively working in the daily processes (or throughputs) of the organization. If you are trying to make the organization more effective (based on the desired outputs), it is only at this second stage that you can focus effectively on the activities and inner workings of the system. This is because each part of a system is not separate. The parts are interrelated, and ideally they work together to achieve the desired outputs and vision.

ENSURE SIMPLICITY OF EXECUTION

Goal 2: Ensure simplicity of execution. In matters of complexity, simplicity wins the game every time.

- Support the enterprise-wide change with departmental plans built around the core strategies—to have everyone accountable for the same game plan implementation.

- Cross-functional project teams are the primary vehicles for execution of enterprise-wide change. However, the teams must be balanced by functional accountability. Building a strong integrated web of both vertical functional differentiation and horizontal project team integration is key to success.

- The roller coaster of change (with its ups and downs) is natural and normal—and the main framework for what you need to know about the process and cascades of change. Relate all learning and change applications to it for simplicity of execution.

WAVE AFTER WAVE OF CHANGE

Enterprise-wide change is a constantly unfolding, discovery, creation, and re-creation process. You cannot know everything in advance. Thus, be guided by the systems thinking approach to living systems. Use the approach to coordinate all the needed traditional OD interventions. Ensure that such interventions are linked to the larger purposes of the enterprise-wide change. Understand that the normal and predictable roller coaster of change is a key to the successful journey.

Stage Three: Check on the System (Outside Again: Sustain Business Excellence)

Goal 3: Build and sustain business excellence (year after year). Key actions at the end of each year include:

- Conducting an updated future environmental scan (Phase E).
- Reviewing and assessing your vision and desired outcomes (Phase A).
- Reviewing and assessing the business results and their success measurements from the last year (Phase B).

- Assessing your organization against your mental model of an organization as a system (Phase C).

- Assessing the results of the first year of the enterprise-wide change process itself.

- Assessing how well you are walking the talk on your core values (Phase C).

- Developing further action plans to correct areas of weaknesses or failures (Phase D).

- Redoing the enterprise-wide change game plan for the next 12 months, adjusting core strategies, and revisiting the key initiatives as necessary (Phase D).

- Evaluating and redesigning the innovative project teams to ensure they continue to be effective vehicles for successful execution (Phase D).

- Adjusting your players of change to ensure the proper infrastructure (Phase D).

Four Absolutes for Success on the ECW Journey

The roller coaster of change begins its downward trajectory and sense of loss as a change begins. In other words, *things get worse before they get better in change.* To manage it properly you need:

1. Regular meetings of the enterprise-wide change leadership team, led by the CEO.

2. Tracking and regular reporting about results achieved and measures of success.

3. Guiding the enterprise-wide change effort on a daily basis by a full-time program management office, supported by SMEs and change consultants.

4. A deep understanding of systems thinking, the roller coaster of change, and all the practical change management applications.

Building Your ECW Capacity

The ability of your players and the roles of change to carry out the enterprise-wide change process successfully depend on their having the *capacity* to do so.

The capacity includes:

- Having the senior management and board *commitment* and readiness to undertake and persevere in the complexity of *cultural change.*

- Using the *competencies* and skills to lead enterprise-wide change effectively.

- Dedicating *adequate resources* exclusively to enterprise-wide change.

- Having effective change processes to facilitate the successful outcomes.

- Installing effective change structures, like the Four Absolutes for Success on the Enterprise-wide Change™ journey.

HOW TO TAKE THINGS APART

Moshe Yudkowsky

Moshe Yudkowsky *has developed high-tech products for 20 years, including stints at both Bell Labs and Intel. Today Moshe is president of Disaggregate, a consulting company that helps people understand, create, and apply revolutions in business and technology. Moshe is author of* **The Pebble and the Avalanche: How Taking Things Apart Creates Revolutions** *(Berrett-Koehler, 2005).*

Contact Information:
Disaggregate
2952 W. Fargo
Chicago, IL 60645
773.764.8727
speech@pobox.com
www.disaggregate.com

An excellent way to create and assess innovative solutions is to take an existing structure or product and break it apart into smaller pieces.

Many of the major revolutions in both business and technology over the past 30 years are the result of breaking things apart. In business, for example, the breakup of AT&T's business structure led to fantastic creativity in telecommunications service—the prepaid phone card would have been unthinkable under the old AT&T. In technology, digital music is the result of breaking the physical connection between the music and the storage medium: Music is no longer tied to a phonograph record, a tape, or a CD. The result is an upheaval in the music industry and a slew of creative tools to enhance the consumer experience of music. The open-source business methods that IBM and other companies are using to challenge Microsoft's monopoly are all based on carefully breaking things apart—on the disaggregation of business infrastructure.

But what, exactly, gets broken apart to unleash creativity? How do we find all the implications of an interesting idea? The what of breaking something apart falls into five general categories: authority, ownership, mechanics, space/time, and concepts. In this guide, we see how to use this concept to brainstorm new, innovative solutions or to evaluate and improve existing ideas.

RUNNING THE BRAINSTORMING SESSION

Follow the usual rules for a brainstorming session: Set the agenda, discuss the objectives, and present the ground rules for discussion. If the group is large, you might wish to break up into small teams of two to four individuals to permit the free exchange of ideas.

Instead of tackling the entire problem at once, have the teams discuss the problem category by category, and then report their findings to the group as a whole. If someone suggests an idea that fits best in a different category, record the idea and return to it later.

THE ESSENTIAL POINTS

As each category is discussed, capture three important pieces of information:

1. What is the current state of affairs?
2. What does the innovation do? In what way does the innovation break apart an existing relationship?
3. What is likely to be the outcome of the innovation?

The essential points are best captured on charts. As an example to illustrate what each category means, and to show how to fill in the charts, here is an analysis of technology that created a revolution when it was first introduced: the videocassette recorder.

Authority

Authority means the ability to control something or to determine how a process will work.

Videocassette Recorders: Authority

Before Disaggregation	*The Innovation and What It Does*	*Outcome*
The content of television programs was determined by the television networks.	Videotape cassettes allow viewers to play prerecorded or recorded shows on television.	Viewers control what they see on their television. Other companies (e.g., the movie industry) compete to provide television programming.

Make certain to include each instance of Before, Innovation, and Outcome; it's sometimes necessary to use several copies of the chart to capture all the ideas. For example, in the case of videocassette recorders, we could also discuss the authority of the government to impose decency standards.

Ownership

Ownership includes both the legal idea of ownership—"I own a shirt, or I own a shirt factory"—and the slang meaning—"Acme *owns* the market for widgets."

VCRs did not change who physically owned the television set, but it did introduce radical changes in audience behavior.

Videocassette Recorder: Ownership

Before Disaggregation	*The Innovation and What It Does*	*Outcome*
Major television networks owned the eyeballs of the customers who watched television; they could insert commercials at will.	Customers could obtain prerecorded cassettes that came without commercials, or they could record shows and skip over the commercials.	Television networks suffered a permanent loss. Advertisers created more clever commercials and sought out new, alternative paths to mass audiences.

Mechanics

Breaking a mechanical relationship includes breaking some sort of relationship: the materials something is made out of, how it is put together, what machinery is used to manufacture it, the software it uses, or similar physical elements.

Videocassette Recorder: Mechanics

Before Disaggregation	*The Innovation and What It Does*	*Outcome*
VCRs could only use, mechanically, one type of tape, but two competing types were available (Betamax and VHS). Customers worried about which standard would prevail.	Once everyone switched to VHS tapes, all VCRs became compatible.	One type of tape meant lower VCR and tape costs. More content became available, because content could be released in just one format.

This is an example of a crucial mistake by the videocassette industry: No one broke the relationship between the tape and the *manufacturer* of the recorder. The result was a battle between Betamax and VHS formats, and many potential customers sat on the sidelines and refused to buy until the dust settled. The same battle is about to take place for the next generation of DVD players, with likely the same result. The failure to disaggregate has business consequences.

Space/Time

Innovations in this class break a relationship between an event and its location in space and time. Perhaps the most famous recent invention in this category is the phonograph, which made it possible to listen to a concert without being present at the original performance.

Videocassette Recorder: Space/Time

Before Disaggregation	The Innovation and What It Does	Outcome
Television shows were shown according to a schedule prepared by the networks. Viewers had to see it at that time or miss the show.	Viewers could record the show and watch it at a time of their choosing.	Television shows become less like concerts and more like books: They can be viewed at any time and as often as desired. They are no longer tied to a particular place; a television show from the United Kingdom, from India, or from Australia can be seen in the United States, even if the U.S. networks do not carry it.

Concepts

Sometimes an innovation breaks a relationship that exists not in the real world, but in how people think about technology, business, or society—the concepts that people have about how things relate. Concepts are not "just thoughts," because how we look at the world defines how we act.

As an example, at one time people linked certain jobs to certain genders. A doctor or a police officer was always a male; a librarian or a nurse was almost always a female. In the United States, this conceptual relationship was broken by the new concept of equality: gender, race, and national origin no longer define the jobs a person is allowed to have.

Videocassette Recorder: Concepts

Before Disaggregation	The Innovation and What It Does	Outcome
By definition, movies can be seen only in movie theaters. To see a movie, you must visit the theater during its "run."	Movies can be seen in the home. Tens of thousands of old movies, long gone from the theaters, can be rented from online services.	Customer habits change; new movies must compete not only with current movies, but with all the movies ever made. In response, the film industry institutes radical changes. For example, the movie theater industry builds many smaller theaters instead of single large ones.

These charts can be used in three related modes: innovation, analysis, and improvement. If the goal is creative problem solving, use the charts to generate new ideas: Start by discovering the authority, ownership, and other categories inherent in the problem. Work on ways to break the relationships, and then forecast the possible outcome of the disaggregations.

If the goal is to analyze an already existing innovation, the job is more straightforward. The more disaggregation, the more likely that an innovation is valuable. In that same spirit, it is possible to improve innovations by adding new disaggregations, and especially by filling in blank squares in any of the charts.

Mel Silberman, PhD, is president of Active Training (303 Sayre Drive, Princeton, New Jersey 08540, 609.987.8157, mel@activetraining.com, www.activetraining.com). He is also a professor emeritus of adult and organizational development at Temple University where he specializes in instructional design and team building.

He is the author of:

101 Ways to Make Training Active (Pfeiffer, 2005)

Active Learning (Allyn & Bacon, 1996)

Active Training (Pfeiffer, 1998)

101 Ways to Make Meetings Active (Pfeiffer, 1999)

PeopleSmart (Berrett-Koehler, 2000)

Working PeopleSmart (Berrett-Koehler, 2004)

The 60 Minute Active Training Series (Pfeiffer, 2005)

Training the Active Training Way (Pfeiffer, 2006)

He is the editor of:

The Leadership and Organization Development Sourcebook

The Training and Performance Sourcebook

The Consultant's Toolkit (McGraw-Hill, 2000)

The Consultant's Big Book of Organization Development Tools (McGraw-Hill, 2002)

The Consultant's Big Book of Reproducible Surveys and Questionnaires (McGraw-Hill, 2002)

Active Manager's Toolkit (McGraw-Hill, 2003)

The Best of Active Training (Pfeifer, 2004)

Mel has consulted for hundreds of corporate, governmental, educational, and human service organizations worldwide. Among his recent clients have been:

Merck	Linens N Things
Merrill Lynch	Stockholm School of Economics
BMW of North America	Franklin Covey
Bristol Myers-Squibb	NY State Department of Health
Comcast	US Senate Office of Education and Training
Columbia University	Valero Refining
Virtua Health	New York University
Vanguard Financial	MGM Grand
Conneciv	Wyeth BioPharma
The World Bank	Consolidated Edison

He is also a popular speaker at professional conferences.

Patricia Philips is president of Philips Consulting, Inc. (510 Pamlico River Dr., Washington, NC 27889, 252.975.6795, pphilips@earthlink.net), a management development company that provides management assessment, coaching, meeting facilitation, and customized programs. Philips Consulting, Inc. specializes in the development of new supervisors and managers. She has been the assistant editor of the *Sourcebooks* since 1998 and is a frequent contributor.